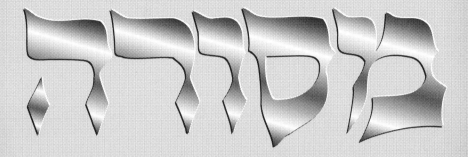

ArtScroll Series®

Rabbi Nosson Scherman / Rabbi Meir Zlotowitz

General Editors

RAV SHACH

Published by
Mesorah Publications, ltd

ON *Chumash*

An anthology collected from
his disciples and those close to him
by his grandson
Rabbi Asher Bergman

Translated from the Hebrew
Lulei Soras'cha
by Rabbi Dovid Oratz

FIRST EDITION
First Impression . . . August 2004

Published and Distributed by
MESORAH PUBLICATIONS, Ltd.
4401 Second Avenue
Brooklyn, New York 11232

Distributed in Europe by
LEHMANNS
Unit E, Viking Business Park
Rolling Mill Road
Jarrow, Tyne & Wear NE32 3DP
England

Distributed in Australia & New Zealand by
GOLDS WORLD OF JUDAICA
3-13 William Street
Balaclava, Melbourne 3183
Victoria Australia

Distributed in Israel by
SIFRIATI / A. GITLER — BOOKS
6 Hayarkon Street
Bnei Brak 51127

Distributed in South Africa by
KOLLEL BOOKSHOP
Shop 8A Norwood Hypermarket
Norwood 2196, Johannesburg, South Africa

Typography by CompuScribe at ArtScroll Studios, Ltd.
4401 Second Avenue / Brooklyn, N.Y. 11232 / (718) 921-9000

Printed in the United States of America by Noble Book Press

❧ Table of Contents

Introduction

The Gemara (*Makkos* 24a) states: "Habakkuk established the basis [for fulfilling the Torah's commandments] on one requirement: 'The righteous person shall live through his faith' " (*Habakkuk* 2:4). My revered grandfather, the late and great master of all the Jewish people, Rav Shach, may his memory be blessed, used to say that Habakkuk clearly did not take away from the Torah; we know that our Torah cannot be changed. Rather, because of the diminishing stature of the generations and their decreasing devotion, Habakkuk was teaching the foundation upon which we must build our spiritual growth, the basis for enabling us to fulfill the Torah and mitzvos. The Torah is the basis for our faith and its inculcation.

He would cite the statement of *Rambam* (*Commentary on the Mishnah,* end of *Berachos*): "I view teaching basic principles of religion and faith as more valuable than teaching anything else." My grandfather was involved in Torah education from the age of 17, and whenever he could, he would share a thought which would lead to greater fear of Heaven. Where there is no fear of Heaven there can be no wisdom, and the start of knowledge is the fear of Hashem. He mined vast stores of faith, a small fraction of which can be seen in the volumes of *Michtavim U'Maamarim*, which my grandfather gave me the merit of publishing, as well as *Shimushah shel Torah* and *Mi-Shulchano shel Rabbeinu*. Like the rest of his Torah, his thoughts on these subjects were deep and penetrating. One of my grandfather's disciples relates that one day he noticed the *Rosh Yeshivah* arrive at the morning study session already deep in thought. He sat in his regular place, but he did not even open his

Gemara; in fact, his Gemara remained shut all morning. The same thing occurred at that day's afternoon study session. He appeared to be totally caught up in some matter. This disciple gathered up the courage to ask just what it was that so upset Rav Shach. The *Rosh Yeshivah* seemed surprised by the question and he answered, "Heaven forbid! I am not upset at all. I was merely contemplating the fundamentals of our faith."

Faith is one foundation for living a Torah life; moral behavior is the other. Thus, the Gemara (ibid.) says, "[King] David came and established eleven [ethical and moral requirements] as the basis *(Psalms 15:2)...* 'One who walks in perfect innocence, and works righteously, and speaks the truth from his heart' etc." He established these requirements because "Moral behavior *(derech eretz)* precedes the Torah" *(Vayikra Rabbah* 60:3). Similarly, the Gemara *(Avodah Zarah* 25a) refers to the first book of the Torah, the book about our forefathers, as "*Sefer HaYashar*" — The Book of Uprightness (see also, e.g., *II Samuel* 1:18).

Rav Shach was a living Torah scroll and a living book of ethics. Through the stories that he told and the advice that he gave, he always encouraged and exhorted people regarding matters of faith and matters of ethics. Most profoundly, however, his dedication to these ideals was evident in his personal conduct; indeed, one could say of his life: "Like everything that I show you ... so shall you do" *(Shemos* 25:9). Each of his conversations, even about pedestrian matters, taught lessons; every action he took was, in effect, a ruling. We, the family members who were close to him, merited to learn from his behavior, a morsel here and a crumb there. And when the sun set and the darkness descended, we set our hearts to collect and organize the material about his life and the stories he told. We were faced with a huge collection of inspiring rulings and enlightening stories. To use some of these in an effective way, we decided to organize them according to the weekly Torah portions. The *Gra* (to *Mishlei* 11:13) explains that the best way to remember something and be inspired by it is to learn it slowly. We therefore arranged this work so that each person can be inspired anew each week, and have his faith more strongly embedded within him.

It once happened that an Orthodox community suffered an unusually large number of tragedies. They came to ask Rav Shach what aspects of their conduct they should undertake to improve, so as to assuage God's anger. He responded that they should accept easy things.

When they asked him what he meant, he explained with a story. "When I studied in Slutzk, I was a Shabbos guest at one of the families in the community. The host was a simple man, and when he began to discuss mundane matters at the Shabbos table, his wife immediately hushed him. This was the atmosphere which infused that community; even a 'simple' wife was a paragon of pious behavior. Can you imagine how wonderful it would be to speak only Torah and sing Shabbos songs at the Shabbos table?

"Of course," added Rav Shach, "this is more difficult in houses with little children, but one can tell them stories from our Sages, and the table will then truly be a Heavenly table!"

We hope that this book will fulfill the wishes of Rav Shach. May it bring merit to his soul, in accordance with the request in his will, that people study Torah and contemplate ethical behavior for the merit of his soul.

The Midrash (*Bamidbar Rabbah* 14:4) expounds on the verse from *Koheles* (12:11): "The words of the wise are like goads, and nails well driven are the sayings of the masters of collections": "When are the words of Torah *well driven* into a person? When they can derive lessons from them. As long as a person's teacher is alive, he can always expansively say, 'Whenever it is necessary, I can turn to my teacher to ask him whatever I need to know.' When the teacher passes away, however, the person must immerse himself day and night in his studies, for he knows that he has no one upon whom to rely." Woe unto us, for we have reached the stage of *masters of collections*. Until the very end, we hoped to be able to stay in the presence of our master. Now that the light has been extinguished, may the *Rosh Yeshivah's* Torah light our way and allow us to see. May he in turn defend us in Heaven.

As my introduction draws to a close, I would like to express my deep gratitude to my revered father, who devoted so much time to reviewing all the material, as well as to my dear mother.

I would also like to express my blessings to my father-in-law, Rav Avram Kolodetzky, and his wife. May it be Hashem's Will that they be granted long and healthy lives and *nachas* from their family.

I offer special blessing to my wife, who has been such a wonderful helpmate in all respects.

I express my gratitude and blessings to the renowned *gaon*, Rav Chaim Kanievsky — who studied under Rav Shach at the yeshivah in Petach Tikvah — who reviewed the entire manuscript and encouraged me to publish this book, in addition to gracing it with his approbation.

I am also grateful to to Rav Shalom Meir Wallach, who helped edit and organize the material.

I express my deepest gratitude to the Davis, Rieder, Glenner, Ray, and Halperin families, who contributed toward the publication of *Lulei Sorascha*, the Hebrew original of this work; to the Adjmi family who contributed toward the publication of the Hebrew companion work, *Sorascha Shaashu'ai*; and to Barry Appel of Miami Beach, Florida, who contributed toward the publication of the new combined one-volume Hebrew edition of *Lulei Sorascha* and *Sorascha Shaashu'ai*.

May this book guide us along the path of our great master, and may his merit protect us and all of Israel to achieve eternal salvation.

Asher, son of the Gaon, Rav Meir Tzvi Bergman.

ספר בראשית &

Bereishis

בראשית — Bereishis

בְּרֵאשִׁית בָּרָא אֱלֹהִים אֵת הַשָּׁמַיִם וְאֵת הָאָרֶץ — *In the beginning of God's creating heaven and earth* (1:1).

*A*new *cheder* (elementary-level yeshivah) in Jerusalem decided that the study of *Chumash* in the first grade would begin with *parashas Lech Lecha*, skipping over the first two *parashios*, *Bereishis* and *Noach*. Rav Shach contacted the *cheder's* administrator and asked why they this approach had been adopted. "The children already know the story of Creation and the Flood from kindergarten," he explained. "And it is pointless to teach young children the account of the births and deaths of the generations between Adam and Avraham. That's why we begin with *Lech Lecha*."

The *Rosh Yeshivah* did not approve. "This is not a new idea," he told the administrator. "One of the congregants in the *minyan* of the Brisker Rav (R' Yitzchak Zev Soloveitchik) brought his young son over to the Rav one Shabbos for a blessing upon the occasion of his beginning to study *Chumash*. He stroked the child's head affectionately and asked him, 'So tell me, what did God create on the first day?' The boy did not know the answer. 'In his *cheder* they don't start with *Bereishis*,' the father explained. 'They begin with *Lech Lecha*.'

"As soon as Shabbos was over the Rav sent for the administrator of that *cheder* and admonished him severely. 'How can you dare to tamper with the traditional system of teaching that has been passed on for generations?' Among the points the Rav made was that a child must not be given the impression that the Torah begins with an account of someone's (Avraham's) 'moving to *Eretz Yisrael*' — a sentiment that plays a central role in the philosophy that the Jewish nationalists strive to inculcate. 'The Torah begins with God's creation of heaven and earth, not with a move to *Eretz Yisrael*!' he said.

"So there you have it," concluded Rav Shach. " 'The sage has already issued his ruling' (*Sanhedrin* 24a)! We may not veer from the traditional method of teaching — starting from *The beginning!*"

בְּרֵאשִׁית בָּרָא אֱלֹהִים אֵת הַשָּׁמַיִם וְאֵת הָאָרֶץ — *In the beginning of God's creating heaven and earth.*

R'Meir Heisler once mentioned to Rav Shach the opinion, advocated by several early commentators, that, although the fate of every human being and the details of his life are controlled directly by God, this does not apply to animals. God's providence watches over the preservation — or lack of it — of species as a whole, but does not concern itself with the fate of each and every butterfly and ant.

Rav Shach told him that this opinion was not accepted in mainstream Jewish thought. The *Talmud Yerushalmi* says otherwise (*Shevi'is* 9:1): "Even a bird is not caught in a trap unless it is decreed so from Heaven."

R' Heisler added that in *Safra Detzniusa*, the Vilna Gaon also explicitly disagrees with this concept, asserting that everything is hinted at in the Torah's account of Creation — all the details of the life of every animal, and even vegetables and plants.

"Why, this is the concept that has fortified me throughout my life!" declared Rav Shach. "The knowledge that every single event that occurs to me is already foretold in the Torah. I am not rootless! I am not abandoned to 'blind fate'!"

בְּרֵאשִׁית בָּרָא אֱלֹהִים אֵת הַשָּׁמַיִם וְאֵת הָאָרֶץ — *In the beginning of God's creating heaven and earth* (1:1).

Rashi to this verse cites the Midrash's question: "Why did God see fit to begin the Torah from the story of Creation, and not from 'This month shall be for you the first of the months' (*Shemos* 12:2) – the first commandment He gave to the Jewish people?"

Rav Shach would frequently quote this Rashi and comment: "How fotunate we are that God did indeed choose to include the story of Creation in the Torah! The Chofetz Chaim used to read the entire first chapter of *Bereishis* each morning after reciting the morning blessings, as a means of strengthening his faith in the Creator. If the Chofetz Chaim found this useful and necessary, how much more so should we!"

וְחֹשֶׁךְ עַל־פְּנֵי תְהוֹם וְרוּחַ אֱלֹהִים מְרַחֶפֶת עַל־פְּנֵי הַמָּיִם — *With darkness upon the surface of the deep, and the Divine Presence hovered upon the surface of the waters (1:2).*

Rav Shach always searched for ways to make faith in God practical and perceptible to people in their everyday lives. As the Alter of Kelm wrote, "Our approach is to expound upon matters of faith in order make them more concrete and tangible."

For quite some time the *Rosh Yeshivah* kept on his desk a page copied from the Rema's *Toras HaOlah*. On that page, the author discusses the origin of *Tashlich* — the prayer for forgiveness that is customarily recited at a seashore or riverbank on the first day of Rosh Hashanah. Rema writes, "This is because it is from the awesome, great depths of the ocean that the concept of the creation of the world can be recognized and felt. This is why we go to a body of water on Rosh Hashanah, the Day of Judgment, so that each person may contemplate the Creation of the world, and the fact that God is the King over all the world. In this manner he will be moved to feel remorse for all his sins, until 'his sins are cast into the depths of the sea' (*Michah* 7:19, one of the verses recited at *Tashlich*). This reason is quite sensible to a perceptive person."

Rav Shach would show this quotation to everyone who came into his study, saying with excitement, "See what it says here!"

נַעֲשֶׂה אָדָם — *Let us make Man (1:26).*

The plural (*us*) is used in this verse, the Sages tell us, to teach that one should always be modest enough to confer with his inferiors. God consulted, as it were, with the angels concerning the creation of man, although He did not need their assistance in any way; He did it just to teach us this lesson.

A student who had studied under Rav Shach many years earlier, and had maintained a close relationship with him, once came to pay him a visit. The attendants had instructions not to let anyone disturb the *Rosh Yeshivah*, for he was preparing remarks that he was to deliver the following day at a mass rally in Yad Eliyahu stadium. In addition to the audience that would pack the hall, his words would reach an even wider audience through the media covering the event.

"Yes, I know the *Rosh Yeshivah* is busy preparing," protested the man. "It is precisely for this reason that I have come to speak with him!" He was allowed in.

The man told Rav Shach, "I believe that this is a tremendous opportunity to sanctify the Name of Heaven in public. It would be quite fitting to speak about faith in God!"

The *Rosh Yeshivah* picked his head up from his papers and listened attentively. "Good! Good!" This man was one of those students whom the Sages describe as "Those who enlighten their own teachers" (*Chagigah* 14a)!

The *Rosh Yeshivah's* positive response emboldened the man further. "And of course, it would be a wonderful chance to speak about the plague of divisiveness and contention within our own camp as well!" he added. "And about the folly of causing needless provocations against the non-Jewish nations."

Rav Shach once again expressed his approval. "Very good! This is excellent advice. Thank you!"

The following day, Rav Shach's speech covered only the topic of faith, leaving the other two suggested subjects untouched. His words had a great impact on the public.

The day after the address, that student came to visit the *Rosh Yeshivah* once again. As soon as the Sage saw him in the doorway, he went to greet him and expressed his apologies. "I am deserving of reprimand (for not following your advice)! Go ahead! Reprimand me! I apologize for mentioning only one of your suggested topics. You see, at first I was told that I was to be the only speaker, so I prepared a speech covering all three subjects. However, I later learned that there were other speakers as well, and I did not wish to burden the audience with endless hours of speeches, so I had to cut my address short!"

The *Rosh Yeshivah* took the lesson of our verse to heart, and heeded the advice of others — even his student — to the point that he felt the need to apologize when he did not fully translate this advice into action!

וַיְכֻלּוּ הַשָּׁמַיִם וְהָאָרֶץ — *Thus the heaven and the earth were finished* (2:1).

A professor once remarked to Rav Shach, "You religious people slavishly follow preconceived notions!"

"And you enlightened, advanced secularists do not," said Rav Shach, pronouncing the logical conclusion to the professor's statement. "Tell me, then," he asked, "how do you explain how the world around us came into existence?"

"It's very simple," responded the professor. "At first there was nothing but a mass of minerals, water, and gases. Then, at some point, these primordial materials began to interact and to form amino acids, which eventually led to the formation of the first primitive organic cell, etc."

"Very well," said Rav Shach. "But where did this original matter of minerals, etc. come from?"

"Well, that's still a mystery for us!" admitted the professor.

"If that's the case," concluded the *Rosh Yeshivah,* "now you tell me — which one of us is encumbered by preconceived notions? It is you who are left with unanswered questions. Among us, every child can tell you how heaven, earth, and all that is contained within them came into being!"

וַיְהִי הָאָדָם לְנֶפֶשׁ חַיָּה — *And man became a living being* (2:7).

The Talmud (*Taanis* 22b) derives from this verse that one is obligated to preserve his life. Saving a life overrides the observance of all commandments in the Torah, except for the three cardinal sins — even if the life that is preserved will last for only a few moments longer (*Yoma* 85a).

R' Leib Chasman observed that when the prophet Yonah asked to be thrown overboard from the ship, he said "'Pick me up and throw me into the sea" (*Yonah* 1:12). Why did Jonah add, "Pick me up"? Couldn't he simply have said, "Throw me into the sea"? R' Leib answered that Yonah wanted them to first lift him high, so he would have a extra few seconds of life before he would be drowned.

Rav Shach retold the following related story, which he had heard from the Brisker Rav:

Toward the end of World War I, morale in the Russian Army was low, and decorum was at the point of total disintegration. Soldiers did whatever they pleased.

The army commanders at the base near Brisk decided to take steps to enforce discipline, and decreed that any soldier caught going AWOL would be shot. As it happened, the first person to be seized violating the new law was a Jewish soldier. He was court-martialed and sentenced to death, with the execution date set for the following day — which was Rosh Hashanah.

Before the execution, the soldier requested that he be allowed to confess to a rabbi, so the commanding officers sent a group of soldiers to summon the local rabbi to comply with the prisoner's last request.

The soldiers arrived at the synagogue as the congregation was reciting the silent *Shemoneh Esrei* prayer, and they waited outside the synagogue until they would be able to speak to the rabbi. Their presence stirred a great deal of curiosity and concern, and some of the congregants, who had already finished their prayer, went out to ask what they wanted.

Upon hearing the nature of the soldiers' mission, some of the men returned to the synagogue, stood near the rabbi, and declared audibly that there was a group of soldiers waiting outside for the Rav, to take him to help a condemned Jewish prisoner with his *Vidui*. But the Rav continued to pray silently, carrying on with the same slow, deliberate pace as before.

As the Rav's prayers dragged on and the patience of the soldiers wore thin, the congregants began to worry that the soldiers would eventually give up, and that the Jewish prisoner would be executed without saying *Vidui*. They placed a watch on the Rav's table, beside his prayer book, as a "hint" that time was of the essence. But it was to no avail; the Rav's prayers continued as before.

Finally, some congregants decided to take matters into their own hands. They chose a distinguished looking Jew, took him out to the soldiers, and told them that this was the rabbi they were looking for. The "rabbi" was taken to the prisoner, he assisted him with his *Vidui*, and accompanied him to the firing squad, where he was executed.

About an hour after the execution, a senior government official arrived at the army base, and when he heard of the decree that prescribed execution for AWOL soldiers, he became furious and ordered that the rule be rescinded immediately.

Following this incident, the Rav declared, "I could have finished my prayers much faster, of course. But it would have been forbidden for me to do so. The soldiers were waiting outside, and the execution was obviously being held up pending the Jewish soldier's *Vidui*. His life was dependent on my prayers; every minute of praying meant another minute of life for that unfortunate soldier. If the congregants had not acted with haste, the man's life would have been saved, for the government official would have rescinded the execution order before I arrived!"

לֹא־טוֹב הֱיוֹת הָאָדָם לְבַדּוֹ — *It is not good that man be alone* (2:18).

The Talmud, basing itself on this verse, asserts that "One who lives without a wife lives without *goodness*."

Some older *bachurim* (unmarried students) once asked Rav

Shach if there was a place in the prayers where they might concentrate on praying to God that they finally meet their proper wife. He responded that they should do so when reciting the words, "satiate us with Your *goodness*" in the Sabbath prayers.

עַל־כֵּן יַעֲזָב־אִישׁ אֶת־אָבִיו וְאֶת־אִמּוֹ — *Therefore a man shall leave his father and his mother* (2:24).

One of the *bachurim* in the yeshivah had chosen to follow the path of practicing "extra stringencies," especially in the area of *kashrus*. He would not eat nor drink anything anyone else gave him, unless he first inquired where it came from, under whose auspices it was declared kosher, etc. The *Rosh Yeshivah* respected the boy's wishes, and when Purim came around and the *bachurim* would visit his house, he poured some wine for everyone except this *bachur*, to avoid embarrassing him.

Eventually the time came for the *bachur* to get married. After his engagement, he came to inform the *Rosh Yeshivah* of the good news. Rav Shach was overjoyed to hear of the young man's *simchah*, and poured him a cup of wine, to drink a "*l'chayim*."

The fellow was puzzled. "The *Rosh Yeshivah* never used to offer me food or drink in the past. What has changed now, all of a sudden?"

"Now you are about to build your own home," answered the *Rosh Yeshivah* warmly. "You will have to develop a relationship with your fiance and deal with your future in-laws. I am trying to tell you that the time has come for you to become more moderate in your behavior!"

וַיֹּאמֶר הָאָדָם הָאִשָּׁה אֲשֶׁר נָתַתָּה עִמָּדִי הִוא נָתְנָה־לִּי מִן־הָעֵץ וָאֹכֵל — *The man said, "The woman whom You gave to be with me — she gave me of the tree, and I ate"* (3:12).

Rashi here cites the comment of the Gemara (*Avodah Zarah* 5a), that, by uttering these words with this attitude, Adam was guilty of ingratitude toward God Who had provided Adam with a wife for Adam's own benefit. Rav Shach often stressed the importance of recognizing one's debts of gratitude toward others, and served as a model for the trait of gratefulness in his own personal life.

R' Meir Heisler relates:

"One time the *Rosh Yeshivah* came into the *beis midrash* and nearly collapsed from exhaustion onto the first bench near the door. Concerned for his health, I ran over and asked him what had happened. 'Don't worry,' he told me. 'I'll be all right. I have just come from Givatayim, from a funeral.'

"Who was it who died?" I asked him.

" 'I'll tell you how I know this man, and then you will understand,' Rav Shach replied.

"He related how, during World War I, he used to sit in the *beis midrash* in Slutzk all day long. He had long since become separated from his parents, and was totally on his own, without any means of support. His clothes became worn out and ripped; his toes could be seen protruding from his torn shoes. 'The lack of food,' he recounted, 'I was able to endure. But when the cold, Russian winter nights arrived, they were simply unbearable. I used to sit on the bench and shiver uncontrollably. One night a local Jew happened to come in, and saw me freezing there. He went home and brought me an old coat, with which he covered me. From then on I was able to sleep at night!'

" 'Today,' he explained, 'was that man's funeral. He deserved that I should walk to attend his funeral; don't you agree?' "

וַיֹּאמֶר הָאָדָם הָאִשָּׁה אֲשֶׁר נָתַתָּה עִמָּדִי הִוא נָתְנָה־לִּי מִן־הָעֵץ וָאֹכֵל — *The man said, "The woman whom You gave to be with me — she gave me of the tree, and I ate"* (3:12).

*T*he Netziv notes that, in this phrase, Adam combines an excuse with a confession. "The woman gave me of the tree" constitutes an excuse. "I ate" is a confession of guilt. The same combination of themes may be seen in the words of the woman, who said, "The serpent deceived me (*excuse*) and I ate (*confession*)." Similarly, Shaul said, "I have sinned, for I have transgressed the word of Hashem and your word (*confession*), for I feared the people and I listened to their voice (*excuse*)" (*I Shmuel* 15:24).

So, too, on Judgment Day in the Next World, commented Rav Shach, we will realize that all of our excuses and rationalizations are worthless, and they will be quickly followed with confessions of guilt. "Imagine this," he cited as an example. "A yeshivah *bachur* will come to Judgment and he will be asked about what he did during the months of Tishrei, Nisan, and Av (when there is no official yeshivah session). What will he answer? 'I didn't learn anything then, because it was vacation time!'?"

Rav Shach noted that the mishnah in *Avos* (3:1) does not say,

"Realize that you will one day give an accounting and reckoning for all your deeds," but, "Realize *before Whom* you will one day give an accounting." Giving an accounting is not so bad if one can present all sorts of excuses and mitigating factors. But because man's future judgment is to be administered by God Himself, such empty excuses will be worthless; only an honest admission of guilt and total surrender will be possible. It is *this* kind of accounting that truly instills fear!

כִּי־עָפָר אַתָּה וְאֶל־עָפָר תָּשׁוּב — *For you are dust and to dust shall you return* (3:19).

The commentary *Yaaros Devash* asserts that the "punishment" God decreed upon Adam — that he would be subject to death, to "returning to dust" — was actually for his own good. For it is only through the realization of one's own mortality that man finds the moral imperative to act properly and to show remorse for his sins. As the Talmud teaches, "In order for a person to conquer his *yetzer hara*, he should ponder the day of his death" (*Berachos* 5a). Mortality is thus, in a sense, the key to a better spiritual life.

When the *Rosh Yeshivah* was quite old, he told one of his closest confidants, "You should know that the Sages' advice to 'ponder the day of death' is something that barely escapes my mind at all these days. I live with it; I eat with it; I learn with it; and even right now, as I talk to you, I am thinking about it. The thought dwells with me constantly, without ceasing."

וְאֵלֶיךָ תְּשׁוּקָתוֹ — *Its desire is toward you* (4:7).

Rav Shach told of a man who was pious and learned, and who made a very nice living from his large fabrics business. His store was always packed with customers, most of them businessmen ordering huge amounts of material for retail sale. The man's worries in life were not about having enough money, but of a completely different nature. He was distressed that he did not spend enough time on Torah study. He devoted nearly all his free time to learning — but this "free time" was such a rare commodity in his busy schedule!

After marrying off the last of his children, he called over the members of his family and told them, "Until now I have worked and toiled so that you should have good lives. Now it is time for me to devote some of my life to my own needs!" He announced that he was retiring, and handing over the business to his sons. The next day he headed for the *beis midrash* and made that the new focal point of his life, supporting himself with his ample savings and investments.

The new owners of the business — as is common when the young generation takes over from the old — were long on ideas but short on experience. They remodeled the entire store, added staff, brought in different lines of merchandise — and stood by the cash registers eagerly waiting to count their money. But the clientele seemed to thin out, and soon the business was in danger of collapse.

The young men discussed the situation with their father, and asked him to share the secret of his success. What economic theories or practical advice could he share with them, after so many years of experience?

The father's advice, much to their surprise, was in a different direction altogether. "Tell me," he asked them. "What do you do when the business is slow, when there are no customers around?"

"We converse, we read the newspaper — things like that," came the reply.

"And when you close for the day, what do you do when you leave the store?"

"We go home, eat dinner, relax, go to sleep. What else should we do?"

The old man sighed. "I figured as much. When I ran the store, I used the slow moments between customers to say some *Tehillim*. When I closed the store I went straight to the *beis midrash* to participate in a *shiur*. The *yetzer hara* (the "forces of evil" personified) saw this, and did his best to bring me plenty of customers to keep me away from my study and prayers. But you waste your spare time and completely ignore your obligations to learn Torah. The *yetzer hara* therefore has no interest in keeping you occupied with business; he is perfectly happy to have you stand around with nothing to do!"

וַיֹּאמֶר קַיִן אֶל־הֶבֶל אָחִיו וַיְהִי בִּהְיוֹתָם בַּשָּׂדֶה וַיָּקָם קַיִן אֶל־הֶבֶל אָחִיו וַיַּהַרְגֵהוּ — *Kayin spoke with his brother Hevel. And it happened when they were in the field, that Kayin rose up against his brother Hevel and killed him (4:8).*

One time there was a sudden surge in the number of students studying at the Ponevezh Yeshivah. The crowding in the *beis midrash* was becoming quite uncomfortable, and many of the newcomers had to settle for seats outside the study hall altogether — in various side-rooms, corridors, and the like. The suggestion was made that some new benches be added to the *beis midrash* to accommodate the new arrivals. The veteran students, however, objected, noting that the additional benches would further crowd the already barely-traversable aisles.

That week Rav Shach alluded to the conflict in his address to the yeshivah:

"The Sages ask (*Midrash Rabbah* ad loc.) regarding our verse (*Kayin spoke with* [lit., *said to*] *his brother Hevel*): 'What is it that Kayin said to Hevel?' One opinion states that the two brothers decided to divide the goods of the world between them — the only two men on earth aside from their parents, at the time. They decided that Hevel would own all the movable property in the world, while Kayin would have ownership of all its real property. Suddenly an argument ensued. Hevel said, 'Your clothes belong to me! Take them off!' Kayin countered, 'The ground you are standing on is mine! Start flying!' The quarrel became heated, until 'Kayin rose up against his brother Hevel and killed him.' According to another view in the Midrash, the brothers split both the land and the movable property of the world evenly between them. What they were arguing about was a different issue altogether: Each one wanted the future Temple of God to be built on *his* portion of land, and not on his brother's.

"It is a known rule that when it comes to Midrashic explanations of verses, varying opinions are not necessarily mutually exclusive. It is quite possible, then, that the Midrash means to say that the deadly argument between the two brothers was over *both* issues — the terms of the material division of property and the desire to be the home to God's Sanctuary.

"Students of the yeshivah! You are presently involved in an argument over the right to use the *beis midrash*. Each group desires to assert its right to a piece of holy ground in which to study the Torah. But the sad truth is that an argument that begins as a dispute over sacred ground can easily degenerate to the point where one group rejects the other totally, telling them, 'You are on my ground. Start flying!' Now, who among you is willing to play the role of a Kayin?"

After that address, the conflict suddenly eased, and a peaceful, amicable solution was found.

נח — Noach

קֵץ כָּל־בָּשָׂר בָּא לְפָנַי כִּי־מָלְאָה הָאָרֶץ חָמָס מִפְּנֵיהֶם — *The end of all flesh has come before Me, for the earth is filled with robbery through them (6:13).*

*T*he Gemara derives from this verse that although the people at the time of the Flood were guilty of many sins (see 6:1-12), it was specifically the sin of stealing that sealed their fate.

Rav Shach related the following story that he heard from the Brisker Rav.

The Rav was once staying in a health spa in Europe. There were several other Torah scholars and *roshei yeshivah* there at the time. As he passed by a group of distinguished men engaged in a Torah discussion, he overheard one of them asserting that the seriousness of committing an act of theft is not dependent on the amount stolen. Whether a person steals a penny or a thousand dollars, he has committed the same sin — stealing. A single act is a single sin; the amount involved is irrelevant.

R' Yitzchak Zev interrupted the discussion to disagree with this assertion. When one steals a single *perutah* (the basic, smallest unit of money in halachah), he commits a single act of theft; when he steals a hundred *perutahs* he transgresses the sin of theft a hundred times. It is comparable, he explained, to a case in which a person eats a hundred *kezeisim* (the basic halachic unit for foodstuffs) of a forbidden food. This person has committed a hundred sins, not one — even if he eats the hundred *kezeisim* at one time.

The scholar who had been corrected then posed a question to the Brisker Rav: Would this fact hold true for a non-Jew as well? Would he also be liable for a hundred acts of theft if he stole a hundred *perutahs* at one time?

The Rav answered that the concept of "minimum amounts" (שיעורין) does not exist in the laws as they apply to non-Jews. The seven kinds of transgressions that apply to them are defined in terms of action, not amount. Thus, for them, any single act of theft, whether it involved a large amount of money or a penny, would indeed be the same.

וּמִן־הַבְּהֵמָה אֲשֶׁר אֵינֶנָּה טְהֹרָה — *And of the animal that is not clean* (7:8).

*T*he usual word used to describe such unclean animals is טמא (*contaminated*). In our verse, however, the Torah uses a circumlocution to avoid this word, describing it instead as an animal "that is not clean." The reason for this, the Talmud (*Pesachim* 3a) explains, is to teach us that one should avoid uttering an expression that is even mildly indelicate or offensive, even if this involves going to the trouble of saying extra words.

Rav Shach recounted that he was once visited by a couple whose daughter had reached the age of *shidduchim* (marriage arrangements), and who sought the *Rosh Yeshivah's* opinion of a certain *bachur* whose name had come up as a prospective match for the girl. The boy learned in the Ponevezh Yeshivah, so it seemed that Rav Shach was the man to ask about him.

"I don't really know the boy, but I'll find out about him for you," he told them.

He asked the appropriate "sources" for information on the *bachur*, and he found out that he had once had a nervous breakdown, and was even hospitalized in a psychiatric ward for a short time.

The next day, when the couple came back to hear the results of Rav Shach's research, he told them, "You know, I think that boy is too young for your daughter! I think it best that you just forget about him!"

But the couple began to argue with the *Rosh Yeshivah,* countering that they believed he was in fact old enough, that age wasn't an important consideration for them, etc.

"What should I do when people don't understand the deeper meaning that lies behind what I am saying to them?" Rav Shach hinted to them.

The hint was taken, and the subject was dropped.

R' Aharon Yeshayah Rotter, a close student of Rav Shach, relates a similar story:

"One time I asked the *Rosh Yeshivah* what he thought of a certain *bachur* in the yeshivah for my own daughter. He replied, 'You know, this is the most difficult question you have ever asked me in all the years that I know you!'

"I understood immediately what he meant to tell me!"

וְיוֹם וָלַיְלָה לֹא יִשְׁבֹּתוּ — *And day and night shall not cease* (8:22).

Rav Shach recounted:

"One time the Chofetz Chaim was walking with another man, speaking with him about matters of faith. He explained to him how it is important for one to look at all matters in the world through the prism of the Torah.

"At one point in the conversation the man asked him, 'How does the Rabbi know this?'

"'How do I know this?!' repeated the Chofetz Chaim. 'Well, how does anyone know anything? Look, now it's daytime; how do you now that in another few hours it will be dark? Just because yesterday and the day before it got dark at the end of the day, this does not prove that the same will happen today! The only true proof we have is the fact that it says in the Torah, "Day and night shall not cease." If not for that, there is no certainty about anything! The Torah is the only source of absolute truth that exists!'"

לך לך — Lech Lecha

וַיֵּלֶךְ לְמַסָּעָיו — *He proceeded on his journeys* (13:3).

On these words, which can also be translated, "He went back along his route," Rashi comments that Avraham returned from Egypt to Canaan along the same route he had taken while traveling *to* Egypt, and he stayed at the same inns along the way. The Torah here teaches us a lesson in proper behavior. Rashi concludes: A person should continue patronizing establishments he has already frequented, and not turn to a competitor without a good reason.

One time Rav Shach suffered from an ailment that required very painful treatments in the hospital. After undergoing the therapy, however, Rav Shach's illness remained. Some people suggested to him that he see a different doctor, who was considered a bigger expert in the field. But the *Rosh Yeshivah* refused to abandon the first doctor, although his illness was causing him great discomfort — all because of his concern that the first doctor might be offended!

הֵן לִי לֹא נָתַתָּה זָרַע — *See, to me You have given no offspring* (15:3).

How could Avraham complain about his childlessness? Did God not promise him previously, "I will make your offspring as the dust of the earth" (13:16)? Did Avraham doubt God's word?! *Ohr HaChaim* explains that certainly Avraham remembered and respected God's promise to him. However, the simile used in that pledge — "as the dust of the earth" — led him to believe that his descendants would be lowly, base people, with little or no spiritual merit. After all, in Hebrew the expression "people of the earth" (עם הארץ, *am ha'aretz*) is used to denote people of low spiritual and intellectual standing. The thought of being "blessed" with a multitude of children of this caliber was most upsetting to the righteous patriarch. This is why he complained, "To *me* You have given no offspring" — that is, *to my satisfaction*. Therefore, God reaffirmed His commitment to Avraham using a more lofty implication: "Like the *stars*" (below, v. 15:5).

Rav Shach used to say that when a yeshivah student feels "pressure" from the *yetzer hara* to waste time with idle conversation, unnecessary trips, unimportant errands, etc., there is no better incentive to overcome this *yetzer hara* and get back to learning, than to contemplate the ultimate result of such *battalah* (time wasting). By wasting time he will end up being an *am ha'aretz*!

The Sages teach us that the most powerful tool to overcome an urge to sin is the fear of the ultimate punishment that will come in the wake of that sin. And there is no worse fate in life than remaining an *am ha'aretz*!

Rav Shach related that, when he was a youngster in Slobodka, the Alter (Rav Nosson Tzvi Finkel) used to urge the *bachurim* to study diligently by warning them, "If you don't learn, you will be *amei ha'aretz*!" The clear implication of this threat was that the fate of *am aratzus* was one of the worst things that could happen to a person in his life! Whoever heard the Alter of Slobodka intone the admonition, "You'll be an *am ha'aretz*!" did not need to attend a *mussar* lecture to have his soul stirred!

וירא — Vayeira

וְהוּא יֹשֵׁב פֶּתַח־הָאֹהֶל כְּחֹם הַיּוֹם — *While he was sitting at the entrance of the tent in the heat of the day* (18:1).

Avraham's hospitality, even in the face of tremendous personal suffering, is astounding. Nothing — his physical discomfort in recuperating from circumcision, the searing desert heat, his advanced age, etc. — could restrain his desire to seek out people in need of help, upon whom he could bestow his beneficence.

Shortly before the death of Rav Shach's wife, she was very ill, and the *Rosh Yeshivah* was totally preoccupied with attending to her needs. A certain *avrech* came to ask his advice as to whether to accept a position teaching Torah in a yeshivah in France. The *Rosh Yeshivah* told him he would look into the matter and give him an answer as soon as possible.

A few days later the Rebbetzin passed away. The *Rosh Yeshivah* was totally distraught, to the point that he had to be given sedatives to calm him.

The *avrech* who had asked about the position in France was among the throngs who came to pay condolence visits at the *shivah*. When the *Rosh Yeshivah* saw him, he told him, "I checked it out! That is a perfect opportunity for you. They really need *avrechim* like you over there! Go, and may you have much success!"

"When did the *Rosh Yeshivah* have a chance to find out this information?" asked the astonished *avrech*.

"Well," Rav Shach explained, "at the funeral I saw one of the *roshei yeshivah* from that institution. I asked him about it. His answers persuaded me that this is the right thing for you."

וְהוּא יֹשֵׁב פֶּתַח־הָאֹהֶל כְּחֹם הַיּוֹם — *While he was sitting at the entrance of the tent in the heat of the day* (18:1).

*A*s Rashi comments, God deliberately "removed the sun from its sheath," making the weather so hot that there would be no wayfarers to disturb Avraham's rest, as he was recuperating from his circumcision. The "plan" did not work, however, for, when the Patriarch saw that the usual travelers were not passing by, he went out to search for them in the scorching sun!

The administrator of one *cheder* relates that during his school's first few years it was desperately short on funds, and its very existence and continued operation were constantly precarious. When Rav Shach found out about this problem, he saw to it that funds were raised for the school. Every month, on the seventeenth of the month, he would personally deliver a check to the *cheder*, enabling them to cover the month's payroll.

"On the seventeenth of Tammuz (a fast day which occurs during the summer), the weather was unbearably hot, even by Bnei Brak summer standards. There was a heat wave the likes of which few people could remember. I was sure that Rav Shach would wait until the following day, for I considered making such a trip in that heat on a fast day to be beyond the realm of possibility. How surprised I was, then, when I heard a knock at the door in the afternoon, and found Rav Shach there, panting from the strain of his arduous walk, reddened by the burning sun, with the usual monthly envelope — right on time!"

אַל־נָא תַעֲבֹר מֵעַל עַבְדֶּךָ — *Please pass not away from Your servant* (18:3).

*A*ccording to one explanation given by Rashi, Avraham is speaking to God in this verse, asking Him to interrupt His Divine communication so that he might attend to his visitors. The Gemara (*Shabbos* 127a) derives from Avraham's conduct that "Receiving guests is greater than meeting with the *Shechinah* (God's Presence)." How much greater it is, then, when a person can do both things at once — entertain guests and communicate with the *Shechinah*!

R' Yosef Fink, who was a neighbor of Rav Shach's in Jerusalem's Ein Kerem neighborhood during the 1948 Arab-Israeli war, relates:

"When Jerusalem was besieged, Rav Shach's apartment was considered relatively safe, for, unlike others, its roof was not made of rafters and shingles, but had a second story built on top of it. Whenever shelling started in the area, many of the neighbors came and crowded into Rav Shach's small apartment. He welcomed everyone warmly. When nighttime came, he even gave up his bed for others, and would stay up all night in the corner of the room, absorbed in his learning, until it was time for morning prayers!"

יֻקַּח־נָא מְעַט־מַיִם — *Let some water be brought* (18:4).

A student once came to see Rav Shach, seeking the Rabbi's advice and blessing for an upcoming important interview in Jerusalem. When the *Rosh Yeshivah* saw him come in, he noticed that he was limping. The student dismissed the ailment. "It's nothing," he reassured the Rav. "Just an ingrown toenail."

"You know," the *Rosh Yeshivah* told him, "my rebbetzin is a registered nurse. She knows how to treat such things! Sit down on the sofa and take off your shoe. She'll be right here!"

The student did as he was told, and sat down waiting for the Rebbetzin to come in.

A few moments later, the *Rosh Yeshivah* himself entered the salon with a basin of warm water for the visitor, in which to soak his feet!

כִּי־עַל־כֵּן עֲבַרְתֶּם עַל־עַבְדְּכֶם — *Inasmuch as you have passed your servant's way* (18:5).

The Ramban explains Avraham's statement: "Since you are passing by, it would not be proper if you did not rest a bit at my place."

R' Eliyahu Mann relates that one year Rav Shach announced that the weekly Tuesday *shiur* would not be given during Chanukah. But then, suddenly, a few minutes before the usual time for the *shiur*, word was circulated among the students that it would, after all, take place. It was quite a shock, for everyone was well aware of the inordinate effort and time that Rav Shach invested throughout the week into his *shiur* preparation, making an impromptu delivery all but impossible. "Most of my days are 'the day before Tuesday,'" the *Rosh Yeshivah* used to quip. How — and why — would he decide to deliver a *shiur* on such short notice?

It was not long before the *bachurim* discovered the reason for the abrupt change in plans. There was a certain man who would travel in from Tel Aviv every Tuesday to attend Rav Shach's *shiur*, both out of respect for the *Rosh Yeshivah* and to partake of the Sage's Torah erudition. When Rav Shach saw that this man had taken the trouble to make the trip from Tel Aviv, he decided that he must deliver the *shiur* on schedule, despite his lack of preparation, rather than allow the man to turn back disappointed and empty-handed!

וַיִּקַּח חֶמְאָה וְחָלָב וּבֶן־הַבָּקָר אֲשֶׁר עָשָׂה וַיִּתֵּן לִפְנֵיהֶם — *He took cream and milk and the calf which he had prepared, and placed these before them* (18:8).

R' Zvi Wolf relates:

"One time, I saw the *Rosh Yeshivah* taking some food from the yeshivah kitchen to bring home for his wife, who was ill. I approached him and asked if I could carry the pot for him.

"He refused, however. 'If you would see me carrying my *lulav* and *esrog* on Sukkos, would you also ask to take them away from me and carry them? Of course not! My wife is sick, and I am now seeing to it that she gets the food she needs. Why should I let you take away this mitzvah from me?'"

וְנָשָׂאתִי לְכָל־הַמָּקוֹם בַּעֲבוּרָם — *I would spare the entire place on their account* (18:26).

Rav Shach recounted this story told about R' Yoel Sirkes (known as "the *Bach*," an acronym for his best-known work, *Bayis Chadash*, a commentary on the *Tur*):

While serving as rabbi of Belz (Galicia, Poland), some people in town gathered testimony from witnesses who testified that, in the dark of night, there was no light to be seen through the windows of the Bach's house, indicating that he did not spend his nights immersed in Torah study. Based on this testimony, he was dismissed from his position as Rav. The Bach himself did not suffer much from the incident, for he immediately moved on to the rabbinate of Cracow, a much more prestigious post. The town of Belz, however, subsequently suffered tremendous tragedies — a punishment from Heaven for their shockingly disrespectful treatment of one of the day's greatest Torah giants.

What was the real reason for the darkness in the Bach's house at night? The explanation lay in the fact that the *Kehillah* (Jewish community council) skimped so much on the rabbi's salary that he simply had no money available to buy candles! This did not, in fact, prevent him from Torah learning, however, for the great scholar was perfectly capable of reviewing and studying the Talmud and other texts from memory.

The behavior of the Belz community seems quite strange. A rabbi is supposed to teach Torah, render halachic opinions and decisions, adjudicate disputes, serve as spiritual leader of the community, etc. Why did the townsfolk consider the Bach's supposed lack of diligence in his private learning as grounds for his dismissal?

The people of Belz apparently took their cue from a statement of the Sages (*Sanhedrin* 99b), who derived from our verse that the Torah study of local scholars supplies a source of merit and protection for all the people in their city. Therefore, they regarded as one of the chief duties of the rabbi to provide them with this protection, and to be engrossed in Torah study day and night.

In those days, Rav Shach noted, the function of the town rabbi was somewhat different from what it is today. The organizational work of the community was completely handled by the *parnasim* (influential, wealthy members of the community) through the *Kehillah*. The major halachic decisions were rendered by the *dayan* (rabbinical judge). The rabbi's main job, then, was to serve as overall spiritual leader and to excel in his scholarly studies. Nowadays, however, all the responsibilities of the community fall on the rabbi's shoulders, and he has many more obligations to bear. As the Gemara tells us, "When there is a rabbinical student in a town, all the town's [religious] affairs are his responsibility!" (*Moed Katan* 6a).

וְנָשָׂאתִי לְכָל-הַמָּקוֹם בַּעֲבוּרָם — *I would spare the entire place on their account* (18:26).

*M*y father (R' Meir Zvi Bergman) once heard the following story:

The great Talmud scholar R' Moshe Soloveitchik (d. 1941) was once being considered as a candidate for the rabbinate in Bialystok (Lithuania). A delegation was sent by the town to Brisk, to seek the advice of R' Chaim Brisker about the matter. They knew that, although R' Chaim was R' Moshe's father, he would give them a completely unbiased opinion as to the latter's suitability for the position.

R' Chaim was enthusiastic about the idea. "You will be most fortunate to have him as your rabbi. Why, just last night I heard from him an absolutely brilliant resolution to a most difficult Rambam!"

One of the Bialystok *parnasim* then spoke up. "I have two problems with that assessment, Rabbi. Firstly, what will the people of Bialystok gain from R' Moshe's tremendous erudition in resolving difficult Rambams? Secondly, why does he need to become rabbi of our town for this kind of activity? He can interpret the Rambam right here in Brisk!"

The others of the delegation chuckled at the man's objection which, they thought, was a valid point, though expressed somewhat irreverently. R' Chaim, however, was not amused. "Gentlemen," he scolded them, "you are amusing yourselves with words of outright heresy!" The men were taken aback, as R' Chaim continued: "Do you think that R' Chaim Brisker, one of the leading Jewish scholars, is not aware of the point this man has made? Nevertheless, this *parnas* has revealed his ignorance, as he seems to be unaware of the Sages' teaching in the Talmud."

R' Chaim took a Gemara off the shelf, opened up to *Sanhedrin* 99b, and read to his visitors: "What is an example of an *apikoros* (heretic)? Someone who says, 'Of what benefit are the rabbis to us? Their study of the Torah and the Mishnah avails only themselves!' R' Nachman noted that this concept can be derived from the Torah, which says, '[If I find fifty righteous people in the midst of the city,] then I would spare the entire place on their account.' "

"So you see," continued R' Chaim, "the level of scholarship of the rabbi — or any other Torah scholar — in a town is, in fact, a major consideration for the people who live there. This is clearly stated in the Talmud, and derived from a Biblical verse!" he concluded, as the *parnas* who had spoken up hid his face in shame.

וְאֶת־הָאֲנָשִׁים אֲשֶׁר־פֶּתַח הַבַּיִת הִכּוּ בַּסַּנְוֵרִים — *And the men who were at the entrance of the house they struck with blindness* (19:11).

*I*n Rav Shach's younger years when he was engaged in full-time study in the yeshivahs of Europe, his wife supported the family with her earnings from her profession as a pharmacist. Because of her work, the Shach home always had on hand supplies of various medical ointments, pills, and the like for sale and emergency dispensation.

When the Communists took over their city, one of their first priorities was the absolute prohibition of any private enterprise. Anyone caught engaging in any sort of commerce was arrested for subversion of the state economy, and was regarded as an enemy of the Revolution. Such charges were treated with the utmost severity; if someone found himself "only" exiled to Siberia after such an arrest he would consider himself quite fortunate!

"One day," Rav Shach related, "the police burst into our house to search for 'contraband.' Bottles and containers of medicine were lying all over, in plain view. When they came in, I was in the living room, sitting at the table near the door, engrossed in my learning. They took one look at this rabbi, surrounded by his numerous books, and 'realized' they had nothing to look for in this house. They didn't even bother looking around the room, which was filled with 'forbidden items.' Or perhaps they did look, but were smitten by mysterious Divine blindness! In any event, they just turned around and left — with an apology, no less!"

לֹא אוּכַל לְהִמָּלֵט הָהָרָה פֶּן־תִּדְבָּקַנִי הָרָעָה וָמַתִּי — *I cannot escape to the mountain lest the evil attach itself to me and I die* (19:19).

Rav Shach related that when R' Meir Simchah HaKohen of Dvinsk (the *"Ohr Same'ach"*) took ill toward the end of his life, R' Elchanan Wasserman, who was by his bedside, suggested that telegrams be sent out to all the yeshivahs and shuls to pray for the Sage's recovery. R' Meir Simchah rejected the idea, however, arguing that he did not wish to be distinguished from the general population in such a manner, for this would only lead to him being held to a higher standard by the Heavenly Court in its decision on his fate. If a person receives preferential consideration in prayer, he is expected to lead his life in a correspondingly outstanding manner!

Rav Shach noted that this idea is echoed in Rashi's comment on our verse. Lot, when he was delivered out of Sodom just before its destruction, asked that he not be forced to go "to the mountain," where Avraham lived. He knew that as long as he was considered "just another one of the Sodomites" he would be judged righteous and deserving of God's protection. However, if he would remove himself from this category and place himself next to the incomparably greater Avraham, he knew he didn't have a chance to survive. Similarly, Rashi continues, the Tzarfatite woman for whom Elisha, as a sign of gratitude, wanted to offer a special prayer, protested, saying, "I dwell among my people" (*II Melachim* 4:13). As long as she was counted "among her people" she felt that she would be judged favorably; singled out in Elisha's prayers, however, she was afraid she would not be so fortunate.

רַק אֵין־יִרְאַת אֱלֹהִים בַּמָּקוֹם הַזֶּה וַהֲרָגוּנִי — *Only there is no fear of God in this place (Gerar), and they will slay me* (20:11).

The word רַק (*only*) implies that this was Gerar's sole shortcoming. Everything else was available there — culture, civility, knowledge, etc. But if "fear of God" is lacking, all these assets are useless: "They will slay me because of my wife."

Rav Shach once observed: "Where is the greatest concentration of educated men to be found? In the university, of course! And who are the most educated and refined of all those in this academic community? Those who have doctorates, of course! And within this group of Ph.D.s, the most accomplished men are the professors. But you have no idea how base some of these people — the crown of the academic world — really are. A professor once examined my grandson who had taken ill, and issued his instructions. I wanted to ask him a question, but he snapped, 'Silence! The professor is speaking!'

"This is an illustration of the Sages' remark that 'Any mouth through which Torah does not pass is not capable of speaking with proper respect.' "

Rav Shach related further that when his wife had to have her foot amputated because of a complication of her diabetes, she suffered tremendous pain after the operation. The surgeon was not present at the time, and another professor took an interest in her plight, prescribing a simple pain killer to be added to her medications. The next day, when the attending surgeon saw that his colleague had added a medication without his permission, he became furious. "If he expresses his opinion in this case again, I will remove myself from continuing to treat the patient!"

וַיַּעַשׂ אַבְרָהָם מִשְׁתֶּה גָדוֹל בְּיוֹם הִגָּמֵל אֶת־יִצְחָק — *Avraham made a great feast on the day Yitzchak was weaned* (21:8).

In *Pirkei d'Rabbi Eliezer*, the word הִגָּמֵל (*weaned*) is interpreted as an abbreviation for ה״ג מל (*he circumcised on the eighth day*). In other words, according to this Midrash Avraham's feast was not held in honor of Yitzchak's weaning, but in honor of his circumcision. This is the source for making a festive meal upon the occasion of a circumcision. Nevertheless, the Gemara (*Eruvin* 40b) teaches that the words "joy is in His Abode" are not added to the *bentching* (Grace after the meal) — as they are at wedding celebrations — out of consideration for the pain suffered by the circumcised child himself. Similarly, *Tosafos* (*Kesubos* 8a) writes that the joyful *Shehecheyanu* blessing is not recited at a circumcision feast, for the same reason.

One time Rav Shach attended the circumcision of the child of a close student, R' Yechezkel Is'chayak. He did not, however, participate in the dancing that took place on that occasion. "Why isn't the *Rosh Yeshivah* dancing?" asked R' Yechezkel. "This is my family *simchah*, a joyous occasion!"

"Yes, indeed it is," answered Rav Shach. "But just today an *avrech* came over to me and tearfully informed me that the doctors have determined, with certainty, that he and his wife will never be able to have children of their own. So how can I dance now?"

וַתֵּרֶא שָׂרָה אֶת־בֶּן־הָגָר הַמִּצְרִית אֲשֶׁר־יָלְדָה לְאַבְרָהָם מְצַחֵק
— *Sarah saw the son of Hagar, the Egyptian...
playing* (21:9).

*A*ccording to Ibn Ezra, Yishmael was simply "playing" like any other normal child.

R' Avraham Yitzchak Kook was once speaking to Rav Shach about maximizing the time potential for Torah learning among *cheder* children. "We have '*Masmidim* clubs' for after-hours learning on Friday afternoon and Shabbos, '*Mishnayos* clubs,' which encourage the children to learn and memorize *Mishnayos* in their spare time, etc.," he told him, beaming with pride.

"But a child needs to play!" demurred Rav Shach.

Surprised by the *Rosh Yeshivah's* lukewarm reaction to these programs, R' Kook objected; "But we always heard from our elders how the schoolchildren used to study from early morning until late at night. In *Shulchan Aruch* (*Y.D.* 245:11) we are told that children should be taught all day and even part of the night, to train them in the precept of studying Torah 'day and night,' and that they should not have any breaks at all except for late in the day on *erev Shabbos* and *erev Yom Tov*!"

"Tell me," responded Rav Shach. "According to your literal under-standing of the *Shulchan Aruch*, when are the children supposed to eat, if they are learning all day long?"

"Well," he answered, "I suppose it means that these hours of learning are *besides* the times for eating. The children must eat, of course, and the *Shulchan Aruch* did not need to mention it."

"Correct!" declared the *Rosh Yeshivah.* "And, by the same token, it means that these hours are besides the times for playing — for children must 'of course' play, just as they must eat! In times past, the

Jew's poverty was so great, while his spiritual Torah heritage was so rich, that the focus of his life was the *beis midrash*. The children also felt this centrality of Torah, and competed with one another in excellence in learning. It was a kind of amusement for them. Nowadays, however, when children do not find learning so entertaining, they must play real games, and it is necessary to allow time for this!

" 'The wise man has eyes in his head,' " (*Koheles* 2:14) concluded Rav Shach. "It is always a good thing to try to raise one's son so that he finds his enjoyment and amusement in learning Torah. However, whether this is the case or not, a child needs to play!"

וַיַּשְׁכֵּם אַבְרָהָם בַּבֹּקֶר וַיַּחֲבֹשׁ אֶת־חֲמֹרוֹ — *Avraham arose early in the morning and saddled his donkey* (22:3).

He hastened to fulfill the commandment as soon as it was possible (*Rashi*).

One time, an acquaintance of Rav Shach from Petach Tikvah came to consult with him regarding a certain *shidduch* (marriage proposal) that had been suggested for his son. The *Rosh Yeshivah* told him that he would find out some information, and clarify a few points about the person involved, before giving an answer.

The man returned to Petach Tikvah, and Rav Shach set himself to the task. That evening, he got the information he was seeking and as soon as the buses started running in the morning, he traveled to Petach Tikvah — a trip that involved taking two buses. Since it was still early in the morning when he arrived, and the *Rosh Yeshivah* did not want to disturb his acquaintance, he wrote down his answer, put it in the man's mailbox, and headed back to Bnei Brak. By 7 o'clock he was in the yeshivah for morning prayers!

חיי שרה — CHAYEI SARAH

תְּנוּ לִי אֲחֻזַּת־קֶבֶר עִמָּכֶם וְאֶקְבְּרָה מֵתִי מִלְּפָנָי — *Grant me an estate for a burial site with you, that I may bury my dead from before me* (23:4).

"Our Torah is a living Torah," Rav Shach remarked, "with practical lessons for us in every situation arising in life. The Midrash, for instance, tells us that when Rebbi prepared himself for a meeting with Roman officials, he would review the story of the encounter between Yaakov and Esav (the progenitor of the Romans) described in *Vayishlach*, and take his inspiration from that passage.

"Similarly, we can learn several lessons from the way Avraham set out to purchase the Machpelah Cave for Sarah's burial. At first he sought permission from the town's residents to be granted the right to bury his wife altogether (v. 4). Next he requested of the townsmen that they speak to Ephron and persuade him to agree to the sale of the Cave (v. 8). Seeing that he was reluctant to sell the Cave alone without the surrounding field (v. 11), Avraham offered to buy the field as well (v. 13). Then, as soon as he heard that the price for the field was 400 *shekels*, he immediately weighed out the specified sum, using the most acceptable and valuable type of currency (v. 16). He made sure to do this while the townsmen were still assembled, so that there should never be any possibility of appeal or denial of the sale. (This analysis of the story is based on Ralbag's commentary.) This careful, deliberate approach to a purchase provides us with valuable instruction for our own business dealings. There is nothing that is not alluded to in the Torah!

"The Chofetz Chaim was known to be an extremely wise person, with knowledge and insights in all walks of life. This is because, in every situation, he conducted himself according to the lessons provided to us by the Torah. The Torah was the source of all his wisdom!"

נָתַתִּי כֶּסֶף הַשָּׂדֶה קַח מִמֶּנִּי וְאֶקְבְּרָה אֶת־מֵתִי שָׁמָּה — *I give the price of the field, accept it from me, that I may bury my dead there* (23:13).

R' Aharon Kotler once sent Rav Shach — who was a *Rosh Mesivta* in his yeshivah in Kletzk — on an urgent mission to the Chofetz Chaim. A certain woman had died in America, and her family wanted to have her buried in *Eretz Yisrael* — an endeavor that cost a very considerable amount of money in those days. The woman's brother, however, suggested that it would be a greater source of merit for his departed sister's soul if she were buried locally and the amount of money saved would be donated to a yeshivah, to further Torah study in her memory. The family members said they would agree to the idea, but only if the foremost Sage of Israel — the Chofetz Chaim himself — would send them a message in writing, that it would indeed be preferable for them to do so. R' Aharon received a telegram about the case, and he hastened to bring the matter up before the Chofetz Chaim.

The Chofetz Chaim responded as follows: "It is true that Avraham paid 400 *shekel* — a huge sum — for Sarah's burial place, which shows the great importance attached to procuring the most fitting and honorable grave, especially in *Eretz Yisrael*. However, there is a rule that we cannot derive halachic conclusions from events described in the Torah that took place before the giving of the Torah at Mount Sinai. Ever since the Torah was given, it has been the truth that the learning of Torah is the highest priority for us. On the other hand, this woman's family obviously does not appreciate this ultimate importance of Torah learning, and is under the false impression that burial in *Eretz Yisrael* is of greater significance. This being the case, they will not listen to me even if I do tell them that their money is better spent in the support of Torah study. And, as the Sages teach, 'Just as it is obligatory to speak up when one's words will be heeded, so it is obligatory to remain silent when one's words will not be heeded' (*Yevamos* 65b)." The Chofetz Chaim therefore declined to send the desired message to America.

Rav Shach thereupon decided that he would seek the advice of the other towering rabbinic authority of the time — R' Chaim Ozer Grodzinsky, the leading rabbi of Vilna. R' Chaim Ozer acceded to his request, and handed him a letter to the effect that the Torah declares that supporting Torah study is of greater importance than burial in *Eretz Yisrael*.

The Chofetz Chaim's reservations, however, proved to be exactly on the mark. The woman's children ignored the letter from R' Chaim

Ozer, and insisted on having her body shipped to *Eretz Yisrael*.

Decades later, Rav Shach would refer to this incident when he wrote in the introduction to his *Avi Ezri*, "I heard it explicitly from the mouth of the Chofetz Chaim that the study of Torah and its support are the most important values we have."

— וַתְּמַהֵר וַתְּעַר כַּדָּהּ אֶל־הַשֹּׁקֶת וַתָּרָץ עוֹד אֶל־הַבְּאֵר לִשְׁאֹב

So she hurried and emptied her jug into the trough and ran again to the well to draw water (24:20).

R' Meir Heisler relates:

"There was once a *bachur* who came to learn in the yeshivah (Ponevezh) from Jerusalem. Toward the end of Elul, the *Rosh Yeshivah* noticed that the boy seemed gloomy and depressed. After keeping an eye on him for a few days, he called me over in the evening of *erev Rosh Hashanah* and said, 'You're from Jerusalem. You are surely familiar with the yeshivah where this *bachur* learned before he came to us. I would like you to arrange a meeting for me with the *rosh yeshivah* of that institution, so that I can inquire as to how this fellow acted when he was there. Perhaps I will get some details about his family background, personal difficulties, etc., that will help me to figure out what's bothering him and help him solve his problem.'

" 'When would the *Rosh Yeshivah* like to speak with him?' I asked, thinking that *Tzom Gedalyah* (the day after Rosh Hashanah) would be the earliest possible time.

"But Rav Shach answered, 'Tonight. I'll go tonight!'

" 'Tonight?' I asked incredulously. 'That's not practical. The man is probably going to say *Selichos* at night — it's *erev Rosh Hashanah*!'

" 'All right, then tomorrow!' he consented. 'Call him now and tell him that I am coming to Jerusalem tomorrow to talk with him. Not at his house — that would make it look too urgent, and might harm the boy's image. I will meet him in the *shtiblach* (a cluster of several small synagogues) in Meah Shearim.'

"Now, in those days traveling from Bnei Brak to Jerusalem was no simple matter. First one had to take a bus to Tel Aviv, then switch to a bus going to Jerusalem — on the old, winding road that was in use before the main highway was built. It was a trip of several hours. Spending several hours going and then coming back again on *erev Rosh Hashanah* seemed like an immensely inconvenient plan. 'What would happen if the *Rosh Yeshivah* postponed his visit until after the holiday?' I asked.

"Of course, nothing at all would happen. But when it came to going out and helping a *bachur*, the *Rosh Yeshivah* simply could not wait. It was against his nature!"

— וַתְּמַהֵר וַתְּעַר כַּדָּהּ אֶל־הַשֹּׁקֶת וַתָּרָץ עוֹד אֶל־הַבְּאֵר לִשְׁאֹב
So she hurried and emptied her jug into the trough and ran again to the well to draw water (24:20).

One time a businessman went to see Rav Shach with a halachic query — something relating to his business activities and Shabbos. The *Rosh Yeshivah* informed him that he was not in the practice of rendering halachic decisions.

"What about Rabbi So-and-so in Jerusalem?" he asked. "Does the *Rosh Yeshivah* think I can rely on him in this matter?"

Rav Shach answered that he thought that that rabbi was indeed reliable, but noted that he was quite busy with his own learning and with giving *shiurim*, and he would be difficult to reach. However, Rav Shach told the man that he would see to it that the rabbi would make time for him and address his question.

The *Rosh Yeshivah* immediately called for R' Yechezkel Is'chayak and asked him to arrange travel for him to Jerusalem the following day, so that he could speak to that rabbi. Rav Shach was quite old already, and his family and confidants pleaded with him not to undertake such a strenuous journey for this matter. Surely it could be arranged over the telephone! The *Rosh Yeshivah* would hear nothing of it, however, replying, "You know very well that you can't get anything done over the phone!"

The next day he set out for Jerusalem and met with that rabbi. He did not discuss any matters at all with him other than to request that the rabbi agree to see the businessman and deal with his question!

עֶבֶד אַבְרָהָם אָנֹכִי — *I am a servant of Avraham* (24:34).

Rav Shach's admiration for the *Mashgiach,* R' Yechezkel Levinstein, knew no bounds. "Our understanding of the term 'piety' goes as far as the *Mashgiach*," he used to say. "Beyond that it is impossible for us to imagine. He was the epitome of the 'true servant of God,' having subordinated his entire being to the service of Hashem."

"The *Mashgiach's* wisdom was immense," he would add. "And all of his wisdom was based on the Torah." The *Rosh Yeshivah* told the following story to illustrate his point:

"Many years ago I served as a *Rosh Mesivta* at the yeshivah in Kletzk, where R' Aharon Kotler was the *rosh yeshivah* and R' Yechezkel was the *mashgiach*. In those dire times R' Aharon considered moving the yeshivah to Volozhin, where the building of the famed — but then defunct — Volozhiner Yeshivah stood empty. He sent me to discuss the plan with the rabbis in whose hands the building and its rights were entrusted.

"The meeting was not successful, and the idea was rejected outright. I returned to Kletzk, and arrived just before Shabbos. I barely had time to wash up and get dressed for Shabbos, and headed immediately to the *Mashgiach's* house, where a weekly *mussar* discourse was given every Friday evening, at the onset of Shabbos. When I entered the house, the *Mashgiach's* lecture was well under way. As soon as he saw me come in he stopped short and said, mysteriously and seemingly apropos of nothing, 'I am a servant of Avraham!' I was puzzled, as were all those attending the speech.

"The *Mashgiach* continued. 'Reb Leizer (as Rav Shach was known to his family and friends — ed.) has just come back from performing a mission for the *Rosh Yeshivah*! Now I'll tell you what happened there in Volozhin. He went in and said, "I have come to discuss the possibility of moving the Kletzker Yeshivah to this place." They asked him, "Who are you? Are you the *rosh yeshivah* in Kletzk?" The answer R' Leizer gave, of course, was, "No." Then they asked, "Well, are you the *mashgiach* of the yeshivah?" To which he replied once again in the negative. "Well, who are you, then?" they asked. "I am a *ram* in the yeshivah; I teach the *bachurim* Gemara. The *Rosh Yeshivah* sent me to speak to you ..."

" 'Now, this is not the way things should be done,' continued the *Mashgiach*. 'From our *parashah* we see that another Eliezer introduced himself immediately to Rivkah's family as "the servant of Avraham." This is how we should present ourselves also — no hesitations, no irresolution. It is the greatest honor to say, "I am a *ram* in the yeshivah. I have been sent on a mission by my *rosh yeshivah*!" Such an introduction makes a favorable impression!

"'All right,' he concluded. 'Now you can ask him yourselves, and see if I did not describe his meeting accurately!'

"Everyone in the room was amazed at what the *Mashgiach* had said — but none more than I, who was aware that this is precisely what had taken place in Volozhin! But this was not an illustration of *ruach hakodesh* (Divine inspiration) on the part of the *Mashgiach*. Rather, this knowledge came from his Torah wisdom — and 'a wise man is on an even higher level than a prophet' (*Bava Basra* 12a). From his immense wisdom in analyzing the Torah and his unique understanding of human nature, he was able to figure out exactly what had transpired."

מֵיהֹוָה יָצָא הַדָּבָר — *The matter originated from Hashem!* (24:50).

This is one of the verses that proves that one's finding of a mate for marriage is ordained from Heaven (*Moed Katan* 18b).

There was once a fellow who was engaged to be married, and who was suffering from a bad case of "cold feet." He went to see the *Rosh Yeshivah* and told him that he wanted to break off his engagement. Rav Shach asked him for the details — what flaw had he suddenly noticed in his fiance or her family? From the boy's answers to these questions, the *Rosh Yeshivah* quickly assessed the situation.

"Don't break the engagement!" he exhorted him. "I can tell you for a fact that this girl is the one who has been designated for you by Heaven!"

The *bachur's* face lit up when he heard Rav Shach's endorsement, and he got up and left.

An acquaintance of Rav Shach who happened to be present during this encounter was surprised by what he had seen. "Doesn't the *Rosh Yeshivah* always speak out against rabbis and others who claim to know what has or has not been decreed in Heaven?" he asked.

The *Rosh Yeshivah* smiled and answered, "You're right about that! But don't you see what happened here? This *bachur* didn't really want to break the engagement. He simply wanted me to tell him authoritatively that he must not break it. So I told him!"

תֵּשֵׁב הַנַּעֲרָ אִתָּנוּ יָמִים אוֹ עָשׂוֹר — *Let the girl remain with us a year or ten months* (24:55).

The request for a year's time was based on the ancient custom that a girl marrying for the first time was given a year to prepare her clothing and adornments for the wedding (*Rashi*).

One time, a week before Pesach, a newly engaged couple came to see Rav Shach and asked him for his blessing. He blessed them heartily, and asked them when the wedding was to take place. They told him that it was scheduled for some four months later, after Tishah B'Av.

"After Tishah B'Av?" asked the Rosh Yeshivah, clearly surprised by this information. "Why are you putting it off for so long?"

"It's true that the Mishnah lays down the rule that for a first marriage a girl should be given twelve months to prepare herself," he said. "In more recent times, I remember that people used to wait several months. But there was a reason for that! Things weren't so easily available back then. They had to buy material and sew it together into a quilt, which they stuffed with feathers by hand. They bought material for a dress and took it to a seamstress to make into a garment. And don't think that there was one seamstress involved, either! There were seamstresses or tailors who specialized in sewing on collars, others that made the buttonholes, etc. They had to buy and prepare all the food for the wedding feast on their own. All this took time. Nowadays, however, thank God, everything is bought ready-made. Even the wedding party takes place in a rented hall, with the food prepared and served entirely by a caterer. There is no longer any reason to postpone a marriage for so long!"

תולדות — TOLDOS

וַיִּתְרֹצֲצוּ הַבָּנִים בְּקִרְבָּה — *The children agitated within her* (25:22).

An *avrech* from a certain city in Israel once came to Rav Shach and asked him advice concerning his young son who was about to begin school. In his town there were two institutions that were possible candidates for becoming the boy's school — a more *chareidi* Talmud Torah (*cheder*), and a school belonging to the well-established *Chinuch Atzma'i* system. The Talmud Torah was just getting under way, and its scholastic level and school discipline were no match for those of the veteran *Chinuch Atzma'i* school. On the other hand, the advantage of the *cheder* was that the children who attended it were exclusively from families in which the father devoted himself to learning or teaching Torah full time. The question this *avrech* presented to Rav Shach was: Which was the more important consideration — the level of learning and efficiency in a school, or the child's development of personal relationships with children who are brought up with purer Torah-true values?

The *Rosh Yeshivah* responded that a lower level of learning is a deficiency that can be overcome: The Talmud Torah would eventually become more established and raise its level; the child's learning could be supplemented with private lessons or other means, etc. But if a child develops unhealthy friendships, it is a situation that has no easy remedy, and can permanently hamper his overall spiritual development. A proof for this assertion, continued Rav Shach, is the story related in our verse. Rivkah's children "agitated within her." The Midrash explains this agitation as follows: Whenever Rivkah would pass a place of idolatry, Esav would begin to kick and try to "escape" from the womb, while when she would go by a *beis midrash*, Yaakov would try to push his way out. Now, elsewhere the Sages teach (*Niddah* 30b) that when a fetus is in its mother's womb it is taught the entire

Torah by an angel (but is forced to forget it upon its birth). We can readily understand why Esav would try to jump at every opportunity to escape such an "unpleasant" (for him) experience. But why should Yaakov try to flee from the womb? How could he possibly expect to learn more Torah in a *beis midrash* than what he was accomplishing with his personal, perpetual lessons with an angel?

"The answer," Rav Shach explained to the *avrech*, "is that Yaakov was faced with the same dilemma that you are experiencing — quality of learning vs. environment. While his level of learning could only decline by escaping from the womb, at least he would not have to suffer the company of Esav! By putting these two statements of the Sages together, we then emerge with a clear position on this issue: A healthy, spiritually positive setting is more vital than maintaining a superior level of learning.

וַיֶּאֱהַב יִצְחָק אֶת־עֵשָׂו — *Yitzchak loved Esav* (25:28).

*S*ifsei Kohen explains that Yitzchak was well aware of the unsavory aspects of Esav's conduct and personality, but he nevertheless showered him with warmth and love, so as not to alienate him even further.

A certain *rosh yeshivah* relates that one time he came across a *bachur* who suffered from extremely strict, demanding treatment from his parents. The *rosh yeshivah* discussed the matter with the parents, and they told him that this was their considered approach to bringing up children. He told them, "It's possible that you are correct in your method, and that this is indeed the best way to raise and educate children. But it is also possible that you are mistaken. Let us go and find out what Torah wisdom has to say on this matter!"

He and the parents went to see Rav Shach. This is what he told them:

"The Torah casts a dual role upon the parent — that of parent and that of educator. These two roles are somewhat contradictory; a parent exudes love and affection, while an educator, the Sages tell us, must 'inject the bitterness of fear into his students' (*Kesubos* 103b). 'The fear of one's rabbi (teacher) must be like his fear of Heaven' (*Avos* 4:12). Even within this dichotomy, however, the Sages tell us which of these two qualities should prevail: 'Let your left hand push away (a wayward child or student), but let your right hand draw him close.'"

The parents reflected on the *Rosh Yeshivah's* message. Then he continued, "This was the situation in Israel in ancient times, before R' Yehoshua ben Gamla, when it was a father's duty to teach the Torah to his children himself. But once that Sage introduced the institution of a school education for all children (*Bava Basra* 21a), the duty of imparting Torah knowledge was removed from the parents' shoulders and delegated to the *cheder* rebbi. The dual role, then, no longer exists; a parent's sole function in a child's upbringing is to lavish him with warmth and love. In the house, the child should experience mainly unhindered affection. Try to be broad-minded in supplying his needs and wishes whenever reasonable. Make sure he gets the food, clothing, and protection that he needs. As far as the educational aspect goes, however — leave that to the school. The *mashgiach* of his yeshivah will see to it that he receives the proper training in conduct and personal development.

"You must supply him with the warmth he needs at home," Rav Shach concluded, "or he is likely to go looking for it elsewhere!"

הַקֹּל קוֹל יַעֲקֹב — *The voice is Yaakov's voice* (27:22).

*T*he "voice of Yaakov" is seen by the Sages as a metaphor for the sound of Torah and prayer that emanates from *battei midrashos* and synagogues.

R' Yitzchak Silberstein, rabbi of Ramat Elchanan in Bnei Brak, and the founder and head of the Beis David institutions in Holon, sought Rav Shach's advice when he was first formulating the idea of Torah dissemination in that city, which is primarily populated by secular Jews whose interest in Torah knowledge was not exactly enthusiastic. He wanted to know whether he should build the yeshivah in the center of the city, or in a more secluded neighborhood on the outskirts of town. Rabbi Akiva, after all, cautioned his son, "Do not sit at the high spot of the city and teach Torah" (*Pesachim* 112a), and Rebbi forbade the teaching of Torah in public places (*Moed Katan* 16a). The advice the *Rosh Yeshivah* gave, however, was that in our day and age we must raise the banner of Torah high, in public, for all to see. "If the *kollel* has a building in the middle of town, where the lights stay on until late at night, and the sweet sound of Torah emanates from its walls, curious people will eventually wander in and become drawn to the Torah as a result," he explained.

Not long after the kollel started, a man who had long identified himself with *Hashomer Hatza'ir,* an extremely anti-religious youth movement, came into the *beis midrash* and inquired as to what was studied and taught there. One of the *avrechim* began to study with him on a regular basis, and the man eventually became a fully observant Jew and a regular member of the *kollel* study sessions. One day R'

Silberstein asked him how it was that he had made such a radical about-face in his lifestyle and religious attitude. From the answer he heard, he realized just how wise and prescient Rav Shach's advice had been.

"Back in 1948," the man related, "I was a member of the battalion that attacked and took over the police station at Beit Dagan, which was an Arab stronghold. The first two times we staged an attack we were repulsed, with heavy casualties. As we were about to begin our third assault, one of the soldiers, a religious fellow, suggested, 'Let's study some *Mishnayos* before we go, as a source of merit on our behalf. Perhaps it will help us to be successful this time.' He took out a book and began reading. Though we did not understand anything he was saying, the haunting, chanting melody captivated and moved us tremendously, and gave us courage. Later that night we took Beit Dagan. Ever since that day, fifty years ago, that seductive melody has laid deep in my mind. I often wondered if I would ever hear it again. One night, as I was passing by the *beis midrash*, I saw the lights burning, and turned my attention to the sounds coming out of the building. It was that same enchanting sing-song that I remembered from so long ago. I found myself being pulled into the building, as if drawn by a mysterious spell. One thing led to another — and that is how that night my life changed for good!"

וישצא — Vayeitzei

***

וַיִּקַּח מֵאַבְנֵי הַמָּקוֹם וַיָּשֶׂם מְרַאֲשֹׁתָיו — *He took from the stones of the place which he arranged around his head* (28:11).

The Midrash, noting that in v. 18 we are told that Yaakov had only *one* stone around his head, explains that the stones began to fight among each other, each one wishing to have the merit of supporting Yaakov's head. God rewarded them all for their desire to serve the righteous Patriarch, and turned them into one large stone, so that in effect Yaakov placed his head on all of them.

Rav Shach related a story that reflects the idea of this Midrash. When the great Torah scholar R' Mattisyahu Strashun passed away in Vilna, R' Yitzchak Elchanan Spektor of Kovno hired a carriage to take him to the funeral. The driver, a simple Jew, urged his horses on, crying, "Nu! Faster! Don't you realize that you are pulling the great Rabbi of Kovno in your carriage?"

וְכֹל אֲשֶׁר תִּתֶּן־לִי עַשֵּׂר אֲעַשְּׂרֶנּוּ לָךְ — *And whatever You will give me, I shall repeatedly tithe to You* (28:22).

The Gemara (*Kesubos* 50a) sees in this verse an allusion to the "Enactment of Usha," which decreed that no person should give away more than a fifth of his income to charity.

One time a wealthy philanthropist from abroad asked Rav Shach whether he, as one who had been exceptionally prosperous, might be permitted to break this law and donate more than 20 percent of his earnings to a yeshivah.

The *Rosh Yeshivah* answered that, in any case, the enactment applied only to "giving away money to charity." When one donates money toward Torah learning, however, he is not "giving it away," for he himself earns a share in the Torah study that was made possible through his grant. In the Next World he will be considered to have personally learned those portions of the Torah which he sponsored for others. Therefore, giving money to yeshivahs is a form of acquisition — a "business venture" (so to speak), rather than an outright gift. The ceiling of 20 percent called for by the Enactment of Usha would thus not apply to this situation.

וַיֹּאמְרוּ שָׁלוֹם וְהִנֵּה רָחֵל בִּתּוֹ בָּאָה עִם־הַצֹּאן — *They answered, "He is well; and here comes his daughter Rachel with the sheep"* (29:6).

*T*he Sages teach that one of the characteristics of a wise person is that he does not venture to provide information about things he does not know. "When asked about that which he does not know, he admits, 'I have not heard [that information]' " (*Avos* 5:7). The Biblical source for this trait, writes the commentator R' Ovadiah Bertinora, is from our verse. The people of Charan, when questioned about Lavan and his situation, answered, *"He is well."* That's all we know. If you want more information, we can't help you; but *"here comes his daughter with the sheep."* She can tell you whatever you need to know!

Rav Shach exemplified this quality in his dealings with all people. When he was asked a question about many a topic, he would answer, "I must look into the matter. Come back tomorrow." If the inquiry pertained to matters of education, he would consult with experts or with men with the most experience in dealing with the issue at hand. And so it was for medical questions, or for any other subject. It was not uncommon for someone who had posed a question to Rav Shach to receive a telephone call late at night, hearing the *Rosh Yeshivah's* voice declare, "I have an answer for you now; come by and I will tell you about it." Seldom did he allow himself to retire at night before ascertaining the relevant information and passing it on to the appropriate party.

One time an *avrech* told the *Rosh Yeshivah* about a *shidduch* that had been mentioned to him for his son. The girl lived in a town in which the *avrech* had no contacts, and he was unable to inquire into her particulars: From what sort of family was she? What were her upbringing and education like? What were her personal characteristics?

"Come tomorrow, and we'll see about all that," the *Rosh Yeshivah* reassured him.

The next day the *avrech* returned, and Rav Shach told him, "I checked it out, and everything is fine. She's from a good family, and she has a very good name in her community."

In response to the amazed look an the *avrech's* face, he explained, "You said that you have no contacts in that town. But I do know someone there — Rav So-and-so. I got up and traveled to that city and asked him all the relevant questions in detail, until I was satisfied!"

וְעֵינֵי לֵאָה רַכּוֹת — *Leah's eyes were tender* (29:17).

As Rashi explains, quoting the Gemara, Leah wept bitterly, because people used to say, "Lavan has two daughters and Yitzchak has two sons; the older Esav will marry the older Leah, and the younger ones, Yaakov and Rachel, will marry each other!" This constant crying caused her eyes to become "tender" and unsightly.

R' Mordechai Bunam Silberberg relates:

"There was a rebbetzin in Bnei Brak who often took into her home troubled girls who were not getting along with their families. She cared for these girls and virtually raised them until they married and began to raise their own families.

"There was one girl who decided that she would marry only a fine, upstanding full-time student of Torah. The rebbetzin tried to explain to her that, considering her background, she should not lock herself to that standard. The girl was stubborn, however, and she refused to consider any of the various *shidduchim* that were mentioned involving boys who were not learning full-time.

"Frustrated, the rebbetzin turned to Rav Shach for advice, taking the girl along with her. Rav Shach spoke to the girl at length, and tried to explain to her that the main thing in life is to build a home in which the Torah is scrupulously observed and given the highest priority. There was no law that dictated that every single household must have a father who is a Torah scholar! Finding a husband who was working, and who dedicated some time every day to Torah study, would be an admirable achievement.

"The girl listened to Rav Shach's words, and when he finished she burst out into uncontrollable, heart-rending tears.

"Taken aback by the girl's reaction, Rav Shach acknowledged, 'If she cries so bitterly over this issue — she will indeed find what she seeks!'

"And so it was. The girl eventually married a fine *talmid chacham* and together they raised a wonderful Torah-true family in Jerusalem."

לֹא־תִתֶּן־לִי מְאוּמָה — *Do not give me anything* (Or, *You will not give me anything*) (30:31).

The Torah commentator Sforno explains these words: "If God decides to grace me [with wealth], this will not result in any loss in your property. As the Sages say, 'No person can take away from that which is destined to belong to his fellow' (*Yoma* 38b)."

R' David Cohen relates:

"One time, when I was still learning in *kollel*, I was offered a position in a well-known yeshivah to serve as a *meishiv,* a teacher available to respond to students' questions, and eventually as a *ram,* a regular teacher.

"I went to consult with Rav Shach about the offer. He asked me if I was learning well and growing in Torah knowledge in the *kollel.* When I responded in the affirmative, he advised me to remain where I was. 'Why would you even consider leaving the *kollel?*' he wondered.

"I explained that the offer was an unusual opportunity, a chance that was not likely to present itself again. But he responded, 'If someone is sitting and learning well, he should not think about anything else. As far as passing up a fabulous opportunity goes — the Sages say, "People will call you by your name; they will put you in your rightful place; they will give you what is due you; no person can take away the slightest bit from that which is destined to belong to his fellow' " (*Yoma* 38b). If such a position is indeed fitting for you, you will eventually fill it!'

"Following the *Rosh Yeshivah's* advice, I stayed in *kollel* for another four years, and advanced further in my Torah knowledge. Then the *kollel* closed down, and I had no choice but to move elsewhere. Exactly at that time, the very same position I had turned down based upon Rav Shach's advice was offered to me again!"

כִּי בְּכָל־כֹּחִי עָבַדְתִּי אֶת־אֲבִיכֶן — *That with all my might I have worked for your father* (31:6).

The Rambam writes (*Hil. Sechirus* 13:11): "A hired laborer must work with all his strength, for you see that the righteous Yaakov said, 'With all my might I have worked for your father.' Therefore he received reward [not only in the Next World, but] even in This World, as it says, 'The man became exceedingly prosperous.' "

Rav Shach followed the Rambam's words of exhortation scrupulously. He spent two *sedarim* (study sessions) each day in the yeshivah's *beis midrash,* encouraging the *bachurim* to learn and think logically, and training them in the proper manner of Talmudic study. He gave daily *shiurim,* and toiled with every ounce of his strength in preparing his weekly yeshivah-wide lecture (*shiur klali*) — beginning the preparation of the next *shiur* the moment the previous one was finished. Yet, despite his boundless dedication he was always concerned that he might not be doing enough to fulfill his obligations as an employee of the yeshivah!

He would arrive in the *beis midrash* before anyone else, and begin arranging the books on the shelf in an orderly fashion, so that the students would not have to waste time locating a particular *sefer.* After the maintainance people cleaned the floor, he would take the *shtenders* (lecterns) off the benches and put them back on the floor, without the slightest concern that it was not in line with his dignified status. Furthermore, he would never allow anyone else to assist him in these chores. He explained: "I receive a salary for the *shiurim* I give, don't I? Now, who knows if all the information I say in those *shiurim* is correct all the time, or if I have truly invested the requisite amount of toil or time in preparing them? Perhaps I do not fully earn what I am paid! These extra acts are how I cover that debt that I might owe!"

כִּי־מִשַּׁשְׁתָּ אֶת־כָּל־כֵּלַי מַה־מָּצָאתָ מִכֹּל כְּלֵי־בֵיתֶךָ — *When you rummaged through all my things, what did you find of all your household objects?* (31:37).

The Midrash comments on this verse: "In an ordinary situation, when a son-in-law lives in his father-in-law's house, is it possible for him not to take even one article, even one knife? Yet here [Yaakov says,] 'You have rummaged through all my things' — you have not even found a needle or a hook!' "

Rav Shach's meticulousness in monetary matters was amazingly rigorous, as well. For dozens of years he presided over *Chinuch Atzma'i* (the independent *Charedi* school network), sacrificed hundreds of hours of his time for trips taken on its behalf, as well as for participating in meetings, assemblies, examinations, etc. Yet he never took a penny in remuneration for his services.

One time, while he was in the *Chinuch Atzma'i* office, he needed to speak to the principal of a school which was not part of the *Chinuch Atzma'i* network. He telephoned the man once, but was told that he had stepped out. He called again several minutes later, but the man was still not available. The *Rosh Yeshivah* promptly took out a half-

lirah from his pocket and gave it to the secretary to pay for his two phone calls!

"Oh, there is no need for that," the secretary told him.

"Why not?" protested Rav Shach, perplexed at the suggestion that he should not pay for a call made on someone else's phone!

He was the president of the organization, and the phone call was related to matters of *Charedi* education, but nevertheless, since the principal was not technically associated with *Chinuch Atzma'i,* Rav Shach could not see any justification for not paying for a "personal" call on "someone else's" phone!

אָנֹכִי אֲחַטֶּנָּה מִיָּדִי תְּבַקְשֶׁנָּה — *I myself would bear the loss; you would exact it from me* (31:39).

Someone once related to the *Rosh Yeshivah* that every night, before the Alter of Novaradok went to sleep, he would go through the entire student body in his mind, pondering each *bachur's* progress (or lack thereof) and what could be done to improve his performance.

Rav Shach's reaction was: "So what? He was a *rosh yeshivah,* wasn't he? That's what a *rosh yeshivah* is supposed to do! If you would tell me that he did *not* do this, *then* I would be surprised!"

One time there was a boy in the yeshivah who could have used some improvement in his personal level of Torah observance and fear of God. Rav Shach set up *chavrusos* for him and arranged for an older *bachur* to get involved with him and speak to him. On the day of the *Rosh Yeshivah's* wife's passing, even before the funeral took place, the *Rosh Yeshivah* happened to see the older *bachur,* and he went over to inquire as to the weaker *bachur's* progress and to discuss possible ways to get through to him!

וישלח — **Vayishlach**

וְרֶוַח תָּשִׂימוּ בֵּין עֵדֶר וּבֵין עֵדֶר — *And put a space between herd and herd* (32:17).

The Midrash (*Yalkut Shimoni* 130) interprets this verse homiletically as Yaakov saying to Hashem, "Master of the Universe! If trials and tribulations are to befall my children, do not afflict them ceaselessly. Rather, leave them space between their troubles."

One young man was getting older and older, yet refused to entertain discussion of marriage. Rav Shach spoke with him, and he promised that he would listen to people's suggestions during the summer break.

The summer break came and went, but Rav Shach found out that he was still not listening to people who were suggesting young ladies he should meet. When this kept up through Yom Kippur, Rav Shach asked one of his students to summon the young man.

When the young man came, Rav Shach said to him, "Why did you not keep your word, that you would listen to suggestions during the summer?"

The young man was silent.

Rav Shach gently said, "You are probably concerned about the difficulties that arise after marriage. Let me tell you that you have nothing to worry about. I am not saying that there are no challenges; of course there are! Nevertheless, it is important to know that the problems do not all come at once. Instead, one challenge arises and a solution is found. Then another difficulty arises and a solution is found for that problem as well, and so on."

His words hit home and it was as if a stone rolled off the young man's heart. "Will the *Rosh Yeshivah* officiate at my wedding?" he asked.

"Certainly," he responded. "And I will dance with you as well!"

Rav Shach got up, took out a bottle of wine, and handed it to the fellow, saying, "Take this. We will use this wine at your wedding!"

וַיָּשֶׂם אֶת־הַשְּׁפָחוֹת וְאֶת־יַלְדֵיהֶן רִאשֹׁנָה וְאֶת־לֵאָה וִילָדֶיהָ אַחֲרֹנִים וְאֶת־רָחֵל וְאֶת־יוֹסֵף אַחֲרֹנִים — *He put the handmaids and the children first, and Leah and her children later, and Rachel and Yosef last (33:2).*

Rav Shach once said, "I have discovered a truly innovative exposition (*chiddush*) in the *Chumash* (Pentateuch), and it is now two weeks that I haven't told it to anyone."

When people insisted that he tell them his exposition, he asked: Is it not strange that Yaakov would so differentiate between his children, apparently endangering the lives of the children of the handmaidens by placing them first and protecting Yosef and Rachel by placing them last?

We find, however, that Yosef would bring evil reports to his father about how the brothers belittled the children of the handmaidens (see Rashi 37:2). Presumably, these children suffered from this belittlement, and we know that suffering atones for sin. Accordingly, we can assume that they had greater merits, which would protect them, and he could therefore put them first. He then put Leah and her children who, feeling less loved than Rachel and Yosef, were more humble and thus more worthy of salvation. Finally, he put Rachel and Yosef who, being the most loved, suffered least and thus had the least merits.

"This," stated Rav Shach, "is the true understanding of the verse."

וַיִּקְחוּ שְׁנֵי־בְנֵי־יַעֲקֹב שִׁמְעוֹן וְלֵוִי אֲחֵי דִינָה אִישׁ חַרְבּוֹ — *Two of Yaakov's sons, Shimon and Levi, Dinah's brothers, each took his sword (34:25).*

Rashi comments, "They were [Yaakov's] sons, yet nonetheless they conducted themselves as 'Shimon and Levi,' like other men who are not his sons, for they did not seek advice from him."

When a store selling offensive material was burned down in Jerusalem, the police arrested three yeshivah students for arson. One of them was sentenced to a year and a half in jail.

In his discourse at the yeshivah, Rav Shach spoke about the matter, saying: "We learn everything from the Holy Torah, based on the principle of 'the actions of the fathers are signs for the children' (see Ramban 12:6). We even learn from the Torah how to fight. One should not use criminal tactics for the benefit of the Torah world. In this regard, on his deathbed Yaakov said about them (49:5), 'Stolen tools are their weapons.' As Rashi there explains, this craft of murder is in their possession by theft; it is from the blessing of Esau."

וַיִּקְחוּ שְׁנֵי־בְנֵי־יַעֲקֹב שִׁמְעוֹן וְלֵוִי אֲחֵי דִינָה אִישׁ חַרְבּוֹ — *Two of Yaakov's sons, Shimon and Levi, Dinah's brothers, each took his sword* (34:25).

Our Sages (*Avos* 5:21) state that 13 is the age for [performing] commandments. Bertinora explains that the source for this is the verse (*Bamidbar* 5:6), "A man (*ish*) or woman who commits any of man's sins." From the use of the same word — *ish* — in our own verse, "Each *ish* took his own sword," when Levi was 13, we can derive that an *ish*, with respect to the commandments, is 13 years old.

A father brought his son to be blessed by Rav Shach before his bar mitzvah. Rav Shach asked the boy, "So, are you prepared?"

"Yes," he replied. "As much as is needed."

Rav Shach explained, "I did not mean to ask if you are prepared now. My question was whether you are completing the thirteen-year preparation period. You see, Hashem arranged the world so that a person becomes obligated in the commandments at 13, so that he will have thirteen years to prepare himself."

וַיִּקַּח עֵשָׂו ... וְאֶת־כָּל־נַפְשׁוֹת בֵּיתוֹ — *Esav took ... all the souls of his household* (36:6).

Rashi, commenting on the verse (46:26) that uses the singular form of soul (*nefesh*) regarding the seventy people coming with Yaakov to Egypt, notes that Esav had six souls in his family, yet the verse calls them *the souls of his household*, using the plural form for soul (*nafshos*), because they worshiped many deities. Yaakov, on the other hand, had seventy family members, yet the verse calls them *soul* in the singular because they all worshiped one God. Chasam Sofer asks: We often find many gentiles worshiping one deity, so what is so unique about Israel? He answers that worshiping the One God unifies the Jewish people to be like one person with one heart. Gentiles, on the other hand, even when they do something together or worship the same deity, each of them has his own benefit in mind, and they remain separate individuals.

There was once a major burglary of a jewelry store in the Abu Tor section of Jerusalem. A fortune in jewelry was stolen as the store was virtually emptied. Considering the probability that the jewelry was used to pay for a major drug deal, the police assumed that the merchandise had already changed hands and there was no chance of locating it. The owner of the store, an Orthodox Jew, was devastated, and Rabbi Moshe Aharon Braverman brought him to Rav Shach for encouragement. Rav Shach heard the details and said, "A Jew should never lose hope. Sometimes one thief gets into a fight with another and informs on him."

"Yes," said the owner, "but the police assume that the merchandise is already out of the hands of the thieves." Rav Shach did not respond.

A few days later, the police summoned the store owner to their headquarters. There was a surprise waiting for him — all the stolen merchandise was there! The investigator explained that one of the thieves had gotten into a fight with the others and turned the rest in! The next day, there was an adveriesment in the newspaper, thanking the One Above. It was signed by the store owner.

וישב — Vayeishev

וַיֵּשֶׁב יַעֲקֹב בְּאֶרֶץ מְגוּרֵי אָבִיו — *Yaakov settled in the land of his father's sojournings* (37:1)

ashi cites a homiletic interpretation of this verse: Yaakov wished to settle [down] in tranquility, but the Holy One, Blessed is He, said, "The righteous do not consider that which is prepared for them in the World to Come to be enough for them, but they seek to dwell in tranquility as well!"

In his advanced old age, Rav Shach found it difficult to speak. When Rabbi Shlomo Lorincz (the Knesset member for the Agudah party) came to visit him, he spoke to him with great difficulty and asked him to write down each word.

This is what he said: "All my life I never had even one good day. All my days were filled with difficulties and sorrow, and yet I am a happy man.

"R' Shlomo, soon — maybe in another year, maybe another month, a few more days, or maybe even now as we talk — I will leave this world. When I reach the World of Truth, I will be expected to give an immediate accounting before the Holy One, Blessed is He. I am well aware that I will be punished for my anger, haughtiness, and love of honor. Afterwards, however, I will hear Him say, 'I have forgiven.' Then — ah then! — I will be able to go in and meet R' Akiva Eiger and all our other Rabbis who were the leaders of their generations. Can you even imagine the pleasure — the unmitigated joy — that it will be to meet R' Akiva Eiger, the *Ketzos,* the *Nesivos,* and all the other greats?

"Since I so anxiously await this happy moment, I already feel happy now. Accordingly, despite the difficult times I have been through and the difficult period through which I am passing, there is no happier person than me, in this world. For I know that the joy there will be greater and more sublime than anything I could possibly imagine here!"

וְעָשָׂה לוֹ כְּתֹנֶת פַּסִּים — *And he made him a fine woolen tunic* (37:3).

The Gemara (*Shabbos* 10b) states that a person should never treat any of his children differently, "For as a result of the extra two-*selaim*-weight of fine wool that Yaakov gave to Yosef and not to his brothers, the brothers became jealous of him and this brought about our forefathers' exile in Egypt."

Rav Shach was especially careful not to bring about jealousy between students. One time, he was invited to test the pupils in an elementary school. Needless to say, there were those who excelled and those who did not. Rav Shach tested each one of them and then gave the teacher a sum of money to divide up equally among them all.

וַהֲשִׁבֵנִי דָּבָר — *And bring me back word* (37:14).

A kollel fellow came to Rav Shach to notify him that his son was engaged. Rav Shach blessed him warmly and then asked, "Do you have enough money for all the expenses?"

His face fell, and he muttered that he hoped for a loan from a certain free-loan fund (*gemach*) in Jerusalem, but was pretty sure that they would turn him down.

Rav Shach said, "In a few days, I will be going to Jerusalem for a meeting of the directorate of *Chinuch Atzma'i*, and at that time I will stop in to see the director of the *gemach* and put in a good word for you."

The father protested that it was unnecessary to go through that bother, as a simple telephone call would be sufficient.

Rav Shach replied, "If I were in need of a loan, I would personally go to him. If I would do that for myself, I can do no less for others."

Several days later, there was much excitement in this man's home as the children ran to their father exclaiming, "Rav Shach is here, Rav Shach is here!"

The man rushed to greet Rav Shach, who happily told him, "I came to tell you that I stopped in to see the director of the *gemach* and he said that he will give you whatever sum you need."

Pleased and relieved, he said to Rav Shach, "But you could have notified me by phone; there was no need to take the trouble of coming to my house!"

Rav Shach did not understand. "You were waiting for an answer with bated breath. It is inconceivable that I would not come to notify you personally!"

מקץ — Mikeitz

וְאֶת־בִּנְיָמִין אֲחִי יוֹסֵף לֹא־שָׁלַח יַעֲקֹב אֶת־אֶחָיו כִּי אָמַר פֶּן־יִקְרָאֶנּוּ אָסוֹן — *But Binyamin, Yosef's brother, Yaakov did not send along with his brothers, for he said, "Lest disaster befall him"* (42:4).

The verse says that Yaakov did not send him along "lest disaster befall him." Rashi asks, "And can disaster not befall him at home?" Why was Yaakov so worried about the journey? His answer: "From here we see that the accuser prosecutes at a time of peril."

When Rav Shach taught at Lomza Yeshivah in Petach Tikvah, he would spend the week in the house of R' Eliezer Mordechai Zaks and travel back to his home in Jerusalem for Shabbos. During the week, he could generally be found at any time in the yeshivah, together with his students. Accordingly, the students wondered why, one week, Rav Shach was leaving for Jerusalem on Thursday.

He explained, "It's a long trip to Jerusalem [in those days one had to travel first to Tel Aviv, then go on to Jerusalem by way of Ramle and Har Tuv] and the roads are perilous [in the old cars and during the War of Independence], and the accuser prosecutes at a time of peril. Through his prosecution, he causes delays and places obstacles along the way to try and cause desecration of Shabbos. Thus, I am leaving earlier."

כִּי הַמֵּלִיץ בֵּינֹתָם — *For the interpreter was between them* (42:23).

Rav Shach recounted the story of the Rabbinical meeting called in response to the Russian goverment's demand that all the Rabbis learn how to speak Russian. Most of those assembled did not see a need to oppose this demand since it was not a decree aimed at uprooting the Jewish religion. The leaders of this group included R' Meir Simchah of Dvinsk and R' Itzeleh of Ponevezh. Only R' Chaim Soloveitchik of Brisk vehemently opposed testing Rabbinical candidates on their knowledge of Russian on an equal footing with testing their greatness in Torah and knowledge of Jewish law. He enlisted the Chofetz Chaim on his side, but the majority disagreed with them and the majority was about to write up a decision in the spirit of the government's demand. R' Chaim rose and announced, "I will be the meeting's secretary, and I will write the decision."

"How can you write the decision?" they asked. "You oppose our decision!"

"So what?" he replied. "The majority has reached a decision, and its decision is binding."

"But," they continued, "you do not understand Russian. How will you write the decision in Russian?"

He replied, "And if I understood Russian, I would still need a pen. But who would write the decision, me or the pen? Why, the pen would write, but since the pen writes only what I want, it would be considered as if I were doing the writing. Now all I need is an interpreter who can write in Russian. He will be like my pen and nothing more."

In this manner, he explained to them — and to the government representative who took part in the meeting — a rabbi has no need to know Russian; all he needs is an interpreter!

לָמָה הֲרֵעֹתֶם לִי — *Why did you treat me badly* (43:6).

A man had lost his fortune in a bad deal and was very depressed. He came to speak with Rav Shach, who told him the following to console him: "A man is short-sighted, and does not know what is truly good for him. The Rabbis have compared man to a baby who screams at the top of his lungs when his mother puts him into a bath, not understanding that he is being bathed for his own benefit and comfort. I have clearly seen this in my own life. When I studied at the yeshivah in Slutzk, I was considered among the better students, both with regard to my diligence and with regard to my understanding. The 'better students' were in great demand, and rich fathers would offer those young men apartments and respectable dowries for marrying their daughters. As soon as one of the better students would get engaged, he would tell everyone the size of his dowry and the apartment that he was given. Now the *Rosh Yeshivah*, R' Isser Zalman Meltzer, proposed his niece to me — with no dowry and no apartment — and I accepted. R' Isser Zalman's daughter and son-in-law lived in a room in his house, and had not yet had children. R' Isser

Zalman divided the room in half, and that half was my 'apartment.' I did not care; I asked for one thing and that is what I sought: 'To dwell in the House of Hashem all the days of my life' (see *Tehillim* 27:4). The other students, however, felt bad for me. My friends looked at me with disdain: They received apartments and became homeowners, whereas I lived in half of a room — and it wasn't even mine. I could say that I didn't care, but I could not say that they were not right!

"Then World War II broke out. The Nazis conquered Poland and the Russians invaded Lithuania. Anyone who could, ran away. My friends, however, hesitated. They were homeowners! How could they leave their homes? They debated their options again and again — until it was too late. Unfettered by a home, I left immediately. First I fled to Vilna and then I came to Israel, saving myself and my family.

"So you see, their homes were an obstacle to them and my situation was to my benefit!

"This is the way the Midrash (*Bereishis Rabbah* 91:10) explains Yaakov's statement, 'Why did you treat me badly': Said Rabbi Chama ben Chanina: This is the only place that Yaakov speaks idle words! [At that time,] the Holy One, Blessed is He, said: 'I am involved in making his son king of Egypt, and he says, Why did you treat me badly?' This is what is meant by the verse (*Yeshayahu* 40:27), 'Why do you say, O Yaakov, and declare, O Israel, My way is hidden from Hashem and my cause has passed by my God?' "

הָאֱלֹקִים מָצָא אֶת־עֲוֹן עֲבָדֶיךָ — *God has found the sin of your servants* (44:16).

*T*he Brisker Rav, R' Yitzchak Zev Soloveitchik, once asked Rav Shach a question with which many have grappled: The Mishnah (*Avos* 3:1) says, "Know ... before Whom you will give a judgment and a reckoning." However, it is the way of the world to first do all the reckoning and only afterwards to make the judgment. So why does the Mishnah mention "judgment" before "reckoning"?

Rav Shach answered that for human justice, reckoning comes first and only afterwards can the judgment be determined. For the Holy One, Blessed is He, however, everything is completely clear and the judgment is already known. Only afterwards, does He set the person's reckoning before him so that he can accept the judgment upon himself and say, "You have judged well, you have correctly found me guilty."

The Brisker Rav praised this answer. (See more on this point in *Parashas Nitzavim*, on the verse, "For what reason did Hashem do so to this land.")

וַיִּגַּשׁ — Vayigash

וְלֹא־יָכְלוּ אֶחָיו לַעֲנוֹת אֹתוֹ כִּי נִבְהֲלוּ מִפָּנָיו — *But his brothers could not answer him because they were disconcerted before him* (45:3).

The Midrash (*Bereishis Rabbah* 93:10) cites Abba Kohen Bardela as saying, "Woe to us from the day of judgment, woe to us from the day of rebuke! Yosef was [among] the youngest of the brothers yet they could not stand up to his rebuke. When the Holy One, Blessed is He, will come and rebuke each person according to what he is, as it says (*Tehillim* 50:21), 'I will rebuke you and lay it clearly before your eyes,' how much more so [will it be impossible to stand up to His rebuke]!"

Rav Shach told the Brisker Rav the following exposition: In the normal order of things, rebuke comes before judgment. Why, then, does it say here, "Woe to us from the day of judgment" before "Woe to us from the day of rebuke"? Because a person generally does not see anything wrong in himself, as Shlomo HaMelech says in *Mishlei* (16:2), "All of man's ways are pure in his own eyes" — not only does a man not see anything "wrong" with his ways, but they are "pure in his own eyes"! When he is rebuked, he will always find excuses to justify his behavior. When Hashem will come to rebuke him, however, He will prove to him the wickedness of his ways and show him exactly where he went wrong. "Rebuke" (*tochachah*), as used here, is a cognate of "proof" (*hochachah*). The brothers claimed to Yosef that he should forgo punishing Binyamin out of concern for the father who will die when he sees that the youth is gone. Then, he said to them, *"I am Yosef* — whom you sold to Egypt — *is my father still alive?* Why were you not then concerned about our father, lest he die?" But his brothers could not answer him because they were left disconcerted before him — for he rebuked them by proving their wickedness.

The Brisker Rav praised this answer.

וַיְדַבְּרוּ אֵלָיו אֵת כָּל־דִּבְרֵי יוֹסֵף אֲשֶׁר דִּבֶּר אֲלֵהֶם וַיַּרְא אֶת־
הָעֲגָלוֹת אֲשֶׁר־שָׁלַח יוֹסֵף לָשֵׂאת אֹתוֹ וַתְּחִי רוּחַ יַעֲקֹב אֲבִיהֶם
*And they related to him all the words of Yosef that
he had spoken to them, and he saw the wagons that
Yosef had sent to transport him, then the spirit of
their father Jacob was revived (45:27).*

ashi says that *all the words of Yosef,* refers to the sign sent by
Yosef concerning the Torah section they studied — the decapi-
tated calf (*eglah arufah*). Thus, it says, "He saw the wagons
[aggalos] that Yosef had sent to transport him," rather than
"that Pharaoh had sent to transport him."

When Rav Shach taught before World War II at the Kletzk Yeshivah,
R' Yoel Kloft, who would later be the chief Rabbinical justice of Haifa,
studied there. R' Yoel became very close to Rav Shach and decades
later, signed a letter of Torah thoughts that he wrote to him, "His
friend who admires and respects him from those days, for we drew
much Torah from him in those days, when our whole focus was in-
depth study." After Rav Shach left Kletzk for teaching in Lunnitz, they
continued writing. Torah thoughts to each other. In his last letter
before the war, R' Yoel asked about the question that Rav Akiva Eiger
had posed on the Talmudic discussion concerning *palginan dibura*
(dividing a testimony so that part of it is believed, although part is
not). Rav Shach wrote back and answered the question. Then the
horrors of World War II began, and the two of them lost contact. Rav
Shach miraculously succeeded in fleeing the land of death and he
finally arrived in Israel, going through some difficult times along the
way. R' Yoel also succeeded in escaping Europe and arriving in Israel.
When he heard that Rav Shach also was saved, he hurried to meet
him. He was overwhelmed with joy and feeling when he actually met
his teacher! They hugged and kissed, and in the midst of it all, Rav
Shach asked him, "I'm sure you received my answer to your question
— so what do you say about my answer?"

R' Yoel was astounded and he cried out, "You went through the
horrors of the war, you barely were saved from the valley of death, the
whole world is in flames, here you are in exile wandering from place to
place, and all you can think of is what you answered 'before the
deluge,' as if we were not apart all these years!"

וִיחִי — Vayechi

וְשָׁכַבְתִּי עִם־אֲבֹתַי... וּקְבַרְתַּנִי בִּקְבֻרָתָם — *And I will lie down with my fathers ... and bury me in their grave* (47:30).

Rabbeinu Bachya writes that this verse is the source for the statement of the Sages that a person should always bury the righteous near the righteous.

Rav Shach's closeness to R' Isser Zalman Meltzer is well known. The latter took him into his own home for the stormy period of World War I, when Rav Shach was in great difficulty and had nothing, and raised him like his own son. R' Isser Zalman arranged the marriage of his niece to Rav Shach, appointed him as a teacher in his yeshivah, and was like a father to him. When R' Isser Zalman passed away and was buried on Har HaMenuchos, Rav Shach bought a plot near his rebbi and teacher, and expressed his wishes to be buried there when the time came.

Several years later, R' Yitzchak Epstein, a Rabbinical judge in Tel Aviv, who had a very close relationship with R' Isser Zalman Meltzer, passed away at a relatively young age. Rav Shach felt a debt of gratitude to him because, when he first arrived in Israel at the Rosh HaNikrah border crossing in Northern Israel, R' Yitzchak was waiting for him there, at the behest of R' Isser Zalman, and accompanied him to Jerusalem. So when Rav Shach heard that R' Yitzchak had expressed his desire to be buried near his teacher, he allowed him to be buried in the plot that he had purchased for himself — to repay his debt of gratitude.

But that was not all. Each Shabbos he would take the long walk to R' Yitzchak's house, to test his children in their studies. He refused to let them come to him, for the debt of gratitude that he felt — for R' Yitzchak's accompanying him at the behest of his rebbi — demanded that he go to them each Shabbos, for years!

וַיִּשְׁתַּחוּ יִשְׂרָאֵל עַל־רֹאשׁ הַמִּטָּה — *And Israel prostrated himself toward the head of the bed* (47:31).

Rabbeinu Bachya writes that the verse mentions *bed* in connection with Yaakov, as opposed to Avraham and Yitzchak, because their "bed" (i.e., their offspring) was not completely pure. The "bed" of Yaakov, on the other hand, was completely pure, for his children were all the tribes of God, and it was thus worthy of mention in the Torah.

Rav Shach related that the Brisker Rav once told him that he had not had a good day in his life. He blamed himself and said, "If only I would have been a better person, things would have been better for me."

Rav Shach said to him, "Who of the Torah greats of this generation was fortunate enough to have a completely pure bed, with all his children studying Torah, as was the case with the Rav?"

The Brisker Rav was consoled. "That is true," he said. But do you have any idea how many tears I shed that they have awe of Heaven — all the way back from the time that they were in the cradle?!"

קָחֶם־נָא אֵלַי וַאֲבָרֲכֵם — *Bring them to me, if you please, and I will bless them* (48:9).

R' Yaakov Eliezer Schwartzman recalls a meeting in Bnei Brak, on an important public matter. Rav Shach was not well at the time and there was great doubt whether he would be able to attend. Ultimately, he arrived, and, with almost superhuman effort, spoke a few words. When he left, he almost had to be carried out. R' Schwartzman went along with his children, because he needed Rav Shach's advice concerning a certain matter. He figured that when Rav Shach would come home he woud rest a bit and then he (R' Schwartzman) would be able to ask his questions.

With great difficulty, Rav Shach came to the door of his house, opened it with the key in his hand, and slowly dragged his feet into the house, followed by R' Schwartzman and his children. Much to R' Schwartzman's surprise, Rav Shach went neither to his chair nor to his bed, but slowly walked to the closet. Because of his poor vision he felt around for the key and then felt around in the drawer. Finally, he found what he was looking for. He stretched his hand out with a chocolate bar in it and asked, "Is this milk chocolate?" When R' Schwartzman replied that it was, he said, "Good! Children like milk chocolate." Still standing, he gave out pieces of chocolate to each child and only afterwards, when he was quite obviously exhausted, he sat down on his chair.

וְעֵינֵי יִשְׂרָאֵל כָּבְדוּ מִזֹּקֶן — *Now Israel's eyes were heavy with age* (48:10).

*O*hr HaChaim comments on this verse, "We see that when a person ages, his understanding lessens and his senses weaken."

In Rav Shach's old age, when he felt very weak, he underwent a comprehensive checkup. A few days after receiving the results, he went to pray in the yeshivah, and on the way told those close to him, "I've been very concerned for several days. As you know, I haven't been feeling well for a while now. I had a comprehensive checkup and this week Professor Bank told me that, other than my eyes, everything is fine. All my systems are working as they should, like those of a young man. I asked him how that could be, being that I do not feel well, feel a lack of balance and terrible weakness. He told me that he does not know what I feel, but that, based on the tests, I was totally fine. I was very disturbed by his answer. I am an old man and can even die today or tomorrow. When I go up to give my reckoning and accounting, they will ask me, 'Why did you not learn as well as you should have?' I thought that I would be able to answer that I was too weak to learn properly. In light of what the doctor says, however, it seems as if I was just talking it into myself!

"This greatly disturbed me.

"Last night, however, it all came together! What does it mean to feel well? What actually feels well? Why, the hand is like an inanimate stone, and how can a stone 'feel' well? It is the Creator Who gives life to this 'stone' and He Who grants it the 'good feeling.' The Creator set rules for this, that for seventy years it should feel well, and then, little by little lose its strength. There is thus no question why I do not feel well, and it has nothing to do with the functions of my systems. It is no wonder that the doctor does not understand this. Why, it is a lesson in faith!"

וְעֵינֵי יִשְׂרָאֵל כָּבְדוּ מִזֹּקֶן — *Now Israel's eyes were heavy with age* (48:10).

*W*hen Rav Shach was approximately 80 years old, he went to a top ophthalmologist because his sight was getting worse and worse. The doctor examined his eyes and told him that in fifteen years he would be blind. Rav Shach burst into tears at the news and said, "What will be? How will I be able to learn in another fifteen years?"

Unbelievable! He cried at what would happen in fifteen years (when he would be 95), but not because "the blind are considered as if they are dead" (see *Nedarim* 64b). Rather, he was concerned about how he would be able to learn!

וּלְבֶן־שִׁנַּיִם מֵחָלָב — *And white-toothed from milk* (49:12).

The Gemara (*Kesubos* 111b) uses this verse as a source for saying that one who whitens teeth to his friend (i.e., shows him a shining countenance) is better than one who gives him milk to drink.

Years back, Ponevezh Yeshivah was going through a very difficult period. They served meager meals to the students, and the staff was not paid for a long time. One of the students could not take the deprivation and he wanted to change to another yeshivah. He went to Rav Shach to say good-bye.

Rav Shach said to him, "You are learning well and you have good friends. You are advancing in Torah and have a good name. Why do you want to change to a different yeshivah? I'm sure you know that the Gemara (*Chagigah* 10a) applies the verse (*Zechariah* 8:10), 'Those who travel back and forth had no peace,' to those who move from one place of Torah learning to another. Only when it is actually bad for a person where he is, does the Gemara elsewhere (*Bava Metzia* 75b) advise him to change places. What is so bad here?"

He replied, "I am ashamed to say this ... but ... there is just not enough to eat."

Rav Shach did not tell him how he hungered for bread in his youth and continued learning. Nor did he tell him how much he suffered from the siege during World War I, when he sustained himself by collecting the crumbs left over in the synagogue by those who came to pray. He never demanded of others what he demanded of himself. Instead, he asked, "If you had milk to drink each morning and evening, would that be sufficient?"

When the youth answered in the affirmative, Rav Shach told him to come to his house each morning and evening for a glass of milk.

It subsequently became apparent that during this period Rav Shach himself did not get paid, and all he had for himself and his family was whatever they would give him from the yeshivah kitchen. No one can determine where he got the milk for that student, thereby fulfilling the directive of showing him a shining countenance as well as literally giving him milk to drink!

וַיַּעֲלוּ אִתּוֹ כָּל־עַבְדֵי פַרְעֹה זִקְנֵי בֵיתוֹ וְכֹל זִקְנֵי אֶרֶץ־מִצְרָיִם — *And with him went up all of Pharaoh's servants, the elders of his household, and all the elders of the land of Egypt* (50:7).

Said Rav Shach: "Come see the difference between the earlier generations and the later generations. It is not just the Jewish people who suffer from a deterioration of the generations. Egypt was the most depraved of nations (see Rashi, *Vayikra* 18:3). Nevertheless, they understood that all royalty and all the elders of the land should give honor to the perfect man, to the choicest of our forefathers. Furthermore, they would show this honor not just for a short escorting, but they would accompany him all the way to the Land of Israel, and all the kings of Canaan and all the princes of Yishmael hung their crowns on the coffin of Yaakov our father (see Rashi, *Bereishis* 50:10).

"Yet the biggest funeral I can remember in Europe, which was written up in all the news media and discussed by everybody, was that of a certain gentile who died after an eating contest in which he ate fifty loaves of bread. He died from overeating, but you should have seen the great honor accorded him at his funeral!"

וַיְנַחֵם אוֹתָם וַיְדַבֵּר עַל־לִבָּם — *Thus he comforted them and spoke to their heart* (50:21).

In Radin (Poland) there was an older fellow by the name of Hershel Kaminitzer who never got married due to a lung disease which he had. He told Rav Shach that one Yom Kippur night, after all the other yeshivah students had left the study hall, he was left alone with his thoughts. The Chofetz Chaim, who was rosh yeshivah, came in, sat down next to him, and began talking to him ... reminiscing about his youth: How he had lost his father when he was 10 years old and how he had exiled himself to a place of Torah. He recalled his trials and tribulations both with respect to the material — poverty and lack — and with respect to the spiritual — the attempts of the *maskilim* to pull him away from Orthodoxy. He told him that he agreed to marry his stepsister (who was older than he) only to keep the peace between his mother and her husband, while his friend happily found a wife with a $10,000 dowry. Ultimately, however, his friend lost all his money in a bad deal and became a peddler who could not make ends meet, whereas his wife helped him dedicate his life to Torah and helping people. "So you see," said the Chofetz Chaim, "What appears at the time to be a problem can sprout salvation, and 'By Hashem are man's footsteps established' " (*Tehillim* 37:23).

He spoke of things of this nature all night. Nothing was said about spiritual accounting on the holy day of Yom Kippur, nothing about the awe of Judgment. He just spoke words of consolation and strength!

ספר שמות

Shemos

שמות — Shemos

וַיָּקָם מֶלֶךְ־חָדָשׁ עַל־מִצְרָיִם — *A new king arose over Egypt* (1:8).

When the corrupt and rotten regime of the anti-Semitic Czar Nicholas was overthrown, many Jews were overjoyed. One Torah scholar, in an obvious play on the words of the blessing a father recites when his son becomes bar-mitzvah, said to R' Baruch Ber Leibowitz of Kaminetz, "Blessed is He who has freed us from the punishment of this one."

R' Baruch Ber gave him a long, hard look and said, "You too are so happy?"

In his wisdom, R' Baruch Ber understood what was in store for the Jews. He knew that the communists that took over would be many times worse and would do everything in their power to wipe out Judaism and those who practice it.

וַיְהִי כִּי־יָרְאוּ הַמְיַלְּדֹת אֶת־הָאֱלֹהִים — *And it was because the midwives feared God* (1:21).

R' Binyamin Lehman cites the following exposition of Rav Shach: An earlier verse (v. 17) says that "the midwives feared God and they did not do as the king of Egypt said to them, and they kept the boys alive." Our verse recognizes the fear of God and continues with the reward that they were granted for this fear. It ignores, however, the fact that they saved lives and deserved reward for that!

"At first," said Rav Shach, " I thought that this proves that the most praiseworthy characteristic is fear of God, and that it is even more important than saving life. Now, however, I say that it comes to prove that a good deed is measured by the amount of God-fearingness it contains."

וַתֵּלֶךְ הָעַלְמָה — *So the young girl went* (2:8).

ashi explains that the verse teaches that she went with the alacrity and vigor of a young girl.

R' Shmuel Markowitz recalls the time that he and others came across Rav Shach while he was deep in thought. When he saw them, he said to them, "Do you know what I am thinking about? I am thinking about the things that I must do tomorrow, and wondering which of them I can already take care of today."

Rav Shach did not generally share his private thoughts with his students. Here, however, he was trying to teach them the importance of acting with alacrity!

וַיִּגְדַּל מֹשֶׁה וַיֵּצֵא אֶל־אֶחָיו וַיַּרְא בְּסִבְלֹתָם — *Moshe grew up and went out to his brethren and saw their burdens* (2:11).

ashi explains, "He focused his eyes and heart to be distressed over them."

Accordingly, the verse teaches the great quality which Moshe manifested from his earliest days: the quality of sharing the burden of his friends. Although Moshe grew up in the palace — and he was also of the tribe of Levi, who were not enslaved in Egypt — he nevertheless could not tolerate the suffering of his bretheren, and he focused his eyes and heart to be distressed over their burden.

The quality of "sharing the burden of his friends" is counted among the qualities with which one acquires Torah (see *Avos* 6:6). It is this very quality which was the foundation of the greatness of Moshe as the leader of Israel.

Leaders of every generation were outstanding in their demonstration of this wonderful quality. They would faithfully carry not only the national burden, but also the burden of each individual, with their eyes and heart focused on the needs of others.

Rav Shach demonstrated this quality as well. He would carry the needs of other people close to his heart and constantly think of them. The following story, told by his grandson, R' Ben Zion Bergman, illustrates this point:

A student of Chevron Yeshivah (whom Rav Shach did not know) once went to ask Rav Shach for advice. In the course of the conversation, Rav Shach asked the young man why he was not married. The young man replied that the time had not yet come, and went on to discuss the matter for which he came. Half a year later, the young man returned. He knocked on the door and when he was buzzed in, he went straight to Rav Shach's room. When Rav Shach heard him enter, he asked, "Who is it?" The young man responded and Rav Shach immediately asked him, "So, has the time come yet to get married?"

That is how clearly the needs of the individual were engraved on his heart, and how good was the spirit with which he shared their burden. This was true even for a student of a different yeshivah whom Rav Shach did not know; half a year after meeting him, Rav Shach still remembered his situation!

וַיֵּצֵא אֶל־אֶחָיו וַיַּרְא בְּסִבְלֹתָם — [Moshe] went out to his brethren and saw their burdens (2:11).

Rashi explains, "He focused his eyes and heart to be distressed over them." Ibn Ezra adds that he was in the palace of the king and from there he "went out." Accordingly, the question arises: Why did he endanger himself, bringing upon himself Pharaoh's wrath? Could he not feel pain for their burden while remaining in the palace of the king? The Alter of Kelm explained that knowing of someone's burdens cannot compare to actually seeing them. Thus, Scripture says (Koheles 7:2), "It is better to go to a house of mourning than to go to a house of feasting, for this is the end of all man, and the living should take it to heart." Everyone knows that "this is the end of all man," but when does one "take it to heart"? Only when he actually goes to the house of mourning and sees it with his own eyes!

There was once a family that adopted an orphan girl and raised her with great devotion. She had been an excellent student, and when she finished school she was offered a good job in a place that was quite far from home. This family did everything according to Rav Shach's instructions and, although they saw no need even to ask, they nevertheless asked him what they should do.

Rav Shach told them that the most important thing in the girl's life at that point was to get married. Accordingly, it was better for her to stay at home, even without a job. Then they would see her each day and it would constantly be on their mind to take care of her future!

וַיַּרְא בְּסִבְלֹתָם — And saw their burdens (2:11).

Rashi explains, "He focused his eyes and heart to be distressed over them."

The principal of one of the seminaries for girls came to Rav Shach for advice about a young man who had been suggested as a potential husband for one of his students. The young man had some problems, but so did the girl, and the principal began enumerating her problems: an unhealthy family environment, learning difficulties, and more. After each problem, a sigh would issue from the bottom of Rav Shach's heart. It was quite clear how Rav Shach felt the burden of all her difficulties. Only then did he give his advice.

After Rav Shach died, that principal said of him, "I knew that he shared the pain of every Jew who came to him to express his problems, but I foolishly thought that he only expressed solidarity with the one complaining in order to help alleviate his pain. In my case, however, the girl was not even present. Thus, he was clearly sharing the burden of others in its simplest sense!"

וַיְהִי בַיָּמִים הָרַבִּים הָהֵם — *And it happened during those many days* (2:23).

*H*ow is it that the Children of Israel — offspring of Avraham, Yitzchak, and Yaakov and the twelve holy tribes — sank to the forty-ninth level of impurity? It did not take just a day, nor a year, nor even a few years.

"Do you know how it is that archaeologists find entire cities buried underground?" Rav Shach asked R' Yeshayah Lieberman. "How did the city sink?

"I'll tell you how," he replied. "First there was a fine layer of dust that covered the city. Then came another fine layer. One layer on top of another until an entire city was buried in the sand."

"That is why," R' Lieberman explained, "Rav Shach was so worried about any change in, or deviation from, tradition. He saw in them the first layer of dust, and who knows what the final result would be!"

וּמֹשֶׁה הָיָה רֹעֶה אֶת צֹאן ... — *Moshe was shepherding the sheep* ... (3:1).

*T*he Midrash (*Shemos Rabbah* 2:2) recounts the story of the lamb that ran away from Yisro's herd in the wilderness. Moshe ran after it until it reached some woods and chanced upon a pool of water, from which it stopped to drink. When Moshe caught up with the lamb and saw it drinking, he said, "I did not know that you were running away because you were thirsty. You must be very tired!" And so he carried the lamb on his shoulders until he came back to the herd. Said the Holy One, Blessed is He, "You have the mercy to treat the sheep of a human being in that manner; by your life, you will be the shepherd for my sheep, Israel!" This is the meaning of *Moshe was shepherding*.

The Rebbe of Strikov told Rav Shach the following thought in the name of his grandfather: What was the test that Moshe under-went? What is so outstanding about treating someone's sheep in this way? The test, he explained, was to see whether Moshe comprehended that a herd is composed of individual lambs, and that one must look out for the lamb with the tendency to run away from the herd!

Rav Shach used to retell this exposition and praise it.

It is told that when the late *mashgiach* of Ponevezh, R' Yechezkel Levinstein, was *mashgiach* in Kletzk, he made a point of learning in the *beis midrash*, though he had a private room. When asked for the reason, he would say that there was one young man in the yeshivah who, if the *mashgiach* would not be present, would be likely to go to his room. As long as the *mashgiach* was present, however, he would continue his studies. "If even one young man will study better because of me remaining," explained R' Yechezkel, "then I am obligated to remain in the *beis midrash*!"

וּמֹשֶׁה הָיָה רֹעֶה אֶת צֹאן ... — *Moshe was shepherding the sheep ... (3:1).*

Moshe was a faithful shepherd. What was his test? To follow a lone lamb and take care of its needs!

Rav Shach was once heavily involved in an important battle to protect a breach in Torah observance. Though Rav Shach did not generally summon anyone — it was against his nature to order people to do anything and he refrained from being a burden on others — he sent someone to summon one of his confidants. The person who was summoned was certain that he was being called to join in the battle for the sake of Heaven.

When he arrived, Rav Shach told him about an older student in a yeshivah in southern Israel who had been trying to get married for several years. The boy finally had found a suitable girl and they were all ready to get engaged, but his financial situation was holding things up. Rav Shach had already obligated himself to raise 20,000 *shekel*, but that was not sufficient. Rav Shach said that he had no peace because of this problem; he could not even sleep at night. All day long he was involved in the vital battle for the sake of Heaven and for the sake of all that is holy to Judaism, but at night he was sleepless thinking about this poor fellow. He called to ask that money be collected so that the young man could finally begin building his family!

וּמֹשֶׁה הָיָה רֹעֶה אֶת צֹאן ... — *Moshe was shepherding the sheep ... (3:1).*

One year, just before the Pesach intersession, the head of a certain yeshivah came to speak with Rav Shach about his yeshivah. Rav Shach asked about the smallest details and the *rosh yeshivah* told him all about the difficulties his yeshivah was facing, including that parents were pressuring their children to leave the yeshivah to go to the army. Why, just the other day, a wonderful young man gave in to his parents' pressure and notified the yeshivah that he would not be coming back after vacation. Rav Shach asked for the name of the youth, and asked the *rosh yeshivah* to try to convince him to stay in the yeshivah. The *rosh yeshivah* replied that he was tired of battling parents, and he was busy with so many other things.

After the spring break, that *rosh yeshivah* was quite surprised to see the young man among the returning students.

"Shalom Aleichem," he greeted the young man. "I am so happy to see you back in the yeshivah!"

"And I thank the *rosh yeshivah*," replied the young man, "for sending Rav Shach to Petach Tikvah to speak to my parents and convince them to let me continue in yeshivah, assuring them that I have a great future awaiting me in the Torah world!"

וְאָמְרוּ-לִי מַה-שְּׁמוֹ מָה אֹמַר אֲלֵהֶם — *And they say to me, "What is His Name?" — what shall I say to them? (3:13).*

The Brisker Rav, R' Yitzchak Zev Soloveitchik, presented a very difficult Talmudic question to Rav Shach, and offered a beautiful resolution. When Rav Shach showed great pleasure with both the question and the answer, the Brisker Rav told him, "*Ihr zent a maven* — you are one who has an understanding in these things. Others, as soon as they hear the question, ask 'What is the practical difference?' "

"Come listen to a story," added the Brisker Rav. The Chozeh of

Lublin [*Chozeh* literally means "seer" — he was one of the great early Chassidic masters] was looking for someone to blow the shofar for the High Holy Days. Many of his disciples, including the very wise Reb Bunim of P'shis'cha, wanted the distinction. The Chozeh chose Reb Bunim and began teaching him the secrets of blowing shofar, according to Kabbalah. When he finished teaching him, Reb Bunim told him, "But I can't blow the shofar."

The Chozeh was upset: "So why did you volunteer to blow?"

"I learned from Moshe," he replied. "When Hashem first asked Moshe to take Israel out of Egypt, he said, 'And they say to me, What is His Name?' — what shall I say to them?' Hashem taught him the Holy Names and taught him the wondrous signs and miracles. Finally, he said, 'I am not a man of words ... send by the hand of whomever You will send!'

"From this we learn," concluded the Brisker Rav, "that regarding Torah, we must learn all about it, even if there will be no practical difference!"

שְׁלַח־נָא בְּיַד־תִּשְׁלָח — *Send by the hand of whomever You will send* (4:13).

*R*ashi explains that "by the hand of whomever You will send" refers to the one whom You are accustomed to send, i.e., Aharon.

As is known, in Rav Shach's early years in the Holy Land, he suffered from poverty and he had to travel a great deal to his various teaching positions. His family lived in Jerusalem, and he taught in Jerusalem, Rechovot, and Petach Tikvah, before he found his place in Ponevezh.

The Torah leaders of the generation — the Brisker Rav, Rav Isser Zalman Meltzer, and the Chazon Ish — knew of his greatness in Torah and felt his pain. One day, the opportunity arose to purchase the building of a yeshivah that had closed, and to establish a new yeshivah with Rav Shach at its helm. How much easier that would have made the life of Rav Shach and his family!

Rav Shach thought about it and rejected the offer. And why? Because noted scholars had taught in that yeshivah before it closed, and if they were to hear that the yeshivah had reopened — under new management and with new students — they would feel very bad. For that reason alone, Rav Shach felt that the yeshivah should not reopen.

שְׁלַח־נָא בְּיַד־תִּשְׁלָח — *Send by the hand of whomever You will send* (4:13).

ashi explains that "by the hand of whomever You will send" refers to the one whom You are accustomed to send, i.e., Aharon. Several verses earlier (v. 10) Rashi explains that all this was because Moshe did not want to assume superiority over his brother Aharon who was both older than him and a prophet. Moshe kept on protesting, until Hashem notified him that Aharon's greatness would not be affected (see Rashi on v. 14).

After Rav Shach founded the *Degel HaTorah* party, people knew that he would walk to the polling station, despite his advanced age and his great weakness. This was interpreted as a sign of his devotion and his wish to show everybody how important he considered this election, in which the honor of Heaven was at stake.

Only those closest to him knew the real reason he walked. One of the top aides, who had done so much to help found the party, offered to drive Rav Shach to the polls. Rav Shach considered answering in the affirmative, but his regular driver, R' Yechezkel Is'chayak, knowing nothing of this offer — took it for granted that he would be driving Rav Shach to the polls. Since Rav Shach did not want to slight either one of them, he preferred walking — although each step involved great suffering.

שְׁלַח־נָא בְּיַד־תִּשְׁלָח. וַיִּחַר־אַף יְהוָה בְּמֹשֶׁה — *Send by the hand of whomever You will send. And the anger of Hashem burned against Moshe* (4:13-14).

orah" is from the same root as *horaah* — teaching. Accordingly, what is the Torah teaching us by telling us how Moshe demurred accepting Hashem's appointment to go and redeem the people of Israel, and that Hashem was angered by this?

Rav Shach explained that this teaches an important lesson: One who is given a task for the physical and spiritual benefit of the Jewish Nation — such as Moshe who took upon himself the task of redeeming Israel and giving them the Torah — must do so without letting any personal considerations interfere, even if the individual might indeed prefer to remain in the study hall and devote all his energies to serving Hashem directly!

He also recounted what he had heard from his uncle, R' Isser Zalman Meltzer. When the Alter of Slobodka sent him to found the Slutzk

Yeshivah, the Alter told him, "It would be a good idea if you went up to the House of *Mussar* (moral ethics) to study some *mussar* for an hour." R' Isser Zalman said that, at the time, he thought that the Alter was asking too much of him. "After all," he said, "there I was, a young rabbi opening up a yeshivah and already I was expected to do it all for the sake of Heaven?! Nevertheless," he concluded, "all the subsequent difficulties I had in Slutzk, I attribute to the fact that I did not listen to the Alter of Slobodka, and did not go up to study *mussar*."

In recounting this story, Rav Shach would conclude, "Young talented scholars who are diligent, brilliant, and good with people, ask me if they should open a yeshivah. They don't understand this important lesson: If they are not completely certain that their intention is for the sake of Heaven, they cannot depend on Divine aid for their project."

וְאַחַר בָּאוּ מֹשֶׁה וְאַהֲרֹן וַיֹּאמְרוּ אֶל־פַּרְעֹה — *Afterwards Moshe and Aharon came and said to Pharaoh (5:1).*

Rashi points out that the Elders who had been accompanying Moshe and Aharon slipped away one by one before they arrived at Pharaoh's palace, because they were afraid to go to him.

Rav Shach told the Brisker Rav a story that he had heard from a Jew from Slutzk: The Russian government was about to issue a decree that would have had a negative impact on the Jewish religion, and only one man had the power to cancel the decree. This person was a very wealthy assimilated Jew by the name of Poliakov, a man who had the commission to build the railroad, and had a great deal of influence. The problem was that he was particularly unfond of religious Jews. Two great Jewish leaders, the Beis Halevi (R' Yosef Dov Soloveitchik of Brisk) and R' Yitzchak Elchanan Spektor of Kovno, went to see Mr. Poliakov. As they stood at his doorway, the Beis HaLevi saw R' Yitzchak Elchanan pause to prepare what he would say to the anti-religious assimilated Jew. He decided to help out his colleague and asked for permission to speak first. He then walked into the house without knocking, went straight to Mr. Poliakov's desk, and called out the words of the prophet (*Yeshayahu* 51:12), "Who are you that you shall be afraid of mortal humans and of men who will be made as grass?"

Mr. Poliakov was speechless from fright. He mutely heard their entreaties and promised to do whatever he could.

When Rav Shach finished relating the story there were tears in the eyes of the Brisker Rav.

תִּכְבַּד הָעֲבֹדָה עַל־הָאֲנָשִׁים — *Let the work weigh heavier upon the men* (5:9).

av Shach cited the *mashgiach* of Ponevezh, R' Yechezkel Levinstein, as stating that the reason we are commanded to remember the Exodus from Egypt all our lives is because a person can find the solution to every one of his problems in the story of the Exodus. In this vein, Rav Shach said that the reason why they were forced to work even harder after Moshe and Aharon came to demand the release of the people of Israel was to teach us not to give up when things do not develop as we expect them to. From this verse we can see that life always works that way.

Rav Shach continued, "I remember that at one point R' Yitzchak Zev Soloveitchik, the Brisker Rav, asked me to help his son R' Berel open a *kollel*. I convinced some top young men to study there, the *kollel* opened, and the Brisker Rav was happy. At the end of the term, several of the students gave notice that they would be leaving, and the Brisker Rav was quite upset. I consoled him by telling him that that is the way a yeshivah is built. You start with five students, go down to two, and finally you see the fulfillment of the verse (*Iyov* 8:7): 'Though your beginning was insignificant, your end will flourish exceedingly.' Ultimately, that indeed happened!"

תִּכְבַּד הָעֲבֹדָה עַל־הָאֲנָשִׁים ... וְאַל־יִשְׁעוּ בְּדִבְרֵי־שָׁקֶר — *Let the work weigh heavier upon the men ... let them not engage (yish'u) in words of falsity* (5:9).

he Midrash (*Shocher Tov* 119) comments on the verse (*Tehillim* 119:92) "Had Your Torah not been my preoccupation [*sha'ashuai*, lit. my plaything], I would have perished in my affliction," that Israel said: "If not for Your Torah that was with me and was my plaything, I would have perished in my affliction." Similarly, the Midrash continues, Moshe said (ibid. 94:19): "When my forebodings were abundant within me, Your comforts cheered [yes-ha'ashu] my soul." So too Pharaoh said, "Let the work weigh heavier upon the men ... let them not engage (yish'u) in words of falsity" They had scrolls and they would take pleasure from them from Shabbos to Shabbos as from a plaything. Thus it says, "Had Your Torah not been my preoccupation [*sha'ashuai*, lit. my plaything], I would have perished in my affliction. I will never forget Your precepts, for through them You have preserved me." They are the preservation of Israel; without them, there would be no life. Similarly, it says (*Devarim* 30:20): "For

He is your life," and (*Mishlei* 8:35): "For one who finds me finds life," and (ibid. 9:11): "For through me your days will be increased, and they will increase years of life for you."

Said Rav Shach: "When I lost my daughter, may she rest in peace, in Vilna, R' Chaim Ozer Grodzinsky said to me, 'Rav Shach' — that is what he called me — 'Had Your Torah not been my preoccupation, I would have perished in my affliction.'

"His words motivated me to delve deeper into the verse. Our Sages say (*Sotah* 35a) that when King David said (*Tehillim* 119:54), 'Your statutes were music to me' (which they interpreted to mean that he drew strength from singing the words of the Torah, in places in which he felt fear), he was punished. Accordingly, why was he not punished for calling the Torah 'a plaything'?

"The answer is that he was not saying that the Torah is a 'plaything'; rather, he was expressing how he derived pleasure by seeing the world from the Torah perspective. This can be compared to a person who visited a jail in which there were two prisoners, one sad and depressed and the other happy and in a good mood. He was surprised at the contrast between the two, until the wardens explained to him that the former was sentenced to life in prison with no chance for parole, and so he was quite depressed at his devoid-of-hope situation. The second, on the other hand, knew that his release was imminent, and the very thought of release brought him joy.

"We can now turn to the scrolls that they had in Egypt. They would take pleasure from them from Shabbos to Shabbos as from a plaything, because they knew that Hashem would redeem them. This knowledge itself made their enslavement feel less oppressive. So, too, regarding King David saying, 'Had Your Torah not been my preoccupation, I would have perished in my affliction.' He who cleaves to Torah knows that the tribulations of this world are merely like the foam on the surface of the water, which leaves the water beneath unaffected. In the words of Rambam: 'A person must cleave to Hashem and awaken from his slumber and erring in the vanities of time, and he should realize that there is nothing permanent other than the knowledge of the Creator.' Such a person can derive joy as from a plaything!"

אֲדנָ״י לָמָה הֲרֵעֹתָה לָעָם הַזֶּה — *My Lord, why have You harmed this people* (5:22).

According to Rabbeinu Bachya, Hashem's Name expressing His Lordship, spelled *alef, dalet, nun, yud* in Hebrew, is based on the quality of judgment (rather than mercy). Moshe would not have been concerned with the quality of mercy, for he knew that any tribulations deriving from the quality of mercy fall under the category of loving discipline, for which it says (*Tehillim* 94:12), "Praiseworthy is the man whom God disciplines." Regarding this, the Gemara says (*Berachos* 5a), "What is considered 'loving discipline'? That which involves no lost Torah time."

Rav Shach once fell and was badly bruised. A doctor was summoned and when he came, he asked, "Are you in pain from the fall?"

"I have no pain from the fall," replied Rav Shach. "I have suffering from it."

"What is the difference?" the doctor asked.

"The fall made me suffer," Rav Shach explained. "My pain is that the suffering does not allow me to delve into my studies properly, but there is no pain from the fall itself."

ואֵרא — Va'eira

וַיֹּאמֶר ה' אֶל־מֹשֶׁה אֱמֹר אֶל־אַהֲרֹן קַח מַטְּךָ וּנְטֵה־יָדְךָ עַל־מֵימֵי מִצְרַיִם — *Hashem said to Moshe, "Say to Aharon, 'Take your staff and stretch out your hand over the waters of Egypt' "* (7:19).

ashi explains that because the river protected Moshe when he was cast into it, it was not smitten through his hand, neither at the plague of Blood nor at the plague of Frogs, but was smitten instead through the hands of Aharon.

Rav Zvi Eisenstein, the *rosh yeshivah* of Yeshivah Tiferes Tziyon and the *chazzan* for the High Holy Day services at the Ponevezh Yeshivah, related how each year Rav Shach would attend the graduation at Tiferes Tziyon Yeshivah and speak there. In 5754 (1994), when Rav Shach was approaching his hundredth birthday, Rav Eisenstein came to invite him once again. Rav Shach apologized, saying that for several months he had not left his house because of his excessive weakness. He asked to be forgiven for not attending that year.

Needless to say, Rav Eisenstein replied that, to the contrary, nothing was more important than Rav Shach taking care of his health and preserving his strength, and they never intended to bother him if he did not have the strength! He blessed Rav Shach with good health and strength, and turned to leave. All of a sudden, Rav Shach called him back and said, "I've decided to go anyhow."

"No! No! No! Please do not let the *Rosh Yeshivah* go through the bother," he responded.

But Rav Shach said, "True, it will be very difficult for me to come, but since you lead the prayer service at the yeshivah for the High Holy Days and put yourself out so much for the sake of the congregation — I am obligated to put myself out in gratitude for what you do, and accept your request."

And so he did. It was probably his last public appearance outside of

Ponevezh Yeshivah. He graced the ceremony despite his great weakness and, when he turned to leave in total exhaustion, he said to Rav Eisenstein once again that he came only as a demonstration of gratitude; he put himself out in recognition of Rav Eisenstein having putting himself out.

וְהִפְלֵיתִי בַיּוֹם הַהוּא אֶת־אֶרֶץ גֹּשֶׁן אֲשֶׁר עַמִּי עֹמֵד עָלֶיהָ לְבִלְתִּי הֱיוֹת־שָׁם עָרֹב — *And on that day I shall distinguish the land of Goshen upon which My people stands, that there shall be no mixture of wild beasts there* (8:18).

One Friday night in the middle of the first Gulf War, missiles flew over Bnei Brak, and the sounds of their explosions were clearly heard in that city. It soon became apparent that a missile had landed in Ramat Gan, the neighboring city. The next morning, one of those close to Rav Shach said with excitement that they had just witnessed a modern-day equivalent of "And on that day I shall distinguish the land of Goshen upon which My people stands!"

Rav Shach replied, "You are also saying that foolishness? It is the ultimate conceit to think that we see miracles similar to those which occurred during the exodus from Egypt! Quite the contrary, instead of thinking that Bnei Brak does not deserve punishment, it would be proper for us to think that this whole storm is because of our sins! Let me tell you that I was thinking about it. Why, most of the missiles fell on Friday night. We thus have to examine our Friday-night activities to determine why Hashem did what He did, and what is expected of us. Well, the Friday night meal [in the winter] ends at 7 or 8. What do young Torah scholars do from then, until midnight? Perhaps that is what is demanded of us — to strengthen our Torah learning on Friday night!"

בא — Bo

כָּל־מַחְמֶצֶת לֹא תֹאכֵלוּ — *You shall not eat any leavening* (12:20).

Rav Shach's son-in-law, R' Meir Zvi Bergman [my father], relates that he grew up with the custom of not eating any *"gebrokts"* (soaked matzah products on Pesach). [This custom was generally accepted in the chassidic community only.] When he was engaged to marry Rav Shach's daughter, he was invited to Rav Shach's house for the Pesach *Seder*, as is the custom. He asked Rav Shach what their custom was regarding soaked matzah, and Rav Shach assured him that they too are careful in the matter, and neither cook nor eat soaked matzah products.

During Chol HaMoed Pesach, R' Bergman went to visit his rebbi, the Chazon Ish. When he arrived there, he ran into R' Yisrael Yaakov Kanievsky, known as "the Steipler," who greeted him and asked him if he ate *gebrokts*. When he replied in the negative, the Steipler asked, "And in the house of your father-in-law?"

"He assured me that they also do not eat *gebrokts*," replied R' Bergman.

The Steipler smiled and said, "I think that he just said that for you. Your father-in-law is no youngster, and I am sure that it is hard for him to refrain from eating his accustomed softened matzah. There is no limit to his indulgence! I advise you to seek annulment for this custom, thereby making life easier for your father-in-law. In fact, why don't you do it while you are here?"

"The Steipler" was known for his keen insight. He was indeed right. When R' Bergman mentioned to his father-in-law that he had annulled his custom, Rav Shach returned to eating the soaked matzah that he was accustomed to eating.

כָּל־מַחְמֶצֶת לֹא תֹאכֵלוּ — *You shall not eat any leavening* (12:20).

ashi explains that *"any"* leavening includes even a mixture of it with other foods.

Rav Shach recounted how, in Poland, they would sell specially denatured grain alcohol for use as fuel in cooking. In the denaturing process they would add a poison, so that humans would be unable to consume it. The purpose of the denaturing process was to free the alcohol from the high duties collected for ordinary alcohol. The local gentiles, who enjoyed their liquor, found ways to distill the poison from it and get themselves drunk.

As Pesach approached, a question arose: Could it be used as fuel on Pesach. On the one hand, in its present state it is unfit for human consumption, so its use should be permitted. On the other hand, perhaps since it can be distilled into a drinkable form, it should be considered *chametz*, the use of which is forbidden.

Rav Shach's uncle, R' Isser Zalman Meltzer, prohibited its use. Another rabbi in Slutzk, R' Yosef, permitted its use. R' Isser Zalman sent the question to R' Eliahu Chaim Meisel, the rabbi of Lodz, whose authoritative rulings were accepted by all. R' Meisel immediately sent back a telegram prohibiting it, in agreement with the ruling of R' Isser Zalman. However, the mailman erred in the address and brought the telegram to the house of the rabbi who permitted it!

R' Isser Zalman saw this as an act of Divine Providence, indicating how Heaven protected the honor of this rabbi. It would not be proper for him to hear from his disputant that the final ruling went against him. Instead, the situation was so arranged that he was able to find out in a way that allowed him to keep his honor by simply "changing his mind."

בשלח — Beshalach

וַיִּירְאוּ הָעָם אֶת ה' — *And the people revered Hashem* (14:31).

Rav Shach asked his grandson the following question: It says (*Tehillim* 58:11): "The righteous one will rejoice when he sees vengeance." Accordingly, when "Israel saw the great hand that Hashem inflicted on Egypt," why did they feel reverence and awe and not love for Hashem? Indeed, they had seen the two hundred and fifty afflictions that befell the Egyptians, then passed through the sea on the firmament with such wondrous miracles, and had the Divine Presence revealed to them to the degree that a servant woman at the sea saw what even the prophet Yechezkel did not see in his visions (see *Mechilta Beshalach*). When they were then Divinely inspired to sing — and Divine inspiration can only affect a person when he is happy with the joy of the commandments — shouldn't they have achieved the level of love for Hashem rather than reverence and awe?

"This teaches," answered Rav Shach, "that the greater the level a person achieves in his understanding of Hashem, the greater his reverence and awe for Him. The Sages of the Great Assembly, who established our version of prayer, said that the angels 'do with awe and reverence the wishes of their Maker ... respond and say with reverence.' Similarly, they said that the luminaries 'do with awe the will of their Maker.' Now, how did the Sages of the Great Assembly know this? Presumably they extrapolated from their own feelings of awe and reverence what great awe and reverence the angels must feel."

He added, "In the *Nesaneh Tokef* prayer recited on the High Holy Days, we say, 'And the angels hasten, fear and trembling seize them, and they say, "Behold, the day of judgment!" ' Now, why should the angels fear the supreme awe of judgment day? Angels do not sin!

Rather, there is a verse concerning Rosh Hashanah which says (*Yeshayahu* 5:16), 'Hashem, Master of Legions, will become exalted through judgment, and the Holy God will be sanctified through justice.' This verse teaches that there is an additional level of exaltedness that is perceived on that day, having to do with God's role as King and Judge. It is this higher level of perception that brings about the additional reverence."

וַיִּירְאוּ הָעָם אֶת ה' — *And the people revered Hashem* (14:31).

According to the *Zohar*, "the people" (*ha'am*) refers to the "great mixture" that went up with them (see *Shemos* 12:38).

One of Rav Shach's attendants relates how he was once approached by a young man for permission to interview Rav Shach. After looking at his bare head and long hair, he replied that Rav Shach does not give interviews. The young man brazenly pulled a yarmulke from his pocket, pinned it on his head, and said, "So I will ask him for a blessing."

Since no one was turned away from receiving Rav Shach's blessing, he could not be stopped from coming in, but he was told that if he remained and became a bother, he would be forcibly evicted. The young man agreed to this condition.

He entered as if he owned the place, grabbed a chair, and sat himself down opposite Rav Shach. Rav Shach was already in his advanced old age, and bent over; his head barely rose above the level of the table.

The attendant who had let him in suddenly realized that the young man appeared to be in shock, perhaps out of reverence for the *Rosh Yeshivah*. He felt pity — affection, even — for the young man. He went over and whispered to Rav Shach the phrase used in the Haggadah regarding the one who does not know enough to ask questions, "You open up for him."

Rav Shach, in his weak, trembling voice, asked, "Have you ever been in a synagogue?"

The question seemed to bring the young man to life. He straightened up and said in a confident voice, "Of course!"

"How many times?" asked Rav Shach. It was obvious that each word that the Sage uttered required great effort.

"Once, on the day of my bar mitzvah."

"Are you *shomer Shabbos* [Shabbos observant]?" asked Rav Shach.

"Sure," he answered. "The way I understand it. I travel with my family to the beach, for Shabbos pleasure."

"And what do you eat on Pesach?"

"We eat matzah, because that is what is available, but in the evening we go out to a restaurant in Nazareth ..."

Rav Shach interrupted him and asked, "And what do you eat on Yom Kippur?"

"Er ... um ... on Yom Kippur I, um ..."

Then, amazingly, it happened. Rav Shach rose up suddenly with strength no one knew that he had, and thunderously said, "You see, after everything, you still have some reverence!"

וַיִּלֹּנוּ הָעָם עַל מֹשֶׁה לֵאמֹר מַה נִּשְׁתֶּה — *The people complained against Moshe, saying, "What shall we drink?"* (15:24).

Rav Shach recounted how, during World War I, most of the Jewish husbands were drafted, and the wives found it very difficult to earn a living. The unfortunate women came to the rabbi of Slutzk, Rav Shach's uncle, R' Isser Zalman Meltzer, to bemoan their plight and to be blessed by him that their husbands should return in good health, and be able to support their families. This is the answer that he would always give: "In the merit of your belief that I am a Torah scholar, and your belief that the blessing of a Torah scholar helps and his Torah brings about your salvation, may you be saved."

עֶרֶב וִידַעְתֶּם כִּי ה' הוֹצִיא אֶתְכֶם מֵאֶרֶץ מִצְרָיִם — *In the evening, you will know that Hashem took you out of the land of Egypt* (16:6).

Sforno explains that Moshe was saying, "May it be His will that Hashem's promise to me that He will give you food will be in such a manner that He will give you each evening for the needs of that evening — so that you realize that Hashem has totally taken you out of Egypt; for He will have taken you out of its customs whereby you sat by the pots of meat at times that were not set mealtimes, like animals." As the Gemara (*Yoma* 75b) says, "At first, the people of Israel were like chickens pecking at garbage, until Moshe came along and set mealtimes for them."

We thus see that, in addition to teaching the people of Israel the laws of the Torah, Moshe, our teacher, also taught them the laws of etiquette. This is incumbent on any teacher. Rav Shach always instilled in his students that a teacher must teach not only Torah, but also the etiquette that precedes it (see *Yalkut Shimoni, Bereishis* 3:34). After Minchah services at the yeshivah, he would personally put up his *shtender,* to make it easier for the cleaner to clean. One time, one of the students beat Rav Shach to it and began putting up Rav Shach's *shtender.* Rav Shach sternly told him, "You are ruining the lesson I am trying to instill!"

בְּתֵת ה' לָכֶם בָּעֶרֶב בָּשָׂר לֶאֱכֹל וְלֶחֶם בַּבֹּקֶר לִשְׂבֹּעַ — *When, in the evening, Hashem gives you meat to eat and bread to satiety in the morning (16:8).*

During the week in which the Torah portion of *Behar* was read in 5754 (1994), when Rav Shach was approaching his hundredth year, he suffered from severe stomach pains and had to undergo medical tests. As preparation for a particularly difficult test, he had to refrain from food for three days, subsisting only on liquids. This fast weakened him further, yet it did not stop him from studying Torah. He even kept to his practice of going to the yeshivah for afternoon prayers. On Tuesday afternoon they performed the test. When he returned home toward evening, he was served some food after his three-day fast.

"It is not mealtime," he said. He sat down to learn until 8 p.m., then he got up to go to the yeshivah for the pre-Maariv mussar study time and Maariv services. But when he saw that he really had no strength, he had a bite to eat — and then went to the yeshivah!

וַיְהִי יָדָיו אֱמוּנָה עַד בֹּא הַשָּׁמֶשׁ — *And he remained with his hands in faithful prayer until the setting of the sun (17:12).*

Mechilta (*Parashas Amalek* 1) derives from here that Moshe was fasting.

On the day on which Ponevezh Yeshivah was dedicated, Rav Shach stayed in the home of his son-in-law, R' Meir Zvi Bergman. He was fasting, and he asked that this fact be kept a secret.

At noon, his son-in-law asked him if it would not be sufficient to fast half a day. Rav Shach responded in the negative, explaining that when a yeshivah is dedicated, much Divine aid is required. He recounted how in Brody, the city of Rav Simchah Kluger, a beautiful yeshivah was founded. It had a magnificent *beis midrash* and it was headed by rabbis renowned for their Torah scholarship and piety, yet the yeshivah did not succeed. When a fund-raiser for Volozhin Yeshivah came to the city, he was asked for the secret of Volozhin's success — despite its location in some unknown village — as opposed to the beautiful yeshivah in the city of Brody which did not succeed. The fund-raiser replied that when the yeshivah in Brody was founded, there was much joy and everyone drank *"l'chayim."* On the other hand, when Volozhin Yeshivah was founded, Rav Chaim of Volozhin (the founder of the yeshivah) was fasting!

This is another possible insight into the custom that the bride and groom fast on the day of their wedding (see *Shulchan Aruch Even HaEzer* 61:1).

כִּי יָד עַל כֵּס יָה מִלְחָמָה לַיהֹוָה בַּעֲמָלֵק מדֹּר דֹּר — *For there is a hand on the throne of God: Hashem maintains a war against Amalek, from generation to generation* (17:16).

Rashi comments that the Hebrew word for "throne" should be *kisei* (literally, chair) but it is written here in the incomplete form, *kes.* Similarly, Hashem's Name is written in its two-letter form, rather than the standard four-letter form. This indicates that Hashem's Name and His throne are incomplete until Amalek's seed is wiped out.

In a letter of thanks that Rav Shach wrote to his uncle, R' Isser Zalman Meltzer, he ended with the following story that he heard from R' Moshe Londinsky, *rosh yeshivah* of Radin Yeshivah: R' Moshe once went to see the Chofetz Chaim (who lived in Radin). The Chofetz Chaim said to him, "Tell me, R' Moshe, are all the chairs in Radin Yeshivah complete?" R' Moshe replied, "Of course. Why shouldn't they be complete?" The Chofetz Chaim burst into tears and said, "Master of the Universe! All the chairs in Radin are complete, but Your 'chair' is incomplete!"

Rav Shach ended the story by writing, "How far we are from this!" How far we are from such sensitivity to holiness and from sharing the pain of the Divine Presence!

נַחַל קִישׁוֹן גְּרָפָם... תִּדְרְכִי נַפְשִׁי עֹז — *Kishon Brook swept them away ... but I myself trod it vigorously* (*Shoftim* 5:21 — from the *haftarah*).

*A*t the time of the first Gulf War, when missiles had already fallen in all the major cities around Bnei Brak, Rav Shach was giving his Talmud lecture to the entire yeshivah. He stated a remarkably innovative exposition and in his excitement he said, "This is a powerful exposition, an unshakeable foundation — it even has the power to fell a missile into the sea!"

Right at the end of the lecture the air-raid siren sounded, indicating an approaching missile. The students hurried to the shelter, while Rav Shach, exhausted from his lecture, stayed where he was, immersed in his studies. When the all-clear sounded, the students returned, briefly studied *Mussar,* and prayed Maariv.

After prayers, Rav Shach went home and asked, "So, do they know where the missile fell?"

"Yes," was the reply. "It fell into the sea!"

"Kishon Brook swept them away ... but I myself trod it vigorously — The only vigor is the vigor of Torah! (*Zevachim* 116a).

יתרו — Yisro

לֶאֱכָל לֶחֶם עִם חֹתֵן מֹשֶׁה לִפְנֵי הָאֱלֹהִים — *To eat bread with the father-in-law of Moshe before God* (18:12).

*R*ashi (from *Berachos* 64a) derives from the Torah's statement that the meal took place "before God," that one who partakes of a meal at which Torah scholars participate is considered as if he has taken pleasure from the splendor of the *Shechinah*, the Divine Presence.

When Rabbis Avraham Kessler and Eliezer Shlesinger were studying at the yeshivah, they went to the wedding of their friend, R' Jonah Zahler. The next day, Rav Shach asked them where they had been the night before.

"We went to the wedding," they replied.

"Too bad you did not tell me you were planning to go," he said with sorrow.

"And if we would have told you," they asked, "then what?"

"Then," said Rav Shach, "I would have asked you to bring me back a piece of cake."

R' Kessler asked, "And if we would have brought it, would the piece of cake have been considered 'remnants of a mitzvah meal'?"

Rav Shach replied, "Of course! Every meal of a yeshivah student is a mitzvah meal and its remnants are 'remnants of a mitzvah meal'! At any rate, I wanted the piece of cake so that I could partake in the wedding meal of a beloved student!"

וַיַּעֲמֹד הָעָם עַל מֹשֶׁה מִן הַבֹּקֶר עַד־הָעָרֶב — *And the people stood by Moshe from the morning until the evening* (18:13).

A certain *rosh yeshivah* once came to consult with Rav Shach, accompanied by a young man. They went to the yeshivah, *davened* Maariv with everyone and waited in line to speak to

Rav Shach. When their turn came, they asked their question — what to do concerning a young man who applied to their yeshivah. Rav Shach replied, "I have already answered that question for you." There were still plenty of people in line, impatiently waiting their turn, and the two men felt compelled to move on. Nevertheless, Rav Shach's reply was disturbing, and the *rosh yeshivah* tried to understand what Rav Shach meant. He remembered that quite a while back he had asked a similar question, and from the answer to that question he could probably deduce the answer to the present question. There were, however, other issues that they wanted to discuss. Therefore, they decided to walk Rav Shach home and talk to him along the way. Others had the same idea first, however, and they had no choice but to walk behind them.

When Rav Shach went into his house, they entered as well. His family signaled them to wait in a side room, so that Rav Shach could eat his supper in peace.

Needless to say, they acceded to the request, and Rav Shach was served supper. No sooner was the food placed before him than he asked, "Where are the people who came in with me?"

The family said to him, "Maybe they went to *daven* Maariv."

A few minutes later, "Where are they?"

Their reply: "They are not back yet."

And again: "Where are they?"

The family called the men in. They saw that Rav Shach's plate was full and his cup of tea untouched. He was not at peace until they came in. Only then was he happy. He sat down to listen, deliberated on their questions, and advised them. When they left, others were already waiting to see him!

וְכָל הָעָם נִצָּב עָלֶיךָ מִן בֹּקֶר עַד־עָרֶב... לִדְרֹשׁ אֱלֹהִים — *With all the people standing by you from morning to evening... to seek God* (18:14-15).

R' Ben-Zion Bergman, Rav Shach's grandson, recounts the story of the time he showed his grandfather what the author of *Yefei Einayim* wrote in his introduction to Tractate *Shabbos*:

"From morning to night the people line up at the opening of the tents ... many, many disturbances. It is unbelievable that the provisional rabbi should have time to come up with any innovative commentary. When those who pass through the gates of my city see me writing down my commentary, while all around me there are constant disturbances, they marvel at how I can pay attention to everything going on around me, answer all the questions and all the while write down my commentary.

"Thank God who makes it possible to compartmentalize the brain; there is someting like a small attic in my brain — a room in which to think of Torah — to which no disturbances can enter. I too marvel at this ability."

When Rav Shach saw this, he said: "Of course! One can be involved in something else while studying Torah in his thoughts!

כִּי יִהְיֶה לָהֶם דָּבָר בָּא אֵלַי — *When they have a matter, one comes to me* (18:16).

R' Refael Wolf recounts the time a high-school girl came to Rav Shach's house saying that she had an important question. She was allowed in and she asked, "Is it permitted to cheat on a test?"

R' Wolf reprimanded her angrily, saying, "How dare you disturb the *Rosh Yeshivah* with such questions!"

Rav Shach said, "There is no reason for anger! Her teachers taught her that everything must be done in accordance with the law and, when in doubt, one should ask, and that is exactly what she did! No, my daughter, one may not cheat on a test."

וְהוֹדַעְתִּי אֶת חֻקֵּי הָאֱלֹהִים וְאֶת תּוֹרֹתָיו — *And I make known the statutes of God and His laws* (18:16).

The Netziv (*Haamek Davar*) explains that all the commandments of the Torah are called "the statutes of God," as seen in *Vayikra* 26:3.

Now, generally, "statutes" (*chukim*) refers to those commandments for which no reason is known. There are very few such commandments, and the Midrash (*Bamidbar Rabbah* 19:5) lists only four. So why are *all* the commandments of the Torah called "statutes"?

Rav Shach used to recount the story of R' Meir Simchah of Dvinsk who had a faithful sexton working for him in his synagogue, who did everything according to his directions. One time, R' Meir Simchah told him to do something, but he disagreed. R' Meir Simchah said to him, "You never listen to what I say!"

The sexton protested, "Why does the Rav say so? After all, this is the first time I ever disagreed with him!"

R' Meir Simchah replied, "That is true, but this time proves that you always followed my directions because *you* agreed. The proof is, when you do not agree, you do not hesitate to voice your disagreement. Thus, you have always listened to the directions that your own mind gives you, not to my directions!

The same can be said regarding the commandments and the statutes. Because our Sages have explained to us the reasons for most of the commandments, we keep them willingly and enthusiastically. So why are the reasons not revealed for certain commandments which are left as statutes? The answer is so that we will fulfill those statutes *without* understanding why, thereby indicating our total subservience to His will. As a result, we show that the rest of the commandments are fulfilled only because that is His will. Accordingly, the entire Torah is referred to as a statute, because we fulfill everything because of His command.

וְהוֹדַעְתָּ לָהֶם אֶת הַדֶּרֶךְ יֵלְכוּ בָהּ — *And you shall make known to them the path in which they should go* (18:20).

The Gemara (*Bava Metzia* 30b) explains: "And you shall make known to them" refers to their livelihood, "the path" refers to kind deeds, "they shall go" refers to visiting the sick.

Years ago, Rav Shach would take a walk after the Friday night prayers in the yeshivah, all the while preparing in his mind the public lecture that he would give in the middle of the next week. He was immersed in the depths of his preparation, yet he would pay attention to the location of the homes of his students who had been absent for several days and who were presumably ill, so that he could visit them.

One of them, R Yosef Roth, tells of the time he had already missed several days because of an illness, when Rav Shach knocked on his door that Friday night. The family had just begun the Shabbos meal and Rav Shach entered, smilingly asked him how he felt, blessed him for a speedy recovery, said "Good Shabbos," and continued on his way.

וְאַתָּה תֶחֱזֶה מִכָּל הָעָם . . . אַנְשֵׁי אֱמֶת — *And you shall see from among the entire people . . . men of truth* (18:21).

Rav Shach would always arrive at events punctually, although he knew that the event would not start at that time. In fact, he would sometimes come at the stated time and find the door locked!

When asked why he wasted his precious time, fully knowing that the event will start late, he replied, "I follow the truth; if that is the time stated, truth demands that I arrive at that time — and it is worth suffering for truth!"

וְאַתָּה תֶחֱזֶה מִכָּל הָעָם אַנְשֵׁי חַיִל יִרְאֵי אֱלֹהִים . . . וְשָׁפְטוּ אֶת הָעָם בְּכָל עֵת — *And you shall see from among the entire people, men of means, God-fearing people . . . they shall judge the people at all times (18:21-22).*

The Gemara (*Yevamos* 109b) states: "A judge should always see a sword lying between his loins and the opening to Gehinnom open beneath him!" Rambam (*Hil. Sanhedrin* 23:8) rules in accordance with this statement, as does *Smag* (208).

Once Rav Shach was asked a question which he refused to answer. When pressed to answer, he said, "Whenever I am asked a question, I hesitate and think: What if I am wrong? The one who asked will certainly come to me in the World to Come with a claim against me for giving bad advice. Accordingly, I only answer when I know that I can tell the Heavenly Court why I answered one way and not another. Then, if my advice does not succeed, it is for reasons that only God knows, and not because of my error. In the case of your question, however, both sides are equally weighty. Regardless of which side I would choose, it could turn out that the other side would have been better, and I would not be able to explain why I chose the side that I did. So I will not answer."

כָּל הַדָּבָר הַגָּדֹל יָבִיאוּ אֵלֶיךָ — *They shall bring every major matter to you (18:22).*

Our Sages teach (*Avos* 6:1): "Whoever engages in Torah study for its own sake merits many things . . . From him, people enjoy counsel, wisdom, understanding, and strength."

Several years ago, one of the synagogues in Monsey, New York, was seeking a suitable rabbi. Several candidates were suggested for the position, among them Rabbi F., the son-in-law of one of the well-known *rosh yeshivahs* in America. At the time, Rabbi F. was the rabbi of a large synagogue in Miami, Florida. Since he already had his present position, it stood to reason that Rabbi F. would not be interested in the Monsey position, which was a less prestigious congregation. Nevertheless, Rabbi F. expressed great interest in the new position and in fact was appointed rabbi of that synagogue in Monsey.

People were very surprised by this turn of events, until they heard the story behind it. Several months earlier, Rabbi F. had come to the Holy Land with his niece to take her to Rav Shach for a *berachah* to find an appropriate match. When they landed at the airport, Hashem arranged matters so that a secular Jew agreed to take them along with him to Jerusalem. For the entire trip, however, the secular Jew complained that *charedi rabbis* do not encourage the Jews of the Diaspora to make *aliyah* and physically fulfill the mitzvah of settling the land of Israel.

Rabbi F. was bothered by this complaint, and when he accompanied his niece to Rav Shach, he raised the issue with him.

Rav Shach replied, "Here in Israel there are great spiritual dangers for observant Jews. What is there here — Jerusalem? Bnei Brak? You, on the other hand, have Monsey! Monsey!"

Rabbi F. did not understand what Rav Shach had said. He had Monsey? But he was a rabbi in Miami! Still he kept silent.

Several months later, when he was offered the position in Monsey, Rabbi F. understood to what the words of Rav Shach alluded. He saw it as a Divine sign.

וּמֹשֶׁה עָלָה אֶל־הָאֱלֹהִים — *And Moshe ascended to God* (19:3).

"And Moshe ascended" — all his ascensions were early in the morning (*Rashi*). Rav Shach used to say in a light vein: All spiritual ascension and growth is achieved through getting up early!

He illustrated this point by recounting, "When I taught at Kletzk Yeshivah, I stayed with the students for all three study sessions (i.e., morning through night), and at night I would write whatever new ideas would come to me. I would write until dawn, and at 7 a.m. I was back for morning prayers!"

He added: "I remember the great R' Itzele of Ponevezh who would study Torah until he was thoroughly exhausted, then fall into bed with his boots on because he had no strength left to remove them. Yet the next morning he was at the morning prayers, praying with intensity!

"The toiling of the evening is no excuse for laziness the next day, as is written (*Yeshayahu* 40:31): 'But those whose hope is in Hashem will have renewed strength.' "

כֹּה תֹאמַר לְבֵית יַעֲקֹב — *So shall you say to the house of Yaakov* (19:3).

Rashi explains that "the House of Yaakov" refers to the women. Rav Shach recounted the story of when the Chofetz Chaim was told of the founding of the first Bais Yaakov school in Cracow. It was presented as a "breach" in tradition, since girls would be taught Torah, in apparent contradiction to several Talmudic dicta (see *Sotah* 20a and *Yerushalmi Sotah* 3:4).

The Chofetz Chaim's response was, "Oy, I am so upset! Such a holy cause, and I have no part in it!"

כֹּה תֹאמַר לְבֵית יַעֲקֹב — *So shall you say to the House of Yaakov* (19:3).

R' Yeshayah Lieberman, the principal of one of the major Bais Yaakov high schools in Jerusalem, cites Rav Shach as saying: "It is worth devoting one's entire life to opening yeshivah high schools for girls in every location, and to educate thousands of girls in the Torah way, even if only to produce one good mother!

"See the power of one mother!" continued Rav Shach, "Think of the woman who gave birth to Rashi. Can you imagine a world without Rashi's commentaries? Rashi on *Chumash* and on *Navi*, and Rashi on the Talmud! What would the world be without him? And all this, thanks to his mother!"

כֹּה תֹאמַר לְבֵית יַעֲקֹב וְתַגֵּיד לִבְנֵי יִשְׂרָאֵל — *So shall you say to the House of Yaakov and tell the sons of Israel* (19:3).

A prominent rabbi recounts the following story: "In the first years after my marriage, I gave classes into the late hours of the night. I was concerned about not spending sufficient time with my family, so I went to Rav Shach for advice and found him immersed in his studies. He said, 'What is the problem? Tell me briefly, for I too must learn.' I told him that I study all day in a *kollel,* and from there I go to lecture *baalei teshuvah* (penitents) until after midnight, and that I was concerned that it bothered my wife, although she never complained.

"Rav Shach said, 'There is no question that it is hard for her, but you have to lovingly explain that it is for her own good! Think of a person carrying a sack of diamonds for a long journey on a scorchingly hot day. It is certainly hard for him, but would it enter his mind to cast away part of his burden?'

"Then he asked me, 'And where is your wife now?'

"I replied that she was at work, and he said, 'She should not be disturbed now. Give me her name and telephone number. Tell me, do you think it would help if I called and gave her some words of encouragement?'

"I happily responded, 'Of course! Certainly!'

"A day or two passed; It was Friday afternoon, 15 minutes before candle-lighting time. The phone rang and it was Rav Shach on the phone asking to speak with my wife. He told her how fortunate she was to have merited to share in the mitzvah of spreading Torah, and how great was her reward in this world and in the next! He then beseeched her to aid her husband in his endeavors to the best of her ability, blessing her that in that merit she should have happiness and sustenance, and she should have fine upstanding children who are involved in Torah. He then wished her a 'Good Shabbos' and hung up.

"That Shabbos, we were hosting people who were getting closer to Judaism. When they heard that this Torah giant was calling, and even more so, when they heard the subject of his conversation, they were deeply moved and they fully accepted upon themselves to keep Torah and mitzvos!"

וַיְהִי בַיּוֹם הַשְּׁלִישִׁי בִּהְיֹת הַבֹּקֶר וַיְהִי קֹלֹת וּבְרָקִים וְעָנָן כָּבֵד עַל־הָהָר — *On the third day when it was becoming morning, there was thunder and lightning and a heavy cloud on the mountain (19:16).*

"When it was becoming morning" teaches that He preceded them. This is unlike human behavior, where the master never waits for the disciples. Similarly we find (*Yechezkel* 3:22-23): "Arise and go out to the valley... So I arose and went out to the valley and behold the glory of Hashem was standing there" (*Rashi*).

Rav Shach would follow the ways of the Creator in this as well. Unlike others, he would stay in the *beis midrash* for the entire morning and afternoon study sessions (the Ponevezher Rav was amazed by this), and, in his modesty, he would say that he has "permission" to miss the night study session to write his books. Besides all this, he would always arrive before the students for study sessions as well as for prayers. In addition, he would return the books that were left on the tables to their proper places in the library and he would take the chairs off the tables (where they were placed before washing the floors) and put them back on the floor!

When he was invited to weddings and bar mitzvahs he would come early, despite knowing that people generally came late. In fact, it once happened that when he came to a wedding at the stated time and the families had not yet arrived, he went home!

Once, Rav Shach was invited to speak to teachers and principals in a convention of the *Chinuch Atzma'i* school system. He arrived at 7, the designated time, and no one was there — the one who accompanied him to the hall turned on the lights! After everybody came fashionably late, Rav Shach was called upon to speak. He said, "I knew quite well that the convention would not start on time, and my time is no less valuable than yours. So why did I come so 'early'? Because I wanted to speak about the obligation to be punctual and the evils of lateness, and I thus had to be especially early!"

וַיְהִי בַיּוֹם הַשְּׁלִישִׁי בִּהְיֹת הַבֹּקֶר — *On the third day when it was becoming morning* (19:16).

A rosh yeshivah recounted his discussion with Rav Shach concerning a Talmud teacher who constantly came late, claiming that it was accepted practice for the teacher to come late to class. Rav Shach vehemently insisted that that teacher was transgressing, "Cursed be the one who carries out the mission of Hashem deceitfully," Heaven forbid! At that point R' Refael Wolf commented, "I can testify that Rav Shach always comes a bit early."

To which Rav Shach replied, "I try to come on time. At any rate, better to come early than to come late!"

וַיִּתְיַצְּבוּ בְּתַחְתִּית הָהָר — *And they stood under the mountain* (19:17).

The Sages derive from the description in the verse ("stood under the mountain") that Hashem held the mountain over them like a barrel, saying, "If you accept the Torah fine, but if not, you will be buried underneath the mountain" (*Shabbos* 88a). In their commentary there, *Tosafos* ask how this can be said about the

Children of Israel, who wanted the Torah and had already said (*Shemos* 24:7): "We will do and we will obey." They answer that there was the danger that they would change their minds upon seeing the great fire at Mount Sinai.

Rav Shach questioned this approach: We find that when the Jews responded to the offer to give them the Torah with the phrase, "We will do and we will obey," a Heavenly voice came forth saying, "Who revealed to My children this secret that the ministering angels use?" Furthermore, after they said this, heavenly angels came down to tie two crowns on each member of Israel. Accordingly, why was it necessary to have such a fearful fire that would risk their regressing and taking back what they said, and that necessitated that they be forced to accept the Torah?

"Rather," explained Rav Shach, "we must say that it is worth forgoing the exalted level of willingly accepting the Torah and of saying, 'We will do and we will obey,' just to receive the Torah with additional awe!

"This is because 'awe' is the proper vessel in which to receive the Torah, as expounded by our Sages (*Shabbos* 31a) on the verse (*Yeshayahu* 33:6): 'Fear of Hashem, that is [man's] treasure' — it is the treasure-chest for containing the entire Torah!"

And he added: "How great a man was R' Akiva Eiger — and all because of his awesome fear of heaven. It is said that when he would study the first Mishnah in Tractate *Beitzah*, for example, he would recite it as follows: 'An egg born on the festival, Beis Shammai says: It is the Will of Hashem that it may be eaten; and Beis Hillel says: It is the Will of Hashem that it may not be eaten!'

"If He prepared such massive receptacles for fear of Heaven, it is no wonder that He filled them up with so much Torah!"

זָכוֹר אֶת־יוֹם הַשַׁבָּת לְקַדְּשׁוֹ — *Remember the Sabbath day to sanctify it* (20:8).

The Gemara (*Shabbos* 119a) describes how the great Sages of the Talmud (*Amoraim*) used to take the trouble to personally prepare for Shabbos. R' Moshe Chaim Luzzatto, in *Mesillas Yesharim* (Chapter 19), explains that honoring Shabbos is a form of "This is my G-d and I will beautify Him" (*Shemos* 15:2), and the more one personally toils to honor Shabbos, the more pleasing he is to his Creator.

During the 1948 war, Rav Shach taught in Lomza Yeshivah in Petach Tikvah. When Jerusalem was under siege, he was unable to return to his home (which was in Jerusalem at the time) for Shabbos, so he stayed in the home of R' Avraham Hillel Goldberg.

On Friday afternoon, Rav Shach was sitting in the guest room allotted to him and studying Talmud, while the hostess was finishing her Shabbos preparations. Suddenly the hostess' infant son began crying loudly. His mother wanted to put a pot on the fire and then quiet her son, but suddenly there was silence. She was frightened by the sudden silence and she ran to see its cause. She saw Rav Shach holding an open Gemara in his left hand, gently shaking the baby with his right. As he was pacing back and forth in his room to pacify the baby, he was quietly saying, "in honor of the Holy Shabbos."

She said to him, "The Rav can put the baby into his carriage and then I will take care of him so that the Rav can return to his studies."

He gently explained, "The Gemara says that everybody is obligated to take part in food preparation for Shabbos. I cannot help you in the kitchen. When I pacify the baby and enable you to cook in a relaxed way, however, I am taking part in Shabbos preparation. Please let me pacify him!"

כַּבֵּד אֶת־אָבִיךָ וְאֶת־אִמֶּךָ — *Honor your father and your mother* (20:12).

O ne of Rav Shach's young married students lost his father. His mother asked him to stay with her on Yom Kippur and pray in the synagogue of his deceased father. The young man was in a quandary and he turned to Rav Shach for advice. "How can I leave Bnei Brak?" he asked. "How can I not pray on Yom Kippur in the yeshivah?"

Rav Shach replied, "If you can persuade your mother to agree with you without causing her any pain — fine. If she will be pained by your reluctance, however, you must go to her. You should just know, however, that if a person does the right thing according to the dictates of halachah, he will never lose, neither spiritually nor materially!"

כַּבֵּד אֶת־אָבִיךָ וְאֶת־אִמֶּךָ — *Honor your father and your mother* (20:12).

A young couple decided between themselves that if their forthcoming baby were male, they would name him after his paternal grandfather, who had recently died. As the due date came close, a great Torah leader died and they considered naming the baby after him. They asked Rav Shach, who informed them that their original decision might have the status of a verbal commitment to do a mitzvah, which becomes obligatory. The mitzvah? "Honor your father and your mother!"

דַּבֵּר־אַתָּה עִמָּנוּ וְנִשְׁמָעָה... — *You speak to us and we shall hear . . .* (20:16).

av Shach related a story that he had heard from some of his students when he was *rosh yeshivah* of Lunitz. These students were chassidim of the Slonimer Rebbe, and when the Rebbe came to the city, they went to visit him on Shabbos. When they returned, Rav Shach asked them what they had heard.

They told him that the Rebbe cited the verse, "You speak to us and we shall hear, let G-d not speak to us lest we die," and he asked in the name of R' Chaim of Sanz, "Why should they not die? Is is not worth giving up one's life to be able to hear the commandments directly from Hashem?"

The Rebbe then put his head down for a few moments, and when he raised it he said, "Of course they wanted to hear directly from the Holy One, Blessed is He, and they were even willing to give up their lives for it! Nevertheless, if they were to die, they would be incapable of continuing to hear more and more. For that reason, they did not wish to die. And thus they said, 'You speak to us' — and why? That we shall hear more and more; 'Let G-d not speak to us' — lest we die and be incapable of hearing more!"

Rav Shach always highly praised this insight.

וּבַעֲבוּר תִּהְיֶה יִרְאָתוֹ עַל־פְּנֵיכֶם לְבִלְתִּי תֶחֱטָאוּ — *So that His fear shall be before you, so that you shall not sin* (20:17).

av Shach raised a question on the Gemara (*Shabbos* 31b) which states that R' Shimon and R' Elazar were sitting, when R' Yaakov Bar Acha passed by. R' Elazar said, "Let us rise for him, for he is sin-fearing." R' Shimon said, "Let us rise for him, for he is very learned." R' Elazar said to him, "I tell you that he is sin-fearing and you tell me that he is very learned? You have decreased his worth!"

Rav Shach asked: In what way is "fear" greater than being learned? His answer was that Torah is wisdom, and Hashem gives us the ability to grasp and understand the Torah. In fact, our Sages teach us that

"Torah is not in the Heavens," i.e., the law is ruled according to our understanding. Yet "fear" is based on a person's perception of the One Who commands, and His greatness is so infinite that we cannot grasp it!

לְבַעֲבוּר נַסּוֹת אֶתְכֶם בָּא הָאֱלֹהִים וּבַעֲבוּר תִּהְיֶה יִרְאָתוֹ עַל־פְּנֵיכֶם — *For in order to exalt you had God come; so that His fear shall be before you* (20:17).

On one of his visits to Israel, R' Eliyahu Ber Wachtfogel, *rosh yeshivah* of the Yeshiva of South Fallsburg, went to Rav Shach, accompanied by R' Shalom Shechter, for a blessing. From the time they came in, Rav Shach held forth on the importance of studying *mussar* (moral ethics), and spoke of the greatness of R' Yechezkel Levinstein, who drew him so much closer to understanding the importance of *mussar* study. He ended the conversation by stating that it is sometimes worth cutting short a Talmud study session in order to study *mussar*.

When they left, R' Eliyahu Ber went to the airport for his flight home and R' Shalom returned to his home in Jerusalem. Soon afterwards, the phone rang in the Shechter home; it was the father of R' Eliyahu Ber, R' Nosson Wachtfogel, the venerated *mashgiach* of Lakewood Yeshivah. He said that an important question arose which required Rav Shach's Torah judgment and, knowing that his son was staying at the Shechters', he wanted to reach him to present the matter to Rav Shach. The question was: Since the students were getting lax in their *mussar* study, as at that time the married students hurried home to help their wives, could the Talmud study session be shortened by 5 minutes so that they could start studying *mussar* earlier?

R' Shalom was dumbfounded! He told R' Nosson, "Your son is already on his way home, but he has your answer!" and he added that Rav Shach answered the question on his own initiative!

When R' Eliyahu Ber returned to America, he checked with the *rosh yeshivah* of Lakewood, R' Malkiel Kotler, if they had sent anyone to Rav Shach to ask the question. The answer was an emphatic "NO!"

וּבַעֲבוּר תִּהְיֶה יִרְאָתוֹ עַל־פְּנֵיכֶם לְבִלְתִּי תֶחֱטָאוּ — *So that His fear shall be before you, so that you shall not sin* (20:17).

Our Sages (*Nedarim* 20a) explain that "His fear shall be before you" refers to shame. Fear is internal, and only shame can be "before you" (lit. on your faces). The verse continues, "so that you shall not sin," to teach that shame brings fear of sin (*Rabbeinu Bachya*).

A noted educator recounts how Rav Shach once asked him, "You are an educator; how do you account for the diminished spiritual level of this generation?"

"Does the *Rosh Yeshivah* really think that I should know the answer," he replied?

"Certainly," said Rav Shach, "An educator must understand such matters!"

He replied, "Each generation is getting worse and worse."

To which Rav Shach responded, "The regular worsening of generations does not explain such drastic deterioration!"

When the educator said nothing, Rav Shach continued, "The answer is lack of shame! When I was younger, the enlightenment movement was running rampant, and various ideological waves swept people asunder to make great changes. Yet shame stood as a bulwark against too-rapid deterioration. Now, however, the pre-redemption curse of lack of shame (see *Sotah* 49b) has befallen us and the deterioration is unchecked! And don't make the mistake of thinking that we have hit rock-bottom. Heaven protect us, for without shame everything is possible, and who knows the abyss we will reach!"

משפטים — Mishpatim

שְׁאֵרָהּ כְּסוּתָהּ וְעֹנָתָהּ לֹא יִגְרָע — *Her food, her clothing, or her time, he shall not decrease* (21:10).

*A*lthough "שְׁאֵרָהּ" literally means "her flesh," here it refers to providing her food needs [which sustain her flesh] (Rashi, from *Kesubos* 47b).

Rav Shach used to tell his married students who studied Torah full time while the burden of earning a living was borne by their wives, to mollify their wives by telling them that the ultimate responsibility of earning a living was on the husband's own shoulders. The students were to assure their wives that they were only helping out temporarily while they, the husbands, were ascending the levels of Torah learning.

The Gemara (*Moed Katan* 16b) says: "Whoever is involved in Torah study within the confines of the study hall can be assured that his Torah [knowledge] will proclaim his [greatness] abroad." This proclamation of greatness will come at the proper time, as it says (*Taanis* 7a) that a Torah scholar is like a seed planted in the ground; once it germinates it will grow to greatness. Accordingly, a Torah scholar must explain to his wife that just as it is impossible to hasten the germination of a seed, and thus, one must wait patiently, she too must wait patiently until her husband's time comes. In this manner, Rav Shach would say, she will willingly take upon herself the responsibility of earning a living, and marital harmony will be maintained.

Once Rav Shach was asked by a young married student, whose wife earned an excellent salary, if he was allowed to accept a stipend from the *kollel*. Rav Shach replied that he *should* bring home the stipend, thereby taking part in supporting the family. In this way, his wife won't feel that she is the sole supporter.

וְכִי־יְרִיבֻן אֲנָשִׁים וְהִכָּה־אִישׁ אֶת־רֵעֵהוּ בְּאֶבֶן אוֹ בְאֶגְרֹף — *If men will quarrel and one will strike his fellow with a stone or a fist* (21:18).

The Midrash (*Shemos Rabbah* 30:18) states: Nothing good can come out of a quarrel. "When men will quarrel" inevitably leads to, "one will strike his fellow with a stone or a fist."

Rabbi Amnon Yitzchak recounts: When a mixed swimming pool was to opened in Rosh HaAyin, many people were incensed. They went to Rav Shach and asked him if they should have a mass protest rally.

Rav Shach answered emphatically, "If there will be no violence and no stones will be thrown, then you can have a protest rally. If, however, there is a possibility of rioting — or even of a single stone being thrown which will hit even just one Jew — don't have a rally!"

וְרַפֹּא יְרַפֵּא — *And he shall heal* (21:19).

R' Moshe Nosson Halevi Jungreiss once went to Rav Shach concerning a sick child. Rav Shach heard the details, and advised the family to go to a certain doctor. Since he knew how poor the child's parents were, and was aware that the doctor was very expensive, he also offered to pay the consultation fee. R' Jungreiss returned to Jerusalem and told the child's parents what Rav Shach had said. The doctor diagnosed the illness, prescribed medicine, and the child was cured. Knowing how busy Rav Shach was, both in teaching Torah and in public affairs, R' Jungreiss couldn't bring himself to return to Rav Shach and trouble him about a problem that was essentially solved.

On Chol HaMoed Pesach, Rabbi Jungreiss went to Rav Shach for the customary holiday visit, and found him surrounded by people escorting him to the Minchah prayers. As soon as Rav Shach saw R' Jungreiss, he called out to him, "I've been waiting for a long time now to hear what happened to the child!"

R' Jungreiss told him that everything was fine.

Rav Shach opened a cupboard and pointed to an envelope on the shelf. "Here is the money I set aside for the doctor. Why didn't you come and take it? Take it to the child's parents!"

וְכִי־יִפְתַּח אִישׁ בּוֹר אוֹ כִּי־יִכְרֶה אִישׁ בֹּר — *If a man will open a pit, or if a man will dig a pit* (21:33).

av Shach recounted the story of when the Alter of Slobodka, Rav Nosson Zvi Finkel, saw a young man walking along the side of the street. The man bent down, picked up a printed sheet, looked at it and threw it back down.

The Alter asked him to explain what had transpired. The young man explained that he saw Hebrew letters printed on the paper and thought that the subject matter might be Torah, thereby requiring the page to be buried respectfully, rather than merely discarded. After picking it up and seeing that it was about mundane matters, however, he threw it back down.

The Alter asked him, "Tell me, what is the law concerning a person who causes another to fall down?"

"Why, he is a 'person who damages' with the ensuing financial obligations," he replied.

"Well, then," continued the Elder, "How can you not have realized that another person might come along and make the same mistake you did, and bend down for no reason to pick up the paper? And if he does so, then by throwing down the paper you have effectively 'opened a pit' in a public place, thereby placing an obstacle before another! What difference is there between causing another to fall down and causing him to bend down? Once you picked up the paper, you should have held onto it until the opportunity arose to discard it properly!"

בָּל־אַלְמָנָה וְיָתוֹם לֹא תְעַנּוּן — *You shall not persecute any widow or orphan* (22:21).

nce, after his spiritually uplifting opening speech to the summer learning program for working people (*Yarchei Kallah*), Rav Shach was physically drained. He had spoken heatedly and with pain about the status of the generation and its problems, and when he finished, he was so exhausted that he required help to go down from the pulpit. He barely had the strength to make his way home, where there were already people waiting to meet with him.

When he came home, he saw a fatherless orphan shyly standing in the doorway. He immediately asked that the boy be brought to him, and requested that they be allowed to meet in private. At the end of their meeting, he asked the boy if he had enough at home to comfortably meet his needs and whether he had a large enough allowance. All this, while he was physically exhausted and while important community leaders were waiting outside the door!

אִם־עַנֵּה תְעַנֶּה אֹתוֹ... וְהָרַגְתִּי אֶתְכֶם בֶּחָרֶב — *If you will persecute him... I shall kill you by the sword* (22:22-23).

Tactate *Semachos* (8) relates the story of when the Romans decreed death by sword for Rabban Shimon ben Gamliel and R' Yishmael the high priest. R' Yishmael cried, and Rabban Shimon ben Gamliel said to him, "Young man, you are two steps away from the bosom of the righteous, and you are crying?" R' Yishmael replied, "I am only crying for being put to death the same way as murderers and Sabbath desecrators are put to death." Rabban Shimon asked, "Perhaps you were sitting at your dinner table, or sleeping, and a woman came with a pressing question and your attendant said: 'He is sleeping,' and the Torah says, 'If you will persecute him... I shall kill you by the sword!' "

Rav Shach once realized that people were not disturbing him at mealtime. He was quite surprised, because he was so used to being disturbed at all hours of the day. He understood that it must be because the members of his household stood guard to notify those who came that he was eating and was not to be disturbed. Thus, he refused to eat in his room, because he was hard of hearing and he would not hear any knocking from there. Instead, he insisted on eating in the hall where he could hear knocking and he could let visitors in immediately.

Furthermore, for a while Rav Shach told his grandson to stay in the apartment while he went to the yeshivah, and if anyone were to come, regardless of who he was, the grandson should not tell him that Rav Shach was not at home. Rather, he should invite the person in with a smile and give him a seat. He should then beg the guest's pardon for a moment and rush to the yeshivah to call Rav Shach.

This grandson testifies that he did this several times each day, and each time Rav Shach would stop whatever he was doing, hurry to his apartment, speak to the person and then go back to the yeshivah!

אִם־כֶּסֶף תַּלְוֶה אֶת־עַמִּי — *When you will lend money to My people* (22:24)

R' Yosef Goldstein was the officer responsible for meeting the financial obligations of the Torah institutions in Ofakim. Many a time, he would find it necessary to borrow large sums of money to carry him through difficult periods. One

December, he found it necessary to borrow a large sum of money to cover some post-dated checks. Because it was the end of the year, when everybody was busy closing their books with their end-of-year balances, no one wanted to lend him any money.

The date to cover the checks arrived, and there was no money to cover them. He had until 12:30 p.m. to deposit a very large sum in the bank; otherwise, all the checks would be returned.

In desperation, he went to Rav Shach and poured out his heart. Rav Shach looked at him, smiled, and said, "Lift the tablecloth and underneath you will find a large sum of money. Take it as a loan and return it in a few weeks."

Rav Shach continued, "You probably want to know what I'm doing with such a large sum of money." [At that time, Ponevezh Yeshivah had serious financial difficulties, and salaries hadn't been paid for months.] "Well," he continued, "I have a good friend, R' Mordechai Shulman, whom I know from when I studied in Slobodka Yeshivah in Europe, and who is now the *rosh yeshivah* of Slobodka Yeshivah here in Bnei Brak. A while ago, I asked him for a loan to publish my next volume in the *Avi Ezri* series. He immediately took out this sum of money and gave it to me as a loan, saying that it is not repayable until I sell all the books I publish and will thus have the money to repay him. I went from there straight to the publisher to give him the money, but he refused to accept it until after publication of the book. As a result, I was forced to hold onto the money and assume responsibility for it, trying to figure out where to hide such a large sum. I finally decided to hide the money under the tablecloth of the table on which I learn. Now that you are here in desperate need of a loan, I am more than happy to lend you that money."

R' Goldstein concludes the story:

"The sum that Rav Shach lent me was a third of the total amount that I needed on that day. As soon as Rav Shach gave me the money, I went straight to the bank and stood near the entrance. I asked each passerby for a loan in exchange for a post-dated check. With God's help, as the clock approached 12:30 p.m. I had collected the entire sum, and I happily went into the bank to deposit all the money. All the while, I thanked Hashem, Whose aid came in the blink of an eye!"

כֹּל אֲשֶׁר־דִּבֶּר יְהֹוָה נַעֲשֶׂה וְנִשְׁמָע — *Everything that Hashem has spoken we will do and we will obey* (24:7).

Rav Shach retold the story of Rav Shimon Shkop's first week as rabbi of Maltz. The *parashah* that Shabbos was *Yisro*, the portion which includes the receiving of the Torah. When he went afterwards to Brisk, he stopped in to visit his rebbi, R' Chaim Soloveitchik. R' Chaim asked him about his first sermon. R' Shimon told him that he spoke about the concept of "We will do and we will obey." "We will do," he explained, refers to the statutes, the purpose of which is obscure, whereas "we will obey" (lit. hear) refers to those mitzvos whose purpose is known and understood, which are generally easier to fulfill. He proposed that the people of Israel accepted the obscure statutes with the same enthusiasm that they had accepted the understandable mitzvos.

R' Chaim told him, "Your idea is right but you mixed up the details. The so-called 'understandable mitzvos,' do not really have understandable reasons for which we willingly and enthusiastically fulfill them. Actually, no one is privy to God's secrets and we cannot grasp His reasons, not even for the mitzvos of the Torah. Rather, Hashem wanted us to fulfill mitzvos enthusiastically, so He gave us the illusion of grasping their reasons and purpose. Thus, mitzvos appear to be understandable so that we will fulfill them enthusiastically. And even that which is revealed by the Kabbalists — how many worlds are dependent upon each mitzvah and how many worlds are destroyed for a sin — still has no bearing on the exalted nature of each mitzvah. The true exaltedness is inconceivable, and whatever knowledge they have in these matters is only to help bring enthusiasm for serving Him."

וַיֶּחֱזוּ אֶת־הָאֱלֹהִים וַיֹּאכְלוּ וַיִּשְׁתּוּ — *They viewed God, yet they ate and drank* (24:11).

In a more literal form, the verse says, "They viewed G-d *and* they ate and drank." *Onkelos* translates this verse, "They were as happy with their sacrifices as if they had eaten and drunk."

One of those close to Rav Shach bought him a beautiful plastic-covered challah cover to replace the old and worn challah cover that he had always used. Rav Shach took it, looked at it, and said, "It's quite beautiful." He then turned to the giver and asked him if he earned a good living. "Thank God," he replied. "I won't become poor from this purchase!" Rav Shach said in a very serious tone of voice, "Thank you very much, but please forgive me and take it back, for I don't want gifts. Please understand me and don't be angry. Again, please forgive me."

Several weeks later, the person who bought the challah cover hit upon the idea of covering the challahs with it without saying a word. Someone warned him that Rav Shach would be angry at him, for there was no way he wouldn't realize that the challahs were covered with a new plastic coated covering! Nevertheless he made the switch.

Everybody was amazed. Rav Shach did not seem to notice a thing, nor did he even hint at noticing any change! His mind was involved with other matters, not with challah covers!

וַיֶּחֱזוּ אֶת־הָאֱלֹהִים וַיֹּאכְלוּ וַיִּשְׁתּוּ — *They viewed God, yet they ate and drank* (24:11).

*S*forno explains that afterwards they made a party out of joy for the exalted level they had achieved.

Toward the end of Rav Shach's life, when he was too weak to leave his house, he was greatly bothered by a question on a Talmudic subject. He had previously addressed the question in his sefer, *Avi Ezri*, but he was now dissatisfied with his earlier answer. Any student who came to visit him was asked this question, and it was constantly on his mind. When he finally came up with a satisfactory solution, he was so happy that he requested cake and wine to be distributed among all those present for this happy occasion!

וְאֶתְּנָה לְךָ אֶת־לֻחֹת הָאֶבֶן וְהַתּוֹרָה וְהַמִּצְוָה אֲשֶׁר כָּתַבְתִּי לְהוֹרֹתָם — *And I shall give you the tablets of stone and the Torah, and the commandment that I have written, to instruct them* (24:12).

*M*inchas Shai writes that "to instruct them," *l'horosom*, is written in Hebrew without the second *vav*, to hint that Rabbinical disputes will increase in the future, and instructive rulings will be incomplete, and nevertheless, these and those are the words of the living God. Accordingly, the word is written incomplete, to hint at the singular form, as if it is all one instruction.

Once, a person asked Rav Shach how what he wrote in *Avi Ezri* (Hil. Ishus 18) fit with the Gemara, *Kesubos* 102b. As soon as he heard the question he said, "You are right, I have to correct what I wrote." Afterwards, he told his family, "When I wrote what I did, I knew what the Gemara said, and I had a way to reconcile the two. Yet, according to the approach used by the questioner, it would sound forced, so I had to tell him that he was right!"

תרומה — **Terumah**

וְעָשׂוּ לִי מִקְדָּשׁ — *They shall make for Me a Sanctuary*
(25:8).

Whom, in Torah study, Rav Shach would hear weak logic or an untrue approach, he would ask the person who said it, "Do you really think that this is the logic Hashem used at Sinai?" For to him it was crystal-clear that the Torah that he studied was the same Torah taught by Hashem at Sinai. He once related that when he studied the following Midrash at the beginning of *Parashas Terumah* (*Shemos Rabbah* 33:1), he was so affected that he couldn't sleep properly for several nights!

> The Holy One, Blessed is He, said to Israel: "I sold you My Torah, and it is as if I were sold along with it!" It can be compared to a king who had an only daughter, and another king came and took her for a wife. The latter wished to take her with him to his native land. Her father, the king, said, "The daughter I gave you for a wife is my only child. To separate from her, I cannot. To tell you not to take her with you, I cannot, for she is your wife. Just do me this favor: Wherever you go, make me a small room so that I can live with you, for I cannot bear to be separated from my daughter."
>
> This, then, is what the Holy One, Blessed is He, told Israel: "I have given you My Torah. To separate from it, I cannot; to tell you not to take it, I cannot; just wherever you go, make me a room in which to dwell, as it says, 'They shall make Me a Sanctuary' [that I may dwell among them].' "

With great excitement, Rav Shach would repeat, "Hashem says concerning the Torah, 'To separate from it, I cannot!' The Torah and The Holy One, Blessed is He, are One — so that one who learns Torah cleaves to The Holy One, Blessed is He! How great is the reward and how awesome the responsibility! Rejoice in trembling!"

וְעָשׂוּ אֲרוֹן עֲצֵי שִׁטִּים אַמָּתַיִם וָחֵצִי אָרְכּוֹ וְאַמָּה וָחֵצִי רָחְבּוֹ וְאַמָּה וָחֵצִי קֹמָתוֹ — *They shall make an Aron of shittim wood, two and a half amos its length; an amah and a half its width; and an amah and a half its height (25:10).*

*B*aal HaTurim explains: All its measurements contained half *amos* to teach that whoever learns Torah must break and humble himself.

The wonderful education organization for the children of Israel, *Chinuch Atzma'i,* was once so short of funds that its very existence was endangered. All the directors, both in Israel and abroad, were summoned for an emergency meeting. Those in charge painted a bleak picture and the atmosphere was charged with gloom.

Rav Shach, who, as president of the board in Israel, had done much to aid them in material and in spiritual needs, also made sure to be present at the emergency meeting.

At the meeting, one of the most active board members from America stood up and said, "Before I left, I went to R' Moshe Feinstein to get his blessing and advice. R' Moshe suggested that Rav Shach come to America for a week. We will take care of comfortable arrangements, and he will not have to knock on doors for donations. We will arrange for the donors to come to where he is staying and donate respectable sums. R' Moshe said that such a visit would raise over a million dollars, which would take *Chinuch Atzma'i* out of its financial difficulties."

This was the only practical suggestion raised, and all eyes turned to Rav Shach. He stood up and said in a trembling voice, "What is this that my ears hear? That I'll be taken to America? People will come to see me? What a shameful disgrace! Doing that to me is like taking a knife and cutting me to pieces! What a shameful disgrace!"

Honor to him was "a shameful disgrace."

תצוה — Tetzaveh

וְלֹא־יִזַּח הַחֹשֶׁן מֵעַל הָאֵפוֹד — *And the Choshen shall not be loosened from upon the Eifod* (28:28).

The *Sefer HaChinuch* (*Mitzvah* 100) explains that people are impressed by beauty and splendor, and thus we were commanded to spare no element of beauty, and the mitzvah of "the *Choshen* shall not be loosened" is part of the splendor requirement of the garments of the *Kohen*.

It is well known that the holy Shelah ruled that young children should learn from new books, for that broadens the mind. R' Akiva Eiger instructed his son (as recorded in the introduction to his responsa), "To make sure that it be printed on fine paper in an attractive font in black ink, for it seems to me that the soul is impressed, the understanding broadened, and intent strengthened through learning in an attractive and splendid book. The reverse is true for the opposite, when the print is blurry. It is almost comparable to what our Sages said (*Megillah* 32a), 'Whoever studies with no melody and learns without song, concerning him Scripture says (*Yechezkel* 20:25): "I too gave them decrees that were not good and laws by which they could not live," for these [melody and song] awaken and gladden the soul.' "

Rav Shach once went to the yeshivah and asked R' Refael Wolf to find him a specific volume of the *Shulchan Aruch* from an old printing and with a torn binding.

R' Wolf asked what there could possibly be in an old printing that the new printing did not have.

Rav Shach replied, "I want to take this volume home to learn from tonight, and I am afraid that the students may come looking for this volume of *Shulchan Aruch*. Accordingly, if I take the newer edition, the students will be forced to take the older edition, and if they can't learn from it properly, I will be responsible for the lost Torah learning. I am therefore taking the old edition, so that the students can take the newer editions."

— וְנָשָׂא אַהֲרֹן אֶת־שְׁמוֹת בְּנֵי־יִשְׂרָאֵל בְּחֹשֶׁן הַמִּשְׁפָּט עַל־לִבּוֹ
Aaron shall bear the names of the sons of Israel on the Choshen of Judgment on his heart (28:29).

Rav Shach had this quality of "bear[ing] the names of the sons of Israel ... on his heart." The problems of the individual as well as of the entire Jewish people — and certainly the problems of the Torah world and the yeshivahs — were forever in his heart and on his mind. Rav Shach treated them like the apple of his eye, and served as the "eyes" of yeshivah heads and their disciples in all their steps.

The following story was recounted by R' Moshe Chodosh, *rosh yeshivah* of *Ohr Elchanan*, in a eulogy that he gave in his yeshivah: "Several years ago, when R' Shmuel Travitz passed away, the yeshivah in Rishon L'Tziyon was in such financial difficulty that there was a real danger of closing it down. I thought that for such an important matter it is appropriate to seek the counsel of Rav Shach, especially since the yeshivah was founded with his encouragement and blessing. At that time, Rav Shach was extraordinarily weak and he stayed home, barely receiving people. I nevertheless decided to try and meet with him for the sake of such an important cause. Indeed, it was not very long before I was allowed in to see Rav Shach, who listened carefully to what I had to say. I worked hard in presenting the question fully, and he answered what he answered.

"As I was on my way out, I heard Rav Shach ask something else. I went closer to hear the question again, and was astounded when he asked, 'And how is the yeshivah in Teveriah?' (He was referring to our branch for young students in Teveriah.)"

That's how carefully he followed the news about the Torah world: he was indeed the heart of the yeshivahs!

כי תשא — Ki Sisa

וּשְׁמַרְתֶּם אֶת־הַשַּׁבָּת כִּי קֹדֶשׁ הִוא לָכֶם — *You shall observe the Sabbath for it is holy to you* (31:14).

R' Daniel Lehrfield, the *rosh yeshivah* of Beis Yisrael in Neve Yaakov, relates the following story: "Our yeshivah used to be in a rented apartment in the Bayit Vegan section of Jerusalem. The rent was very expensive, and the opportunity arose to buy a building for the yeshivah in the nearby neighborhood of Beit HaKerem.

"I went to ask Rav Shach whether to seize the opportunity and move the yeshivah there.

"Rav Shach answered absolutely: 'That neighborhood does not keep Shabbos and there are no Jews who keep Torah and mitzvos living there. Accordingly, it is not a fitting place to establish a yeshivah!'

"I did as I was told, and with the aid of Hashem the yeshivah moved afterwards to Neve Yaakov, where a building was bought and the yeshivah is located there today."

וַיַּרְא אַהֲרֹן וַיִּבֶן מִזְבֵּחַ לְפָנָיו — *Aharon saw and built an altar (mizbe'ach) before him* (32:5).

The Midrash states that he was afraid because of the one slaughtered (*zavuach*) before him. He said, "What can I do? Why, they have killed Chur, who was a prophet; if they now kill me, a *Kohen*, they will fulfill the verse (*Eichah* 2:20): 'Should Kohen and prophet be killed in the Sanctuary of the Lord,' and they will immediately be exiled. He therefore chose the lesser evil.

In the early years of the State of Israel, yeshivah students traveled all around the country to enroll children in *Chinuch Atzma'i* schools. There was no *Chinuch Atzma'i* school in Dimona, nor was it likely that there would ever be one. The question was, should the young men encourage parents to register their children in the State-sponsored religious schools run by Mizrachi, so that the local children would not attend totally secular schools. Some of the leaders of the registration drive, among them R' Shalom Schwadron, turned to Rav Shach to ask R' Yitzchak Zev Soloveitchik, the Brisker Rav, for a ruling.

Rav Shach went to the Brisker Rav and presented the question. The Brisker Rav answered angrily, "I should help those wicked ones? I should lend a hand to aid them?" He spewed fire and brimstone about Mizrachi and their activities, citing the words used by the angels as the people of Israel, chased by the Egyptians, stood facing the sea: "Why, these are idol-worshipers and those are idol-worshipers!"

Rav Shach was astonished. "Is it really possible to compare the Mizrachi education system to the secular education system?" he asked. "Why, after all, they educate the children to pray, to keep kosher, and to keep Shabbos!"

The Brisker Rav would not budge. "These and those! And especially after all the damage that they have done, they should not be aided in any way!"

Rav Shach went out to those who had sent him and said, "I cannot tell you what we discussed. The conclusion, however, is to work toward registering the children in the State-sponsored religious schools."

"What!" they asked in astonishment? Why, we heard him bang on the table and express himself emphatically!

Now Rav Shach would not budge. "What he said, he said to me. The conclusion, however, is to work to register the children in the Mizrachi schools."

They did as he said.

Several days later, Rav Shalom Schwadron went to the Brisker Rav, who asked him, "So what did you do in the end?"

"We encouraged them to register in the Mizrachi schools," he replied.

"And who told you to do so?" asked the Brisker Rav.

"Rav Shach."

The Brisker Rav smiled and said, "R' Leizer [Shach] is a smart man."

R' Shalom, all confused, told this over to Rav Shach and asked for an explanation. Rav Shach explained that if the Brisker Rav would have been of the opinion that it is in fact prohibited, he would have said outright that they should stop the registration drive. Instead, he went into a diatribe agains Mizrachi, stating their faults in a general way and asking how he could possibly help them. Rav Shach understood from this that he did not want the permission to be given in his name, so that it not be said that their education system is acceptable and even the Brisker Rav permits it. Nevertheless, since it was the lesser of the two evils available in Dimona, it was, of course, the proper choice. Thus, the Brisker Rav was pleased that Rav Shach understood his true intentions.

וַיַּשְׁכִּימוּ מִמָּחֳרָת — *They arose early the next day* (32:6).

The Talmud (*Yerushalmi, Shekalim* 1:1) states: "Can we read this and not take fright? Regarding evil, it says, 'They arose early,' whereas regarding good, it says (*Shemos* 36:3), 'They brought to him additional free-willed gifts every morning,' but not that they arose early." This can be explained by noting that the same Evil Inclination that wakes one early for an evil deed imposes laziness and lassitude for good deeds. No matter how hard a person tries to overcome this inclination, he will find it difficult to achieve the same level of alertness and enthusiasm for a good cause as for an unworthy one.

Rav Shach would recount how a fund-raiser once came to Volozhin to collect charity, and R' Chaim of Volozhin did not give him a penny. People were very surprised, but they had too much reverence for R' Chaim to say anything. Before very long, it became known that this fund-raiser was collecting for missionary causes, and thus all who had helped him had unwittingly aided his mission.

The people came to R' Chaim and said, "We now know that the Rav has *ruach hakodesh* (the holy spirit), but we have a complaint: If the Rav knew that he was raising funds for this purpose, why did he not reveal this shame before all? Why did he allow us to give the man money?"

R' Chaim smiled and replied, "You give me credit for powers that I do not have. I knew nothing, but I inexplicably felt an overwhelming desire to give him money. I thus understood that it could not possibly be a good cause, for if it were a good cause, the Evil Inclination would be working with all its might to produce laziness and lassitude and make me not want to give money!"

וַיַּרְא אֶת־הָעֵגֶל וּמְחֹלֹת . . . וַיַּשְׁלֵךְ מִיָּדָו אֶת־הַלֻּחֹת — *And he saw the calf and the dances . . . he threw down the Tablets from his hands* (32:19).

Sforno explains that although Moshe had heard in Heaven that they made the Calf, he did not break the Tablets until he actually saw the dances, "When he saw their joy in their debauchery."

R' Eliezer Ozer once went into Rav Shach and saw him sitting in front of a Gemara, absorbed in his thoughts, crying and muttering, "They are crazy, crazy."

He asked, "To whom is the *Rosh Yeshivah* referring?"

Rav Shach explained that some Israeli sports team had just won a big game abroad and a huge welcome was being organized for them. Since there was insufficient space at the airport for such a welcome, they were going to be taken as soon as they arrived to a huge park, and a 100,000 people would be there to cheer for them, led by government ministers — crazy!

R' Ozer said, "Let them do their thing and we will do ours. What upsets the *Rosh Yeshivah* so? It is well known that 'they run and we run, but we run to life in the World to Come!' "

Rav Shach's whole body was wracked by his sobs, "But 100,000 thousand Jews will be there!"

מְחֵנִי נָא מִסִּפְרְךָ אֲשֶׁר כָּתָבְתָּ — *Erase me now from Your book that You have written* (32:32).

R' Aharon Yeshayah Rotter relates: "In 1986, before leaving to the United States for an operation on my son, I came to Rav Shach for a blessing that my son be healthy and that I successfully sell my books. We then traveled to Boston for the operation, and when I spoke to the surgeon, I told him that I had received a blessing from Rav Shach. He told me, 'It is unbelievable, but whenever I operate on a religious Israeli, I feel as if an additional hand is guiding my hands!' This was said in front of other doctors, and it brought about a Sanctification of Hashem's Name.

"While there, I tried to sell my books. The director of the educational institutions of a certain group told me that he would be willing to buy a large quantity of my books, if only it did not have Rav Shach's approbation. If I would agree to publish an edition without the approbation, he would agree to buy hundred of sets!

"Although I was quite pressed for money in light of the expenses of the operation, I said to him, 'What would you do if I would propose that you take out the approbation of your rabbi from your book?' He readily admitted that he would not agree to do so, but he added, 'What won't people do to make a living?'

"I replied that I nevertheless would not accept his conditions and that Hashem provides one's living expenses.

"Several days later I sold my entire stock to a store at a good profit.

"When I returned home, I went to Rav Shach and told him that I had to tell him about two miracles: one his and one mine. I told him what the surgeon in Boston said — his miracle. Then I told him how I refused to take out his approbation and yet did not lose from it.

"Before I had the chance to say that I did not lose anything, he interrupted me and said with great feeling, 'R' Aharon, I don't understand what your problem was? What was even the question? Of course you should have torn out the page with my approbation, and sold the books!'"

וּבְיוֹם פָּקְדִי וּפָקַדְתִּי עֲלֵהֶם חַטָּאתָם — *And on a day that I make an accounting, I shall bring their sin to account against them (32:34).*

Rashi (*Bamidbar* 14:33) explains that when Israel sinned with the Golden Calf, it was the Divine intention to decree that they not be allowed to enter the Land [of Israel], but He waited until they filled their measure of evil through the sin of the spies. Thus it says, "And on a day that I make an accounting" — after the spies — "I shall bring their sin to account against them."

Rav Shach used to say that his greatest fear was filling up the measure of evil, Heaven forbid. It was following such "filling up of the measure" that the Holocaust occurred, he said, and from then until now there has been a great increase of evil. If the measure is filled, God forbid, regardless of whether in Israel or abroad, who knows what could happen! It is therefore incumbent upon us to increase our good deeds as a balance agains the evil, he would conclude, and to repent to prevent filling the measure.

וְהָיָה כָּל־מְבַקֵּשׁ יהוה יֵצֵא אֶל־אֹהֶל מוֹעֵד — *And it would be that whoever would seek Hashem would go out to the Tent of Meeting (33:7).*

In 1972, Rav Shach went through a difficult operation to remove a growth, and he required an extended period of recuperation and rest. His family decided not to allow any visitors, and they arranged for a guard to stand by the door of the building and not let non-residents in, regardless of who they were. The guard did his job faithfully, and Rav Shach invested all his efforts in studying restfully and in peace.

A week later, the guard left his post for a moment and someone managed to take the opportunity to enter the apartment. Rav Shach was happy to see him and received him as graciously as he always received guests, asking him where he had been, in light of the fact that he generally came to visit frequently.

The visitor replied, "I wanted to visit last week, but the guard would not let me in."

This was the first that Rav Shach heard about the guard. "Where is there a guard?" he asked.

"Downstairs, at the entrance to the building," he replied. "Only residents of this building are permitted to enter."

Rav Shach immediately got up, ran down the stairs, and got rid of the guard!

וְהָיָה כָּל־מְבַקֵּשׁ יְהֹוָה יֵצֵא אֶל־אֹהֶל מוֹעֵד — *And it would be that whoever would seek Hashem would go out to the Tent of Meeting* (33:7).

There were many guests at the wedding of one of Rav Shach's grandchildren. When Rav Shach arrived, the crowd surged forward to see him and wish him *"mazal tov."* Upset by the crowding, Rav Shach cried out, "Please, don't push, and leave me be! I am available each day at the yeshivah. Whoever wants to see me can see me there!"

When that did not help, he turned around and left.

וְהִבִּיטוּ אַחֲרֵי מֹשֶׁה — *And they would gaze after Moshe* (33:8).

According to one opinion, their gaze was of a critical nature (*Kiddushin* 33b) to find fault with his actions (*Meshech Chochmah, Devarim* 4:15). Yet, whoever questions his rebbi's actions is considered as if he is questioning the *Shechinah* (*Sanhedrin* 110a).

Rav Shach would recount the story of the important person who went into the room of the Chofetz Chaim during Chol HaMoed and saw him writing Torah commentary. That person expressed his astonishment at the fact that he was writing during Chol HaMoed. Upset, the Chofetz Chaim asked him, "Do you really think that I would do something without first clarifying that it is permitted?"

כִּי עַל־פִּי הַדְּבָרִים הָאֵלֶּה כָּרַתִּי אִתְּךָ בְּרִית וְאֶת־יִשְׂרָאֵל — *For according to these words have I entered a covenant with you and with Israel* (34:27).

The Gemara (*Gittin* 80b) states that words presented orally may not be written down. And why not? R' Baruch Shmuel Deutsch heard the reason from Rav Shach.

It is well known that Rav Shach would deliver weekly lectures on those tractates studied in yeshivahs in a cycle. He taught eighteen cycles of these tractates, plumbed their depths, sharpened his delivery, and even published several works on them. Nevertheless, he would start preparing the next lecture as soon as he completed his last lecture, and he was wont to say, "Most of my days are Monday nights" — Tuesday was the day of his weekly lecture. He would also say that he knows only two days of the week: Shabbos and Tuesday! In fact, when people would come over to him on a Tuesday to talk Torah, he would ask in amazement: "Did you not say the daily psalm today? Why, it is Tuesday, and the whole day is devoted to the *shiur* I will be teaching!"

He was once asked why he was so tense about the lecture; after all, he is merely restating that which is already in print! Rav Shach explained, "You should know that transmitting Torah from generation to generation can only be done orally, from rebbi to disciple. The disciple, for his part, must hear the lesson from his rebbi, and not from a text. If it would indeed be acceptable to transmit from a book, there are better books than my *Avi Ezri*. I could say over the questions and answers developed by R' Akiva Eiger, or an approach of *Ketzos HaChoshen*. But then it would not be 'me' talking, and that is not the way the Torah is transmitted. Even if I were to say what I remember from the past, that would merely be a quote, and not something emerging from myself. Accordingly, I immerse myself again in the Gemara and comment on it — even if the same comment was made in the past. Only in this way does it come straight from my heart, and the student receives it straight from the rebbi."

וַיִּירְאוּ מִגֶּשֶׁת אֵלָיו — *And they feared to approach him* (34:30).

Rav Shach once said that if he were told that the Vilna Gaon were inside the yeshivah, he would run away from him, feeling only fear and shame!

When the Satmar Rav visited the Holy Land, Rav Shach went to visit him. Rav Shach said to him, "They speak of the beginning of the redemption and the footsteps of the Mashiach. The Chofetz Chaim said that it is closer than we think — and we await it each and every day — but when the Mashiach comes, who is to say that we will merit to see him, to come into his presence?"

The Rav shot back, "Maybe that was the fear of R' Yosef (*Sanhedrin* 98b) when he said that, despite the hardships of that time [which led Rabbah and Ulla to say they did not want to see the Mashiach come], he wanted to see the Mashiach, even if only in the shade of his donkey's dung — anything, just to merit seeing the Mashiach."

וַיְכַל מֹשֶׁה מִדַּבֵּר אִתָּם וַיִּתֵּן עַל־פָּנָיו מַסְוֶה. וּבְבֹא מֹשֶׁה לִפְנֵי ה׳
לְדַבֵּר אִתּוֹ יָסִיר אֶת־הַמַּסְוֶה — *Moshe finished speaking with them and placed a mask on his face. When Moshe would come before Hashem to speak with Him, he would remove the mask* (34:33-34).

Chizkuni explains that when Hashem spoke to Moshe or when Moshe himself spoke to Israel he would not place the mask on his face, because of the verse (*Yeshayahu* 30:20), "Your eyes will behold your teacher." With respect to Moshe, Hashem was the teacher, whereas with respect to Israel, Moshe was the teacher.

A handicapped person once went to Rav Shach for a blessing, before beginning his rehabilitation. Rav Shach asked him where he would be going and when his rehabilitation would begin. After the man left, Rav Shach turned to one of his attendants and said, "Hurry, buy some framed pictures of the Chofetz Chaim, R' Chaim Ozer, and the Chortkover Rebbe. Then take them to that rehabilitation center, find out which room he will be assigned to, and hang up those pictures."

"Is all this really necessary?" asked the attendant.

"When you get there, you will understand," Rav Shach replied.

He did as he was instructed, bought the pictures of those great rabbis, went to the rehabilitation center, and was told a room number. When he went into the room, he was shocked: The walls were covered with indecent pictures!

When he returned to Rav Shach, he said, "The *Rosh Yeshivah* has *ruach hakodesh* and knows the future!"

Rav Shach smiled and said, "I just used my head. Hospitals are filled with sick people who cannot get out of their beds, and all they can think about is their suffering. In rehabilitation departments, however, there are bored people who are kept busy only a few hours a day, and their enforced inactivity makes them even more bored. Furthermore, since they are not home surrounded by their social circle, barriers often fall down."

The attendant asked, "If so, why didn't you just send me to 'clean up' the room before he came?"

Rav Shach replied, "No, no! When barriers fall they must be re-erected! We must create a spirit of Torah and sanctity by fulfilling 'Your eyes will behold your teacher.'"

ויקהל — Vayakhel

וַיַּקְהֵל מֹשֶׁה אֶת־כָּל־עֲדַת בְּנֵי יִשְׂרָאֵל ... שֵׁשֶׁת יָמִים תֵּעָשֶׂה מְלָאכָה וּבַיּוֹם הַשְּׁבִיעִי יִהְיֶה לָכֶם קֹדֶשׁ — *And Moshe assembled the entire assembly of the Children of Israel ... for six days work may be done, but the seventh day shall be holy for you (35:1-2).*

*T*he Midrash here (*Yalkut Shimoni*) states that from the beginning of the Torah until its end, this is the only Torah portion beginning with the command to assemble the nation. The Holy One, Blessed is He, said, "Assemble great assemblies ... so that future generations learn from you to assemble assemblies each Shabbos and gather in study halls to study Torah." *Tanna d'Vei Eliyahu* (*Rabbah* 1) adds, "Shabbos should be devoted exclusively to Torah."

During the lifetime of the Ponevezher Rav, one of the top yeshivah students made a *Kiddush* one Shabbos in honor of his *aufruf,* being called up to the Torah in advance of his forthcoming wedding. Rav Shach and the Ponevezher Rav also attended the *Kiddush.* Afterwards, the Ponevezher Rav went to his home in the yeshivah, and Rav Shach escorted him. At that time Rav Shach lived on Wasserman Street, and the Ponevezher Rav told him that he need not escort him all the way home; instead, Rav Shach could go home for lunch and he would make his own way home.

Rav Shach, ever the honest one, told him, "I am escorting the Rav because I, too, am going to the yeshivah, so that I can continue learning Torah."

שֵׁשֶׁת יָמִים תֵּעָשֶׂה מְלָאכָה וּבַיּוֹם הַשְּׁבִיעִי יִהְיֶה לָכֶם קֹדֶשׁ — *For six days work may be done, but the seventh day shall be holy for you (35:2).*

*M*ishnah Berurah (*Hilchos Shabbos* 250:3) cites earlier sources who mandate repenting in one's heart before every Shabbos, since the Shabbos is called a Queen, and thus accepting the Shabbos is like accepting royalty. Is it proper to accept royalty dressed in the rags of sin?

Rav Shach's family noticed that every Shabbos he was weaker than the rest of the week. They asked him for an explanation and he said, "Friday is a time which is designated for a spiritual accounting, since the week ends then. When I do my spiritual accounting on Friday it causes me great angst, and this weakens me for the Shabbos!"

רְאוּ קָרָא יְהֹוָה בְּשֵׁם בְּצַלְאֵל בֶּן־אוּרִי בֶן־חוּר לְמַטֵּה יְהוּדָה —
See, Hashem has proclaimed by name, Betzalel son of Uri son of Chur, of the tribe of Yehudah (35:30).

*T*he Gemara (*Berachos* 55a) states that a leader is not appointed over the community without consulting the community, as it says, "See, Hashem has proclaimed by name, Betzalel."

There was once a public figure who did everything possible to benefit the public (and each and every individual). Everything he did was always done in a clean, above-board manner, and he never showed any expectation of receiving anything in return. Nevertheless, he was not well liked, and the public showed no appreciation for all his hard work. Rav Shach said that although he deserved to be nominated for office as a result of his hard work, he should not be nominated if the public does not like him!

וְלַחְשֹׁב מַחֲשָׁבֹת — *To make artistic designs (35:32).*

R' Yitzchak Zev Soloveitchik, the Brisker Rav, told Rav Shach that for years his grandfather, R' Chaim Volozhin, raised funds to sustain the yeshivah that he established, until he appointed a fund-raiser to take his place. The fund-raiser would go from town to town and from village to village, writing down how much each one gave, so that R' Chaim could bless the donor.

The fund-raiser once returned from his trip, brought R' Chaim the money, gave him the list of donors, and said, "It seems to me that I spend most of my time on the roads between towns and villages. The traveling is very difficult and tiring, in the summer because of the heat and in the winter because of the snows and cold. If you give me a wagon, I will be able to cut quite a bit of my travel time, and I will be able to visit more potential donors and raise more money." R' Chaim acceded to his request and bought him a horse and wagon from yeshivah funds. Indeed, the fund-raiser returned in half the time and gave R' Chaim the money and the donor list. R' Chaim perused the list and noticed that the name of one regular donor was not on this list. He asked what happened and was told, "He slammed the door in my face, saying, 'I give for Torah, not for horses.' "

R' Chaim told him that he wanted to go along on the next fund-raising trip so that he could speak with that donor. Needless to say, when that donor saw R' Chaim, he welcomed him profusely and accorded him great honor. R' Chaim said to the donor, "The Holy Torah lists the praises of Betzalel son of Uri son of Chur, saying that he 'makes artistic designs [lit. thinks thoughts] to work with the silver and with the gold.' Now what were these 'thoughts'? Well, we know that regarding the *Mishkan,* Hashem demanded 'generosity of the heart' (see 35:5), for 'Hashem requires our heart.' The more pure the heart that gave and the more generously it was given, the more it was desired and accepted by Hashem. All of Israel donated what they could, each according to the purity of his soul. It was up to Betzalel, who was blessed with the ability to read hearts, to know who gave with all his heart, and to decide that such gold belonged for the Holy Ark in the Holy of Holies. One whose intent was a bit less pure had his gold designated for the covering of the ark, then for the Menorah, for the Table, all the way down to the pillars; it all depended on the purity of his motives when giving.

"Now," continued R' Chaim, "We have no *Mishkan* nor Temple, and no Betzalel who knows the thoughts of people. Our Sages, however, say that the study halls are our miniature temples (*Megillah* 29a, from *Yechezkel* 11:16). It is there that the *Shechinah* dwells, for Hashem has in this world only the four *amos* of Torah law (*Berachos* 5a), and those who study Torah are like the Ark of the covenant (*Yoma* 72b), like the Tabernacle, the Temple and the Altar (see *Mesillas Yesharim* 26).

"Divine Providence hovers over the donors who donate for the Tabernacle of our time, those who support Torah in each generation. They need only give their donation with a completely pure heart and their money will go toward the food and drink of those who study, which in turn is considered like sacrifices and wine libations (*Mesillas Yesharim* ibid.) This food and drink will give them the strength to study the Holy Torah, which is like the Tablets placed in the Ark of the covenant (*Berachos* 8a). If the donor's heart is less pure, however, his money is directed from Heaven to maintenance and salaries of the workers, the janitors, and the landlords. And when money is donated with a bitter heart, out of stinginess, then that money is directed to buying a horse and wagon.

"I am certain," concluded R' Chaim, "that your pure-hearted donation was directed exclusively to studying Torah, and it was not your money that was used for purchasing the horse and wagon!"

פקודי — **Pekudei**

וְהָיָה הַמִּזְבֵּחַ קֹדֶשׁ קָדָשִׁים — *And the Mizbe'ach shall be holy of holies* (40:10).

Ramban (*Vayikra* 8:11) derives from this verse that the *Mizbe'ach* required greater sanctification than the other utensils (see *Gur Aryeh* ibid.). Our Sages (*Berachos* 55a) teach us that while the Temple stood, the *Mizbe'ach* atoned for Israel, but now a person's table atones for him. Accordingly, a person's table requires sanctification more than all his other utensils!

A young man came to Rav Shach to speak with him in Torah subjects. At the time, Rav Shach was deeply immersed in a Torah subject of his own. He apologized for not being able to give full concentration to the subjects the young man wished to discuss, and asked him to return some other time.

The young man apologized for the disturbance and turned to go.

Rav Shach wanted to make him feel better, so he said to him, "That you can learn well, I know from the past, but tell me, do you know how to eat as well?"

The young man was puzzled and he replied, "To eat? Everybody knows how to eat!"

"You are mistaken," said Rav Shach. "True, everybody eats — but only few know *how* to eat the way the Torah wants — how to eat and for what purpose, to eat so that one's table is like an atoning *Mizbe'ach!*"

ספר ויקרא ﷽

Vayikra

ויקרא — Vayikra

בָּל־חֵלֶב לַהי — *All the choice parts for Hashem* (3:16).

Rambam (end of *Hil. Issurei Mizbe'ach*) writes: "Anything for the sake of the Hashem should be attractive and good. If one feeds the poor, he should feed from the best and the sweetest on his table. If one wishes to consecrate something, he should consecrate from his finest possessions. And thus it says, 'All the choice parts for Hashem.' Furthermore, if one slaughters a skinny animal for the Sabbath *tamid* offering, he should bring another, fatter one, and slaughter that one (*Menachos* 64a)."

The same is true regarding benevolence and doing favors. R' Meir HaLevi Birnbaum went to Rav Shach to get an approbation for his book. Rav Shach, who was then over 90 years old, began writing slowly and painstakingly. After writing two lines, letter by letter, he noticed that he had forgotten to write the author's name. He put the page away and began writing all over again, rather then simply insert the name between the lines.

צו — Tzav

זֹאת הַתּוֹרָה לָעֹלָה לַמִּנְחָה וְלַחַטָּאת וְלָאָשָׁם וְלַמִּלּוּאִים וּלְזֶבַח הַשְּׁלָמִים — *This is the law of the olah-offering, the meal-offering, the sin-offering, and the guilt-offering; and the inauguration-offerings, and the sacrifice of the peace-offering (7:37).*

The Gemara (*Menachos* 110a) derives from, "This is the law [lit. Torah] of the olah-offering, the meal-offering, the sin-offering, and the guilt offering," that one involved in Torah [study] needs neither olah-offering, meal-offering, sin-offering, nor guilt-offering.

One of Rav Shach's students was once absent from the daily lecture. When the student returned in the afternoon, Rav Shach expressed concern and asked how the young man was feeling, as he had not attended the lecture. The student replied that he was fine; he had just attended the *pidyon haben* (redemption of the firstborn) festive meal for his nephew.

When he saw the consternation on Rav Shach's face, he hurriedly added that he had heard that attending such meals was considered very important, capable of atoning as if one had fasted eighty-four fasts.

Well, that was like pouring kerosene on a fire! Rav Shach got very excited and retorted emphatically, "Don't you know that one hour of Torah study is also worth eighty-four fasts, at the very least?!"

שמיני — Shemini

וַיְהִי בַּיּוֹם הַשְּׁמִינִי קָרָא מֹשֶׁה לְאַהֲרֹן וּלְבָנָיו וּלְזִקְנֵי יִשְׂרָאֵל — *It was on the eighth day, Moshe called to Aharon and his sons, and to the elders of Israel (9:1).*

*T*he Hebrew word for "it was" — וַיְהִי — is generally a term reflecting sorrow (*Megillah* 10b). *Ohr HaChaim* explains that in this case it refers to the sorrow of Moshe. He was originally designated to be Kohen (see *Shemos Rabbah* 3:17) and it was he who performed the sacrifices during the eight days of inauguration. Now he saw it all taken away from him. Yet, despite everything, he hid and repressed his feelings.

Rav Shach was always sensitive to the feelings of others.

R' Moshe Portman led the High Holiday services at the yeshivah. He had a beautiful voice and everyone loved to hear him. Then he developed heart problems and was forbidden to lead the services. Everybody was very disturbed by this turn of events, and the administration had to choose someone else to lead the services.

The very next Rosh Hashanah, after the service, Rav Shach went to eat a little something, and then called his grandson to accompany him.

Where did he go on that Day of Judgment, when every second is so precious? He went to the home of Rabbi Portman, the former leader of the services, to honor him with his visit, to wish him a year of good health, to lift his spirits, and to give him encouragement!

וַיִּשְׁמַע מֹשֶׁה וַיִּיטַב בְּעֵינָיו — *Moshe heard and he approved (10:20).*

*O*ur Sages (*Zevachim* 101b) explain that he approved, saying, "That is what I heard and what I forgot."

Rav Shach recounted an amazing story concerning the humility of the great decisor of Jewish law, R' Yitzchak Elchanan Spektor, Rav of Kovna. The rabbi of a small town was asked a question of Jewish law and he answered contrary to the authoritative opinion of the

Shach [a 17th-century commentary on *Shulchan Aruch*], which he had forgotten. The town had a small group of people who opposed the rabbi, and they caught the rabbi in this mistake. They decided to send a letter to R' Yitzchak Elchanan in Kovno, and they asked him to rule on this question, as if the question were their own. He immediately sent them an answer which was also contrary to the opinion of *Shach*, as ruled by their rabbi. Rav Yitzchak Elchanan sent his answer by mail, knowing that it would not arrive until the next day. A few hours later, he sent out an emergency telegram stating that he found that the *Shach* rules contrary to what he had written, and thus, he defers to the *Shach*'s opinion. Accordingly, he said, when his letter arrives, be aware that he has changed his mind and no longer agrees with what he had written.

What happened? R' Yitzchak Elchanan knew the *Shach*'s ruling and when the question arrived he was surprised to be asked such a straightforward question, especially since there was a respected Rav in town. In his great wisdom, he discerned that the local Rav must have made a mistake, and the questioners were merely waiting in ambush to pounce on the man. He decided to foil their plans and show them that even the leading rabbi of the day could make this mistake!

And to that end, he was willing to forgo his honor and appear to have made a mistake!

וַיִּשְׁמַע מֹשֶׁה וַיִּיטַב בְּעֵינָיו — *Moshe heard and he approved* (10:20).

The Midrash (*Vayikra Rabbah* 13:1; *Targum Yonasan*) relates that Moshe had it proclaimed throughout the camp that he had been mistaken and that his brother, Aharon, came and taught him the correct law.

R' Chaim Kanievsky tells the story of the lecture that Rav Shach gave in Lomza Yeshivah in Petach Tikvah. One of the pupils, R' Refael Yitzchak Wasserman, asked a question which challenged a basic premise of the lecture. Rav Shach immediately stopped in the middle of his lecture and stepped down from the pulpit.

Afterwards, he went from group to group of study partners saying, "I want you to know that I was mistaken in my logic, and your friend set me straight!" In this manner he hoped to make them respect their friend more and to motivate them, in accordance with the Talmudic dictum (*Bava Basra* 21a), "Jealousy among scribes increases wisdom."

וַיִּשְׁמַע מֹשֶׁה וַיִּיטַב בְּעֵינָיו — *Moshe heard and he approved* (10:20).

*A*mong the characteristics of the wise man cited by the Mishnah (*Avos* 5:7) is that he admits to the truth; it is also one of the methods to acquire Torah knowledge. Bertinora, in his commentary to the Mishnah, states that this applies even when one has the opportunity to back up his view with logical arguments, as we find concerning Moshe, who admitted without shame to the words of Aharon.

In the middle of one of Rav Shach's lectures in Ponevezh Yeshivah, one of the students posed a question. Rav Shach immediately offered a rejoinder, and the student admitted that he had been mistaken. The other students agreed that Rav Shach's response was on the mark. Rav Shach, however, stood deep in thought, his keen mind quickly analyzing the various possibilities, until he said, "No, the question is correct," and he closed the Gemara and sat down.

After several hours, though, Rav Shach found what he felt was the true answer to the student's question. He happily announced the answer to the students.

וְשֶׁקֶץ יִהְיוּ לָכֶם — *And they shall be an abomination to you* (11:11).

*O*hr HaChaim states that the previous verse ends with the words, "they are an abomination to you," and so this verse begins, "and they shall be an abomination to you." As to the addition of "and," it can be explained based on the Talmudic dictum (*Chullin* 5b), "Hashem does not allow a mishap to occur to the animals of the righteous, and certainly not to the righteous themselves." *Tosafos* (ad loc.) apply this only to prohibited food. It would be shameful for a righteous person to consume prohibited food — even if only accidentally. The additional "*and*" of this verse comes to include even such accidental consumption; it too "shall be an abomination to you."

Rav Shach used to express his surprise that all those years that he was in Lithuania, many people tended to be lenient regarding butter produced from gentile milk (see *Shulchan Aruch, Yoreh Deah* 118:3; *Chochmas Adam* 67:9). He himself was always stringent in this regard and would use only butter made from Jewish milk, even though it was much more expensive. He recalled that on several occasions people tried to trick him into using butter from gentile milk, and there was always some reason that he did not eat it, although he had no suspicion about the butter. Presumably it was Heaven holding him back from violating his practice.

תזריע — Tazria

בְּגָדָיו יִהְיוּ פְרֻמִים — *His garments shall be rent* (13:45).

*T*zaraas comes as punishment for the sin of gossip (*Arachin* 16a). *Charedim* (61) points out that the reason for the garment having to be rent is — since he shamed other people, he, too, should be shamed. Since it is a person's clothing that give him honor (R' Yochanan would call his clothes "my honorers"; *Bava Kamma* 91b), his clothes must be rent.

Rav Shach used to say that in the olden days, when people were more serious, they wore clothing of honor: coats, suits and hats. Even the gentiles understood this "secret." "Once," said Rav Shach, "I entered a courtroom abroad, and I saw that the judge was wearing special robes. And why? So that there would be a serious atmosphere and reverence for justice. You can tell the spirit of a community, their level of seriousness, and their respectability, just by looking at their clothing. When you see that fashion dictates wearing torn and faded clothing that are worn with abandon, you can understand that there is a lightness, a lack of seriousness, and lack of respectability."

מצורע — Metzora

אוֹ עַל־הַכְּלִי אֲשֶׁר־הִוא יֹשֶׁבֶת־עָלָיו — *Or on the utensil upon which she is sitting* (15:23).

The Talmud (*Pesachim* 15:23) derives from the fact that the word used for the male (in verse 9) is *ride*, while *sitting* is used for the female, that one should always speak with pure language. Rashi explains that it is not proper to speak of a female "riding," although the laws for riding and sitting are identical.

After an exceptionally horrible accident in which several young men lost their lives, Rav Shach cited the Gemara (*Shabbos* 33a) which states: "For the sin of degenerate speech many sorrows [befall us] and difficult edicts are newly imposed; young men of Israel die, orphans and widows cry out but are not answered, as it says (*Yeshayahu* 9:16): 'Therefore, my Lord shall not rejoice over their young men, and he shall not pity their orphans and widows, for they are all hypocritical and evil, and every mouth utters degeneracy. Yet despite all this, His anger has not subsided and His hand is still outstretched.' "

He then recounted how, in the city of Pinsk, one young man after another was dying. The people blamed an evil person who sullied the souls of the youth with his filthy tongue and his disgustingly degenerate speech, and they wanted to demonstrate in front of his house. They were afraid, however, because this person had connections with the authorities and they feared that he would call upon them to unfairly punish the protesters. The decision was not to demonstrate openly at that time, but that if another young man were to die, they would hold the funeral in front of his house. When the next young man died, all the Jews of the city gathered in front of this evil man's house for the funeral. One after another, the eulogizers got up and exhorted the people to greater modesty and to watch over their speech, and everyone knew at whom the words were directed. As expected, the man took the community to court for defamation of character.

As soon as the court case began, the revered Rav of Pinsk, R' Elazar Moshe Horowitz, got up and pleaded guilty. He took full responsibility on himself, saying that it was he who ruled to hold the funeral there, being that the plaintiff was responsible for the terrible fate that had befallen the community. The Rav said that it was the plaintiff's degenerate speech that brought about so much misfortune to so many families.

The judge could not hide his astonishment: "What possible connection could there be between his manner of speaking and the misfortunes that befell the young men?" he asked. "Can you prove your strange accusation?"

The Rav replied, "I have brought documentary evidence along with me." He then recited the Gemara mentioned above, using the services of a Russian interpreter. When he reached the citation from *Yeshayahu*, he presented the judge with a Russian-language Bible open to the appropriate verse. The judge listened, read the verse, and ruled that the Rav had acted correctly. Indeed, it was his obligation to stand in the breach and stop the plague!

אחרי מות — Acharei Mos

כִּי־בַיּוֹם הַזֶּה יְכַפֵּר עֲלֵיכֶם לְטַהֵר אֶתְכֶם — *For on this day* [Yom Kippur] *he shall provide atonement for you to cleanse you* (16:30).

Every year, each person comes beore Hashem for judgment, and for a decision regarding whether he will live or die that year. Rambam (*Hil. Teshuvah* 3:3) explains that if person's good deeds outweigh his bad deeds, or his bad deeds outweigh his good deeds, Hashem renders the verdict on Rosh Hashanah. If, however, the good deeds and the bad deeds bear equal weight, the decision regarding that person's fate remains in abeyace until Yom Kippur. If he repents, he is granted life; if not, he is sealed in the "Book of Death."

Rav Itzel Peterburger asked: Since we are referring to one whose good and bad deeds are equal, why must he repent to be able to live? Why, even if he does only one good deed, the scales will be tipped toward the side of merit!

Rav Shach offered the following insight: At this stage, the one good deed is of no avail in changing the balance, because — now that it is after Rosh Hashanah — the good deed that he does belongs to the new year's account. Only an additional good deed *before* Rosh Hashanah could have tipped the scales. Now, however, only repentance can change the outcome of last year's account!

וּשְׁמַרְתֶּם אֶת־חֻקֹּתַי וְאֶת־מִשְׁפָּטַי אֲשֶׁר יַעֲשֶׂה אֹתָם הָאָדָם וָחַי בָּהֶם — *You shall observe my decrees and my judgments, which man shall carry out and live by them* (18:5).

This verse is the Gemara's source (*Yoma* 85b) for ruling that sustaining life supersedes the restrictions of the Sabbath, for we are commanded to *live by them*, and not die by them. Rambam (*Hil. Shabbos* 2:3) codifies this law and says, "And when one does these things [transgresses Sabbath prohibitions to save life], he should not do them by means of a gentile, nor by means of a minor nor a woman, so that they not treat the Sabbath lightly. Rather, they should be done by the elders of Israel and their Sages."

Rav Shach related that when a fire broke out on Friday in a town neighboring Ponevezh (in Europe), many Jews were left without a roof over their heads and, in those days before supermarkets and prepared foods, with literally nothing to eat. The Rav of Ponevezh, Rav Itzeleh Ponevezher, arranged for a wagon to drive around to the Jewish homes of Ponevezh throughout the Sabbath day, collecting food. While the wagon was driven by a non-Jew, Rav Itzeleh himself followed the wagon on foot and encouraged everybody to donate as much food as they could.

וּשְׁמַרְתֶּם אֶת־חֻקֹּתַי וְאֶת־מִשְׁפָּטַי אֲשֶׁר יַעֲשֶׂה אֹתָם הָאָדָם וָחַי בָּהֶם אֲנִי ה' — *You shall observe my decrees and my judgments, which man shall carry out and live by them, I am Hashem* (18:5).

Rashi explains: *live by them* — in the World to Come, *I am Hashem* — who faithfully pays reward.

The was once a complex Talmudic question that was troubling Rav Shach, and he traveled to Jerusalem to discuss the matter with R' Yitzchak Zev Soloveitchik, the Brisker Rav. The Brisker Rav reviewed the related section of the Gemara with Rav Shach, and he explained it a way that obviated the question. Rav Shach was very excited, and he went back to the yeshivah where he explained the new approach to his students. Still inspired by the resolution, he remarked, "I do not know if my Torah and mitzvos are worth anything in Heaven's eyes. I do not know how they will weigh my sins — especially since we know that the depth of the Ultimate Judgment is beyond mortal comprehension. If I did deserve a portion in the World to Come, however, I am afraid that my joy at learning this novel approach was so great that I have already received my entire reward in this world, thereby losing my portion in the World to Come!"

וּשְׁמַרְתֶּם אֶת־מִשְׁמַרְתִּי — *You shall safeguard My charge* (18:30).

The Gemara (*Yevamos* 21a) teaches that this enjoins us to make safeguards to safeguards protecting the Torah. *Ohr HaChaim* explains that we must place a safeguard around the safeguard, *to safeguard us from the pitfalls of abominations* — even by accident.

Rav Shach recounted a story told of a simple Jewish villager who went into the bookstore and asked for a *siddur*. The seller gave him a standard *siddur* and told him that the price was 30 kopeck.

"I don't want a *siddur* like this, I want a thick *siddur*, with extra prayers and with commentaries!" The seller brought out a *siddur* with the commentary of *Shelah*, and the man's eyes lit up. However, when the seller explained that the price was a ruble, the simple man exclaimed, "So expensive!"

"I knew that you did not need a *siddur* like this, take the regular *siddur* for 30 kopeck," the seller said. "This *siddur* is for rabbis and learned people!"

The Jew said, "I still want the second one. True it costs a whole ruble, but it is worth every kopeck! I have already been harmed by the thin *siddur*."

The seller seemed confused about how one could get "harmed" by a *siddur*, so the villager explained, "Look, I had a standard *siddur* and my neighbor had a nice thick *siddur*. As time went on — you know how it is — pages became torn and they fell out. In my *siddur*, when one page was torn — there went putting on *tallis* and *tefillin*. Another page fell out — no more morning blessings. Another few pages, and the *siddur* began with *Yishtabach*, and I must buy a new *siddur*. With my neighbor's *siddur*, on the other hand, page after page fell out, and it still starts with the midnight prayers mourning over the destruction of the Temple. Not a single page of actual prayers fell out!"

That is the intention of setting up safeguards for the safeguards. Even if a safeguard is mistakenly beached, at least the actual sin remains far away!

קדושים — Kedoshim

לֹא תִּגְנֹבוּ — *You shall not steal* (19:11).

*T*he *Tosefta* (*Bava Kamma* 7:3) says that there are seven forms of "stealing." First and foremost is the one who cheats and "steals" an improperly earned favorable opinion. The *Tosefta* continues and concludes, "However, one who steals behind the back of his friend and goes to study Torah, although he too is considered as 'stealing,' he achieves merit for himself, and ultimately he becomes a community leader who brings merit to the community." Rav Shach was asked to explain this apparently praiseworthy category.

He explained with a story that took place when Rav Yitzchak Elchanan Spektor, later the Rav of Kovno and leading halachic decisor of his generation, was a young man. At that time, R' Yitzchak Elchanan was studying in Volkovisk under the tutelage of the *Av Beis Din* of the city, Rav Binyamin Diskin. His study partner was Rav Baruch Mordechai Lipshutz, who would later become the Rav of Novaradok. R' Yitzchak Elchanan and R' Baruch Mordechai studied together diligently until late into the night and they would then walk home together. R' Baruch Mordechai would say good night to his friend and go into his house, whereas R' Yitzchak Elchanan would "steal" back to the study hall for several more hours of study. These "stolen" hours of extra study resulted in his becoming the leading halachic authority of his time and a leader in a generation of Torah giants.

לֹא־תַעֲשֹׁק אֶת־רֵעֲךָ וְלֹא תִגְזֹל — *You shall not cheat your fellow and you shall not rob* (19:13).

*I*n his advanced old age, after decades of unceasing devotion to Ponevezh Yeshivah and its students, Rav Shach became too weak to lecture in the yeshivah. He was very disturbed by his inability to present his lectures, and he went to Jerusalem to discuss the matter with Rav Yosef Shalom Elyashiv: Since he was no longer lecturing, there seemd to be no justification for him to draw a salary from the yeshivah, nor to live in an apartment that belonged to the yeshivah. He worked out that he could live very frugally on the old age benefit given by *Bituach Leumi* (the government's social security), and he already began looking for a room to rent.

Rav Elyashiv told the Rosh Yeshivah that he could relax, because he was still contributing to the yeshivah far more than he was receiving from it. He was contributing to the staff, to the students, and even to the financial well-being of the yeshivah by simply remaining at its helm.

"Before long, I will be facing the Heavenly Court," Rav Shach argued in a choked-up voice. "They will ask me the primary question 'Did you conduct your affairs honestly?' (see *Shabbos* 31a). I do not want to be quilty of the slightest possibility of wrongly taking the money of others, and especially the money of the yeshivah. Besides, I have an opportunity to rent a room of my own."

Rav Elyashiv repeated that Rav Shach should not leave the yeshivah, which truly needed him, for his simple presence contributed immeasurably to the yeshivah's welfare.

"Are you absolutely certain?" Rav Shach asked. "I want to know if Rav Elyashiv is telling me this as a halachic ruling or only as his opinion."

"It is a halachic ruling!" Rav Elyashiv replied.

לֹא־תַעֲשֹׁק אֶת־רֵעֲךָ וְלֹא תִגְזֹל — *You shall not cheat your fellow and you shall not rob* (19:13).

*R*av Shach used to suggest that a good way to avoid the pursuit of honor is for a person to say to himself, "True, I covet honor, but I am not a thief! If I want other people to honor me when I do not truly deserve it, or if I want them to forgo their right to an honor in favor of giving it to me, why, I would then be cheating them by taking something that they have no reason to give me!"

וְלִפְנֵי עִוֵּר לֹא תִתֵּן מִכְשֹׁל — *You shall not place a stumbling block in front of a blind person* (19:14).

A young man, whom Rav Shach did not know, turned to Rav Shach for advice about whether he should take a job offered to him at a yeshivah in Bnei Brak, or a similar job offered in a yeshivah in Jerusalem. Rav Shach told the fellow to return in five days.

The young man was surprised by the answer, but he did as told. Five days later he returned and was told to take the position in the Jerusalem yeshivah.

When he called to notify them that he was accepting their job offer, they were quite pleased and closed the conversation by saying, "We did not know that you were related to Rav Shach."

Well — nor did he.

"What makes you say that," he asked?

"Because," they replied, "over the last four days, Rav Shach called several times to clarify various details about our offer to you."

וְלִפְנֵי עִוֵּר לֹא תִתֵּן מִכְשֹׁל — *You shall not place a stumbling block in front of a blind person* (19:14).

Rashi explains that one should not give advice that would mislead a person who is "blind" in that matter.

A young man who was strengthening his commitment to Torah observance asked Rav Shach which one of two yeshivos he should attend. Rav Shach demurred and would not answer. The young man did not give up, and he returned the following day with the same question. Once again, Rav Shach would not answer. The young man left quite upset.

Rav Shach's family was surprised. Rav Shach was prepared to help anybody, even deciding questions of life and death. Was this so difficult a question that Rav Shach could not answer it?

When they asked Rav Shach to explain, this is what he said: "The truth is that both yeshivos are good for him, and he would become more committed to Torah observance in either one of them. I just do not know in which of the two he will become more committed. The difference between the two yeshivos will affect how solidly Jewish his home will be and will impact how his children will grow up. If he goes to the 'wrong' yeshivah, he will grow somewhat less, his children will grow up in a slightly less committed home and, as a result, they may slacken in their observance of mitzvos. The wrong answer to this man's question may lead to his grandchild 'leaving the fold' — and who can accept such a responsibility upon himself?"

וְלִפְנֵי עִוֵּר לֹא תִתֵּן מִכְשֹׁל — *You shall not place a stumbling block in front of a blind person* (19:14).

A Torah scholar who was close to Rav Shach was offered the Rabbinate of an important city. He refused the offer, saying that the position would interfere with his Torah study and spiritual growth. The members of the selection committee went to Rav Shach to discuss the matter. Rav Shach encouraged them, saying, "A Torah scholar like that will bring blessing to your city."

They responded that they already knew this, but that the man refuses to accept their offer. Rav Shach told them not to give up and to continue their efforts to persuade the man to accept the position. They replied that they would do whatever they could, but that it might be best if Rav Shach himself would get involved, since the man would certainly listen to Rav Shach.

Rav Shach explained why he would not speak with him: "When I talk to you, I consider what is best for you and for your city. For you, a Torah scholar will bring immediate blessing, as the Gemara (*Berachos* 42a) states. When I speak with him, however, I consider what is best for him — and I am not so sure that it is a good idea for him!"

וְלִפְנֵי עִוֵּר לֹא תִתֵּן מִכְשֹׁל — *You shall not place a stumbling block in front of a blind person* (19:14).

A Bais Yaakov high school for girls opened under the guidance of Rav Shach, and they would not make any decisions without first getting his advice. The administration turned to one of the most popular and experienced teachers in the city, and asked her to accept a senior teaching position in their school. Her husband, a Torah scholar who was close to Rav Shach, went to him for advice. Much to his amazement, Rav Shach began asking him some basic questions: Where was the school located and did they have a building? Was the building rented and how do they pay the rent? The husband admitted that he did not know any of the answers.

"Find out," said Rav Shach tersely.

The man left all confused, but as he considered the matter he understood what had happened: Rav Shach was interested in the good of the school, and there is no question that the school would benefit from an experienced teacher with an excellent reputation. Despite this, Rav Shach was not convinced that the school would succeed, for it was facing some formidable financial problems.

Accordingly, if the man's wife would accept the new position, someone else would be hired to replace her at her current job. If the new school would then fail, she might find herself without a job altogether. Rav Shach was highlighting the risks involved so that they could make an informed decision.

הוֹכֵחַ תּוֹכִיחַ אֶת־עֲמִיתֶךָ — *You shall reprove your fellow* (19:17).

Our Sages (*Tanna D'vei Eliyahu Rabbah* 18) derive from this verse that it must be *your fellow* — i.e., one who likes you and will listen to you. Otherwise, say the Sages elsewhere (*Yevamos* 65b), "Just as there is an obligation to say that which will be heard, so too there is an obligation not to say that which will not be heard but ignored."

Every summer, the Ponevezh Yeshivah holds a *Yarchei Kallah*, an event that attracts hundreds of working people who dedicate their summer vacation time to study in the yeshivah. Rav Shach would give the opening lecture, and he would generally use the opportunity to discuss important contemporary issues.

He once mentioned that there was a topic he had wanted to raise, but that he then decided not to talk about it. Why? Because although he had no reservations about discussing a matter that he knew to be true — even though some people would object and even if it would cause controversy — he would do so only when there was a problem that could be addressed and remedied. Concerning the issue he chose not to discuss, however, he felt that even if he would speak about it, in the end nothing would change.

הוֹכֵחַ תּוֹכִיחַ אֶת־עֲמִיתֶךָ וְלֹא־תִשָּׂא עָלָיו חֵטְא — *You shall reprove your fellow, and you shall not bear a sin because of him* (19:17).

A rosh yeshivah once saw Rav Shach approach a very studious young man who would delve in great depth into the Talmudic passage being studied in the yeshivah. Rav Shach told the fellow, "I want to offer you reproof, and I know that you will not listen to my guidance. Apparently I should follow the advice of our Sages who say, 'Just as there is an obligation to say that which will be listened to, so too there is an obligation not to say that which will not be listened to.' So why did I decide to offer you reproof anyway?

Because I know that the day will come when you will understand that your approach was wrong, and you will be bitter about it. You might want to lay the blame on your teachers saying, 'Why did nobody ever offer me guidance? If they said nothing, they obviously agreed that what I was doing was proper — but they were wrong!'

"I am therefore telling you now to change your way of study!"

The young man was spending a great deal of time achieving an in-depth understanding of Talmudic discussions and topics, one at a time, but not attaining a broad knowledge of Torah.

Of course, Rav Shach was right. The boy did not immediately change. As time passed, however, he regretted not listening. But by then, the time spent was lost forever.

מִפְּנֵי שֵׂיבָה תָּקוּם וְהָדַרְתָּ פְּנֵי זָקֵן — *You shall rise in the presence of an old person and you shall honor the presence of an elder* (19:32).

*T*he Gemara (*Kiddushin* 32b) explains that *elder* (*zaken*) refers to one who acquired (*zeh kanah*) wisdom. Elsewhere (*Makkos* 22b), the Gemara says, "How foolish are those who rise in the presence of a Torah scroll, but not in the presence of a great man."

Whenever Rav Shach used to visit the Chazon Ish, the latter would excort him to the gate of his house, saying, "I am escorting a Torah scroll."

אֱמֹר אֶל־הַכֹּהֲנִים בְּנֵי אַהֲרֹן וְאָמַרְתָּ אֲלֵהֶם לְנֶפֶשׁ לֹא־יִטַּמָּא בְּעַמָּיו. כִּי אִם־לִשְׁאֵרוֹ הַקָּרֹב אֵלָיו לְאִמּוֹ וּלְאָבִיו — *Say to the Kohanim, the sons of Aharon, and you shall say to them: To a [dead] person he shall not become impure among his people; except for the relative who is closest to him, to his mother and to his father (21:1,2).*

Rambam (*Hil. Eivel* 2:6) points out the stringency of the mourning requirement: We see that the prohibition of impurity for a Kohen is superseded by the requirements of mourning for close relatives, as indicated by the verse "except for the relative who is closest to him."

At a *shivah* visit to a mourner, Rav Shach was asked why a mourner is prohibited to study Torah, based on the verse (*Tehillim* 19:9), "The orders of Hashem are upright, gladdening the heart," whereas meat and wine are permitted despite the Gemara's dictum (*Pesachim* 109a) that there can be no joy without them. In fact, the contrary is the case, as Scripture says (*Mishlei* 31:6), "Give strong drink to the woebegone and wine to the embittered soul." Would it not have made more sense to prohibit joy in material matters such as food, and exhort mourners to study Torah in honor of the soul of the departed?

Rav Shach answered based on the verse (*Devarim* 14:1) which states, "You are children to Hashem, your God — you shall not cut yourselves ... for a dead person." Sforno explains that since Hashem, your Father, exists eternally, it is not proper to mourn excessively for any dead person.

Nevertheless, Scripture says (*Tehillim* 19:10): "The judgments of Hashem are true, altogether righteous," and thus, if the mourner was not supposed to suffer, his loved one would not have died.

Accordingly, the Gemara (*Moed Katan* 15a) teaches that a mourner is required to overturn his bed, for Bar Kappara taught: (The Holy One, Blessed is He, said), "I put my image in them, and in their sins they overturned it — let them overturn their bed!" And thus, "If one of the group dies, the entire group shoul be worried." This is why Torah study is not permitted: so that there should be time for introspection and for spiritual accounting in order to improve one's ways!

As a byproduct of this answer, we can see what immersion in Torah meant to Rav Shach: If Torah study would have been permitted, there would be no opportunity for spiritual accounting!

לְנֶפֶשׁ לֹא־יִטַּמָּא בְּעַמָּיו. כִּי אִם־לִשְׁאֵרוֹ — *To a [dead] person he shall not become impure among his people; except for his relative* (21:1-2).

Rambam, in his *Sefer HaMitzvos* (Asei 37) and *Sefer HaChinuch* (*Mitzvah* 264), includes in this mitzvah of a Kohen becoming impure for his relatives, the mitzvah of mourning that is incumbent upon every Jew when his close relatives die.

When Rav Shach was sitting *shivah* for his wife, R' Yehudah Addes made a *shivah* call to console him. It was a Sunday, and Rav Shach told him that he was thinking of going to the yeshivah on Tuesday — right in the middle of the days of mourning — to give his weekly lecture. He opened up the *Shulchan Aruch* to the laws of mourning (*Yoreh Deah* 384), and showed R' Addes the paragraph that states that a mourner who is needed by many from whom to learn is permitted to teach them Torah (the commentary of *Shach*, ad loc., writes that the teacher of children is considered "one who is needed by many"). In Rav Shach's great modesty, he turned to R' Addes and asked, "And what is your opinion on the matter?"

R' Addes was quite surprised at the very idea of having the strength to deliver a lecture in the middle of the days of mourning, but since he was given the opportunity to answer, he said: "And who is to say that the community will not understand this as disrespect for the laws of mourning rather than as honoring Torah study?"

Rav Shach replied, "If so, then it would be better not to deliver a lecture."

It should be noted that several months after the Rebbetzin passed away, Rav Shach wrote to a Torah scholar, "It is quite a while that I have not written to you. I am sure that you know that the reason is because it was difficult for me to concentrate enough to write, and I have still not recovered from my anguish, but, "Had your Torah not been my enjoyment ..." (see *Tehillim* 119:92).

If he still had not recovered from his anguish several months later, how great must his anguish have been in the midst of the *shivah*. Nevertheless, he considered going to the yeshivah to teach Torah to the public!

מֵעֶרֶב עַד־עֶרֶב תִּשְׁבְּתוּ שַׁבַּתְּכֶם — *From evening to evening shall you rest on your rest day* (23:32).

Once, when Rav Shach had already passed his 80th birthday, he returned home from Yom Kippur services and was immediately called to an important meeting on community matters. He listened carefully to all the speakers, weighed their words, and asked for clarifications, until he formed his Torah-based opinion as to what should be done concerning the matter at hand. When the meeting ended, he finally went home, recited *Havdalah*, and had a bite to eat!

בַּסֻּכֹּת תֵּשְׁבוּ שִׁבְעַת יָמִים — *You shall dwell in booths for a seven-day period* (23:42).

According to the Mishnah (*Sukkah* 28b), the Hebrew word "teishvu," should be translated "dwell," rather than the more literal "sit." Since one does not dwell in discomfort, there is no obligation to dwell in the *sukkah* in situations of discomfort. Accordingly, when it is raining, one may eat in his own home, rather than in the *sukkah*. He should nevertheless realize that the Gemara (*Sukkah* 28b) compares this to a servant who pours a cup for his master, who then throws its contents in the servant's face saying, "I have no need for your service."

Rav Shach recounted the story that he heard from R' Aharon Kotler who had himself witnessed it: A Jew wanted to eat in the *sukkah,* but was unable to do so because of rain. He took his food and ate in a dark corner of the kitchen, as a servant would when reprimanded by his master. The Jew said, "We are being reprimanded by the Creator. We wanted to eat in His shadow and He told us that He had no interest in our mitzvah. How could I possibly eat the holiday meal in luxury? I must, at the very least, show that I recognize that I was being reprimanded!"

וַיְדַבֵּר מֹשֶׁה אֶת־מֹעֲדֵי ה׳ אֶל־בְּנֵי יִשְׂרָאֵל — *And Moshe declared the appointed festivals of Hashem to the Children of Israel* (23:44).

bn Ezra points out that it was declared to "the Children of Israel," and not to *all* the Children of Israel," for it is not possible to speak with them all.

Rav Shach said that *maggidei shiur,* Talmud lecturers, should not aim their lectures at the brightest and quickest of the class. On the other hand, one should also not wait until the weakest and slowest understand everything. Rather, the lecture should be aimed at the average level of the class.

The lecturers should, however, be present in the study hall during the time alotted for independent study, taking care of everyone's needs: repeating and patiently explaining to the weakest and slowest (see *Sanhedrin* 91b, and Maharsha ad loc., and *Eruvin* 54b), and adding whatever is necessary for the advanced students who can delve deeper!

וַיֵּצֵא בֶּן־אִשָּׁה יִשְׂרְאֵלִית וְהוּא בֶּן־אִישׁ מִצְרִי — *The son of an Israelite woman went out — and he was the son of an Egyptian man* (24:10).

ashi explains that he "went out" from the court of Moshe, where he was found guilty. He had pitched his tent in the midst of the tribe of Dan, and when asked what he was doing there, he told them that he was from the tribe of Dan. They replied that Scripture says (*Bamidbar* 2:2), "The children of Israel shall encamp, each man by his banner according to the insignias of their fathers' household." He then went to the court of Moshe, which ruled against him. It was then that he stood and blasphemed.

The Alter of Kelm asks: The tribe of Dan numbered over 60,000 people. Would it really make such a difference to them if that son of an Egyptian would pitch his tent in their midst? He answered that this episode teaches that all it takes is one evil person to ruin an entire tribe!

A father took his soon-to-be bar-mitzvah son to Rav Shach and asked him the following question: The Chazon Ish, when he became a bar mitzvah, accepted upon himself to study Torah lishmah, for its sake, and for no other ulterior motives. This helped make the Chazon Ish what he was. What should a bar mitzvah boy accept upon himself in our times?

Rav Shach told the youth, "Two things. First, stay away from bad friends. Second, do not hang around outdoors, but just go straight from the house to the *beis midrash* and from the *beis midrash* to the house. If you do so — and you eat and sleep according to your needs — I am certain that you will become a Torah scholar!"

בהר — Behar

וְלֹא תוֹנוּ אִישׁ אֶת־עֲמִיתוֹ וְיָרֵאתָ מֵאֱלֹקֶיךָ כִּי אֲנִי ה' אֱלֹקֵיכֶם —
Do not harass one another, and you shall fear your God, for I am Hashem, your God (25:17).

This is the source for the prohibition against causing anguish to another Jew. It is not possible to enumerate all the different things that cause anguish to others, but each person must be careful according to his understanding. "For Hashem, Blessed is He, knows all one's steps and his intentions, for, as Scripture says (*I Shmuel* 16:7): 'Man sees what his eyes behold, but Hashem sees into the heart' " (*Sefer Chinuch, Mitzvah* 338).

Rav Shach was once the *sandak* (the one who holds the baby) at a circumcision. Meanwhile, someone was moving a bench from one place to another and accidentally banged the bench into the back of Rav Shach's neck.

All the guests cried out in alarm, but Rav Shach did not even turn around to see who had inadvertently hit him, so as not to embarrass the person!

אַל־תִּקַּח מֵאִתּוֹ נֶשֶׁךְ וְתַרְבִּית וְיָרֵאתָ מֵאֱלֹקֶיךָ — *Do not take from him interest and increase; and you shall fear your God (25:36).*

The Rebbetzin once complained to R' Moshe Zivyon about her husband: "What should I do with the *Rosh Yeshivah*! Please speak to him; maybe you will have some influence on him."

"What is the problem?" he asked, quite surprised.

"Well, my neighbor's son is getting married, and they asked him to officiate at the wedding. He refuses! He just won't hear of it! I tell him that he must honor their request. Why, they have been so good to us!

When the salaries are late, they lend us money. When we run out of groceries, we turn to them. Even now we owe them money, and despite the expenses of the wedding they are not asking for it! At the very least, he can honor their request. If it is so important to them, how can he refuse?

"But he just says that for that very reason he cannot come, for that would be a question of interest!"

בחקתי — Bechukosai

אִם־בְּחֻקֹּתַי תֵּלֵכוּ — *If you will go in My statutes* (26:3).

Rashi explains that "going in His statutes" refers to toiling in Torah.

Rav Shach's toiling in Torah was legendary. He once said about himself that from the time he was 18, his whole existence was immersion in Torah study!

Once Rav Shach was walking on the porch before the main sanctuary of the yeshivah, deeply immersed in his Torah thoughts. One youth hurried by, and accidentally bumped into the *Rosh Yeshivah* and knocked him down. Two others immediately rushed to help him up. The first youth was mortified, and he went to Rav Shach and begged his forgiveness.

Rav Shach's response: "I don't know what you are talking about."

The youth understood from this that Rav Shach would not forgive him, and he was afraid to have the *Rosh Yeshivah* angry with him. He was so upset that he turned to one of those who were known to be close to Rav Shach and begged him to ask for forgiveness.

The latter asked Rav Shach to forgive the youth, and Rav Shach said to him, "Again about that? Why, he himself already asked me, and I told him that I do not know what he is talking about!"

Seeing that he was not going to get his forgiveness, he asked Rav Shach to explain this great anger against the youth.

"Now I don't know what *you* are talking about," said Rav Shach, in obvious confusion.

"I am asking the *Rosh Yeshivah* to forgive that youth for knocking you down," he replied. "It was purely by accident."

"What in the world are you talking about?" wondered Rav Shach aloud. "Nobody knocked me down!"

So deeply was Rav Shach immersed in his Torah thoughts, that he did not even realize that he was knocked down and that he was helped up!

אִם־בְּחֻקֹּתַי תֵּלֵכוּ — *If you will go in My statutes* (26:3).

R' Eli Munk recounted the time that he asked Rav Shach a question regarding the section of Talmud being studied. At that moment, Rav Shach was deeply immersed in a long difficult passage elsewhere. At first, he apologized and said that he was in the middle of some other matter — but he immediately recanted, his sense of duty to his students overriding all else — and said, "Let's hear the question."

R' Munk asked his question, and when he was finished, Rav Shach apologized for not fully concentrating, and requested that he repeat the question. He repeated the question, and again Rav Shach apologized and asked him to repeat the question. After asking the question for the third time, Rav Shach smiled sadly and said, "You see, it just is not going in, for I am in the middle of thinking about something else!"

אִם־בְּחֻקֹּתַי תֵּלֵכוּ — *If you will go in My statutes* (26:3).

Rashi explains that "going in His statutes" refers to toiling in Torah.

An example of Rav Shach's toiling in Torah was provided by R' Menachem Pertzowitz, whose family lived in the same building in Jerusalem which Rav Shach used to live. Though he was just a young boy at the time, he clearly remembers the incredible diligence of Rav Shach's deep immersion in Torah. R' Pertzowitz recalls, "There were many large families living in the building. I was part of a boisterously loud group of boys. We would all run into his room to play catch. Rav Shach would be sitting at his desk, surrounded by his books, deeply immersed in his studies. We would run all around, bang into his chair, move the table, and who knows what else. He, however, was oblivious to everything!"

אִם־בְּחֻקֹּתַי תֵּלֵכוּ — *If you will go in My statutes* (26:3).

Rashi explains that "going in His statutes" refers to toiling in Torah. How is the lifestyle of one who toils in Torah described in *Pirkei Avos* (6:4)?

"Bread with salt shall you eat, and water in measure shall

you drink, and you shall sleep on the ground; and you shall live a life of difficulty and in Torah shall you toil" — this teaches that toiling in Torah requires total detachment from mundane matters.

R' Refael Wolf recalls that when they built Rav Shach his new apartment on the top floor opposite the yeshivah, Rav Shach insisted that they bring the old and broken-down bed that he had originally been given by the Jewish Agency. They complied with his request, but decided to exchange the old straw mattress for a new innerspring mattress.

That night, when Rav Shach got into bed he cried out, "*Oy*, the bed is jumping!"

On that note, when he moved into that apartment, they placed a sofa in a corner of the hall for his comfort. Two years later he turned to R' Wolf to ask, "Why did they just add a sofa here?"

וְאִם־בְּזֹאת לֹא תִשְׁמְעוּ לִי וַהֲלַכְתֶּם עִמִּי בְּקֶרִי, וְהָלַכְתִּי עִמָּכֶם בַּחֲמַת־קֶרִי — *If despite this you will not heed Me, and you behave toward Me with casualness, I will behave toward you with a fury of casualness* (26:27-28).

R ambam (*Hil. Taanis* 1:3) writes that when misfortune occurs, if people do not cry out and call for repentance, but say that it is the custom of the world for such things to happen, and this misfortune is merely a casual happenstance, then they are following a cruel path. They cause themselves to be caught in their evil ways, and the misfortune will lead to further woe. Thus, the Torah says, "If... you behave toward Me with casualness, I will behave toward you with a fury of casualness." In other words, when I bring upon you misfortune so that you repent, if you say that it is casual happenstance, then I will add to you a fury of that casual happenstance.

During the Second World War, Kletzk Yeshivah moved to Vilna, and from there to Janova. Rav Shach was in Vilna as a refugee, and the *rosh yeshivah*, R' Aharon Kotler, asked him to lecture in his yeshivah. At the same time, a telegram came with the tragic news that R' Chaim Ozer Grodzinsky had passed away, and the yeshivah hired a truck to take the students, led by Rav Shach, to the funeral. When they returned, R' Aharon asked Rav Shach to address the yeshivah.

This is what he said: "I would like to ask you. What is more severe, transgressing a negative commandment or transgressing a positive commandment? Everybody knows that transgressing a negative commandment is more severe — despite the fact that a positive commandment is 'stronger' than a negative one, as can be seen from the fact that a positive commandment supersedes a negative one. The Gemara (*Yoma* 86a) teaches us that whoever transgresses a positive commandment and then repents is forgiven immediately, whereas one who transgresses a negative commandment and repents is left waiting until Yom Kippur for the atonement to be complete. Why is this so? Because one transgresses a positive commandment by refraining from action, whereas one transgresses a negative commandment by doing an act, and that is worse.

"We may then ask why one who transgresses a negative commandment — which we have established as more severe — is punished only by thirty-nine lashes, whereas one who refuses to fulfill a positive commandment is lashed until his soul leaves his body (see *Kesubos* 86a).

"The answer is that the thirty-nine lashes are indeed a punishment for transgressing a negative commandment, which is, in fact, more severe than transgressing a positive commandment. On the other hand, one who refuses to fulfill a positive commandment is lashed only once. If he learns his lesson and fulfills the commandment, fine. If not, he is lashed again, and so on until he does as he should or until his soul departs his body.

"To what am I referring? The ascendance of our Nazi enemy in Germany was the first blow. When that failed to wake us up, the war broke out. When that did not wake us up, the Russians captured Lithuania. When we still did not wake up, our great master and teacher was taken from us. What more do we need before we wake up?!"

ספר במדבר 🙠

Bamidbar

במדבר — Bamidbar

וַיִּפְקֹד אֹתָם מֹשֶׁה עַל-פִּי ה' — *Moshe counted them according to the word of Hashem* (3:16).

Rashi explains the expression, "according to the word of Hashem:" "Moshe asked the Holy One, Blessed is He: 'How can I enter their tents to count their suckling infants?' The Holy One, Blessed is He, replied: 'You do yours, and I will do mine.' So Moshe went and stood before each tent, and the Divine Presence preceded him, and a Voice would emerge from each tent saying: 'This number of suckling infants are in this tent.' It therefore says that he counted them 'according to the word of Hashem.'"

Rav Shach would use this as the source for saying that Hashem does not have impossible expectations of a person. Each person is required to try his best, and from there it is in His Hands, as it says (*Tehillim* 57:3): "God Who fulfills for me," and (ibid. 138:8): "May Hashem complete on my behalf."

Once, the son of a person close to Rav Shach fell ill and was in danger of losing his sight. The doctor stressed how he could lose his sight at any moment, and that time was of the essence. The father ran to Rav Shach to ask what to do. Rav Shach told him to consult with a certain surgeon who would examine the child and advise what to do. They called, but were unable to secure an appointment before the next day.

The father cried out in fear, "Who knows what can happen until tomorrow morning!"

But Rav Shach calmly said, "We have done everything that we can, we have fulfilled our obligation to try, now Hashem will do His — and He is the Healer of all flesh Who does miraculous things. I take it upon myself to guarantee you that the boy's situation will not worsen before tomorrow morning!"

מִשְׁפַּחַת בְּנֵי־קְהָת יַחֲנוּ עַל יֶרֶךְ הַמִּשְׁכָּן תֵּימָנָה — *The families of the children of Kehas would encamp on the side of the Tabernacle, to the south (3:29).*

Rashi states that they were next to the division of Reuven, who also encamped to the south; "woe to the wicked and woe to his neighbor." Thus, Dasan and Aviram, as well as two hundred and fifty others [from the tribe of Reuven], were punished along with Korach (from the children of Kehas) and his group, for they were drawn along with them in their dispute. Subsequently, Rashi comments on the verse (3:38) which lists "Moshe and Aharon and his sons," that they were near the division of the camp of Yehudah and their neighbors, Yissachar and Zevulun, for it is "good for the righteous and good for his neighbor." Thus, the neighbors of Moshe, who was involved in Torah study, became great in Torah — "Yehudah is My lawgiver" (*Tehillim* 60:9); "Of the children of Yissachar, men with understanding for the times" (I *Divrei HaYamim* 12:33), who produced two hundred heads of the Sanhedrin court (see Rashi, *Bereishis* 49:15); and "from Zebulun, those who ply the scribal quill" (*Shoftim* 5:14).

Rav Shach would recount the story about a dybbuk in the time of the Vilna Gaon. The dybbuk went to the courtyard of the synagogue and screamed mightily in a horrifying, strange voice, revealing many hidden secrets. The people thronged to see the awesome sight and the tumult was great.

The tumult disturbed the Gaon's Torah study, and he opened the shutters to see the cause of the uproar. The dybbuk saw him and called out, "Are you the one concerning whom it is proclaimed in the Heavens, 'Take heed of Elijah and of his Torah'? If you decree from your own mouth that I must exit from this person, I am willing to leave."

The Gaon replied, "I never wanted to have anything to do with them, and now too, I want nothing to do with them," and he slammed the shutters shut!

Rav Shach added that he later saw that the *Rosh* of Amitzislav writes in the Introduction to his commentary to the *Midrash HeChadash* on *Ruth* a continuation to this story that he later heard from the Gaon's disciple, R' Chaim of Volozhin. The Gaon's answer spread among the denizens of the powers of evil. When an evil spirit entered a youth from Novaradok and he was warned that they would bring him to the Vilna Gaon, he replied, "True, we fear him greatly, but we know that he wants nothing to do with us."

They then asked him, "Why are you so afraid of him? He does not even afflict himself by fasting, as do other Kabbalists!"

"His very eating is like eating sacrifices in the Temple," the spirit replied.

Rav Shach would end the story by noting, "There is much we can learn from the tough stand of the Gaon — not to have anything to do with 'them' even if they will take advantage of that situation. This is similar to the words of our Sages (*Avos* 1:7): 'Do not become attached to the wicked,' which is amplified in *Avos d'Rav Nassan*: 'Not even for Torah!' "

וְהִתְוַדּוּ אֶת־חַטָּאתָם אֲשֶׁר עָשׂוּ — *And they shall confess their sin that they committed (5:7).*

*P*recious is Israel, for Scripture permitted each and every individual to pray for himself, as it says (*I Melachim* 8:38): "Each man knowing the affliction of his heart, when he spreads out his hands [in prayer] toward this Temple," rather than obligating prayer by means of an agent (*Yoma* 52a, cited in Rashi).

"In earlier times," stated Rav Shach, "people did not run to the leaders to ask for advice and blessings in every matter. Even to the Chofetz Chaim — whom everybody knew to be like a son to Hashem, for whom He would do anything — people did not come with every little question."

His grandson asked him if that was a good quality of today or a bad quality. Perhaps the generation became more aware of the need to consult our leaders?

"No," replied Rav Shach. "The reason for the change is that people are too lazy to think for themselves or to pray for themselves!"

וְהֵבִיא הָאִישׁ אֶת־אִשְׁתּוֹ אֶל־הַכֹּהֵן — *The man shall bring his wife to the Kohen (5:15).*

*R*ashi notes the juxtaposition of this subject with the previous subject, where it says (5:10): "A man's holies shall be his." The connection between them is to teach that if one holds back the gifts of the Kohen (by keeping his holies to himself), he will be forced to come to the Kohen to bring the *sotah*-woman. The Midrash (*Bamidbar Rabbah* 9:13) completes this idea with the statement, "If a gate is not opened for charity, it will be opened for the doctor."

Rav Shach was given $5,000 to use for charity. He inquired as to the source of the money, and was told the following: R' Zvi Genauer had to undergo an eye operation. The surgeon he chose to perform the operation told him that it would cost $5,000. He went to R' Chananya Chulak for advice, and the latter was able to arrange for the operation to be performed by the same surgeon, but under the standard *Kupat Cholim* health fund, so that it would be done at no charge to the patient. After successfully undergoing the operation, R' Genauer sent $100 to be given to Rav Shach for charitable purposes. An hour later, R' Genauer rushed back in explaining that when he told his wife that he gave $100, she said, "If you saved $5,000, it is only right to give the entire sum to charity." So he added another $4,900!

Rav Shach was so impressed that he said, "Please bring that couple to me. If this is the way they think, I must bless them!"

מֵחַרְצַנִּים וְעַד־זָג לֹא יֹאכֵל — *From pips to skin he shall not eat* (6:4).

*R*ight before the yeshivah boys were to leave for intersession, Rav Shach read to his students from *Shaarei Teshuvah* of Rabbeinu Yonah (3:80): "And if you ask in your heart, where do we find in Scripture that the Torah erects a fence? We can answer that regarding the *nazir*, whose main purpose is not to drink wine (and drinking itself is a fence) 'lest he drink and forget the statute [of the Torah]' (*Mishlei* 31:5), or be enticed to immorality — the Torah forbids him 'anything made from wine grapes,' and all as a fence and a distancing from drinking wine." Rabbeinu Yonah continues that this is behind the need to distance oneself from those with whom he is forbidden to have relations, a sin for which one must sacrifice his life rather than commit.

Rabbeinu Yonah's source for this is the Gemara (*Shabbos* 13a) which states that any form of closeness to such people is prohibited because of the principle that, "We tell the *nazir* to go all the way around but not to draw near the vineyard." In other words, the Torah prohibits grapes for a *nazir* because of wine, which is prohibited "lest he drink and forget the statute [of the Torah]," and our Sages prohibit him to enter the vineyard, lest he come to eat grapes, which itself is prohibited — as a fence to a fence. Furthermore, the *nazir* must go "all the way around!" This is Rambam's source for saying (*Hil. Nezirus* 5:10), "It is Rabbinically prohibited for the *nazir* to stand among those sitting and drinking wine, and he must distance himself greatly from them, for they are a potential obstacle. The Sages say that he shall not come near the vineyard."

Rav Shach concluded by saying, "Can there be any greater example of 'sitting and drinking wine' than the streets of the big city?"

בהעלותך — Beha'aloscha

וְכִי־תָבֹאוּ מִלְחָמָה בְּאַרְצְכֶם עַל־הַצַּר הַצֹּרֵר אֶתְכֶם וַהֲרֵעֹתֶם בַּחֲצֹצְרֹת — *When you go to wage war in your land against an enemy who oppresses you, you shall sound short blasts of the trumpets (10:9).*

Rambam (*Hil. Taaniyos* 1:2) explains, "This is one of the ways of repentance, that when misfortune falls and people cry out about it and blast the trumpet, they should all know that misfortune befell them because of their bad deeds, as it is written (*Yirmiyahu* 5:25), 'Your sins have overturned these, and your transgressions have kept goodness away from you,' and this will cause them to remove the misfortune from themselves."

During the Gulf War in 1991, R' Nachum Kook went to Rav Shach's house to discuss something. Suddenly, the air-raid siren sounded; a missile had been fired, and people were afraid. Where would the missile fall? What havoc would it wreak? Would it be a conventional warhead, or perhaps a chemical or biological warhead?

As the siren wailed, R' Kook asked Rav Shach, "What do we do now? Is there a sealed room, or do we go to the shelter?"

Rav Shach replied, "Each person has his own matters to fix."

כַּאֲשֶׁר יִשָּׂא הָאֹמֵן אֶת־הַיֹּנֵק — *As a wet nurse carries a suckling (11:12).*

The Gemara (*Sanhedrin* 8a) states that a judge must bear his community. And how much? Said R' Chanan: "As a wet nurse carries a suckling."

A young man once approached R' Mordechai Appolion and told him that his parents had reserved a vacation room and, for whatever reason, cancelled their reservation. A short while later, they changed their mind, but it was too late; the place would no longer accept their reservation.

R' Appolion asked the youth what help he wanted from him. The youth replied that since the rabbi was known to be close to Rav Shach, perhaps he could ask Rav Shach to intercede on their behalf. Since Rav Shach was so fatherly in his relationships, R' Appolion felt that he could indeed approach Rav Shach concerning the matter.

Rav Shach asked what the parents did, and was told that they work for a living. "If so," he said, "then they need a vacation."

He took R' Appolion to a private room, and asked him to find the phone number of the place and to dial the number (Rav Shach was extremely near-sighted). When they answered the phone, Rav Shach introduced himself and asked them to accept the reservations of the couple. After the conversation, he turned to R' Appolion and assured him that the matter would be resolved.

כַּאֲשֶׁר יִשָּׂא הָאֹמֵן אֶת־הַיֹּנֵק — As a nurse carries a suckling (11:12).

Years ago, there was no private telephone in Rav Shach's residence on R' Wasserman Street. When Rav Shach had to make a telephone call, he would go to the public telephone on R' Dessler Street. R' Eliyahu Steinberg once passed by as Rav Shach spoke animatedly into the phone, while being thoroughly soaked by a pouring rain. R' Steinberg approached and held his umbrella over Rav Shach, wondering all the while what matter of earth-shattering importance had pulled Rav Shach into the torrential downpour.

Then he heard Rav Shach implore the person on the other end to accept a girl into his school!

כַּאֲשֶׁר יִשָּׂא הָאֹמֵן אֶת־הַיֹּנֵק — As a nurse carries a suckling (11:12).

A family from Rishon L'Tziyon became newly Orthodox after attending a seminar for baalei teshuvah. They asked Rav Shach if they should move to Bnei Brak, and he encouraged them to do so. They moved to Bnei Brak, but when they went to register their daughter in the local school, she was rejected.

They went to Rav Shach and broken-heartedly told the story. Rav Shach immediately phoned R' Shraga Grossbard, the director of the Chinuch Atzma'i school system, and asked him to intercede on the girl's behalf. R' Grossbard did so, but could not change the principal's mind. She explained that her adamant refusal was based on sound educational principles, and nothing could budge her.

Rav Shach himself called the principal and asked her to please accept the girl. The principal replied that her hands were tied; there was a parents' council and they threatened that if this girl were to be accepted — and this was not the only girl who wanted to be accepted — the parents would withdraw their daughters from that school.

Rav Shach asked for the telephone numbers of the entire parent council, phoned each one, and asked them as a personal favor to withdraw their objection to accepting the girl!

וַיִּשָּׁאֲרוּ שְׁנֵי־אֲנָשִׁים בַּמַּחֲנֶה... וְהֵמָּה בַּכְּתֻבִים — *Two men remained behind in the camp ... they had been among the recorded ones* (11:26).

ashi cites *Sifri* that Eldad and Meidad were chosen for prophecy but, out of their great modesty, did not come forth, and they allowed others to go in their stead.

When Rav Shach published his first work, his uncle, R' Isser Zalman Meltzer, was ready to publish another volume of his works. R' Isser Zalman told Rav Shach at the time, "Times are difficult now and there is great poverty. People cannot afford to buy two books. I am old, but you are young, and it is the time for people to see your scholarliness in Torah. If people buy my work, they will not be able to afford yours." So he did not publish his book until after *Avi Ezri* was on the market for a while!

וַיִּשָּׁאֲרוּ שְׁנֵי־אֲנָשִׁים בַּמַּחֲנֶה — *Two men remained behind in the camp* (11:26).

ashi explains that the two remained behind from among those selected [to be among the seventy elders], because they felt themselves unworthy of such greatness.

R' Moshe Friedman once saw Rav Shach leave his seat in the middle of praying and finish his prayers in the back of the *beis midrash*. After the services, he asked Rav Shach why he had changed his place.

Rav Shach explained, "All of a sudden, right in the middle of the services, a thought passed through my mind: 'What am I doing standing at the eastern wall? What is so special about me?' Now, I know that, in truth, sitting at the eastern wall is meaningless, but instead of having to fight that thought, which would mitigate the purity of my prayers, I decided to change places, thereby eliminating the problem."

אֲדֹנִי מֹשֶׁה כְּלָאֵם — *My lord Moshe, make an end of them* (11:28).

hat is meant by "make an end of them"? The Gemara (*Sanhedrin* 17a) explains that he told Moshe to make them responsible for the needs of the community, which would "make an end of them" — make them self-destruct.

When R' Simchah Kook was offered the chief rabbinate of Rechovot, he went to Rav Shach for advice. R' Kook expressed his fear that the problems of the big city would not leave him any free time to study Torah.

Rav Shach told him that even the rabbinate of the smallest town requires attention 24 hours a day but, on the other hand, even the largest city cannot stop its rabbi from setting specific study times. Accordingly, the size of the city is immaterial!

Rav Shach related that after the marriage of the Chofetz Chaim's son, R' Leib, the latter moved to the small village in which his father-in-law lived. From time to time he would come to Radin, and the Chofetz Chaim would tell him to learn specific sections to help him in writing the portion of *Mishnah Berurah* relating to those sections.

Once, he came unprepared. He did not bring any notes on the specified sections for his father to review and put into his work. R' Leib apologized, saying that the villagers consider him a big rabbi, and they constantly come to ask him for advice and help, so that he was forced into community work. Since there was no one else who could fulfill his role, he was forced to stop his Torah study.

The Chofetz Chaim replied: "That is not the way! You should know that a village of fifty families can keep its leader busy day and night and make him forget all his Torah knowledge!" (See *Berachos* 18b, concerning the children of R' Chiya forgetting their Torah study when they moved to the city.)

הֲלֹא גַם־בָּנוּ דִבֶּר וַיִּשְׁמַע ה'. וְהָאִישׁ מֹשֶׁה עָנָו מְאֹד — *Did He not speak with us, as well? And Hashem heard. Now the man Moshe was exceedingly humble* (12:2-3).

forno explains that this accords with the statement of our Sages that Hashem demands retribution for slighting the honor of Torah scholars. He apparently refers to the Gemara (*Berachos* 19a) which states that a person once spoke against one of the Sages, who neither heard nor cared what was said, and a wall fell on the speaker breaking his skull, for Hashem stands up for the honor of scholars. Accordingly, although "Moshe was exceedingly humble," Miriam had to be punished in deference to Moshe's honor.

Once, the son of a young Torah scholar was ill and required hospitalization. The boy's father told his friend, a disciple of Rav Shach, that he feared he was being punished for being disrespectful about Rav Shach. The friend attempted to put him at ease, telling him that we cannot know the accounts of Heaven. The father nevertheless insisted that he go to Rav Shach and ask, in his name, to be pardoned.

He did so, but Rav Shach was upset that his disciple hadn't made clear that there was no connection. The disciple clarified that he did make it clear, but that the friend insisted. Accordingly, even if there is no connection, he felt that it would be worth putting his friend at ease.

Rav Shach said, "Look, it is inconceivable that he was disrespectful for no good reason. Rather, he probably disagrees with me in some matter. He is probably a Torah scholar and he has a right to disagree with me. Besides, how can I say that I pardon him when I never felt slighted?" Finally Rav Shach told the friend to tell him what to say, and that he would repeat it after him.

The friend said, "I pardon So-and-so, and hold no grudge against him," and Rav Shach repeated each word after him.

The child had been in critical condition, and they even made a name change for his speedy recovery. Suddenly, the boy's condition stabilized and he recovered completely!

וְהָאִישׁ מֹשֶׁה עָנָו מְאֹד מִכֹּל הָאָדָם אֲשֶׁר עַל־פְּנֵי הָאֲדָמָה — *Now the man Moshe was exceedingly humble, more than any person on the face of the earth (12:3).*

The question arises: Did Moshe really not grasp his own greatness? Did he not realize that he was a "man of God," and that no one else would ever reach his level? Rav Shach was asked a similar question about the extreme modesty of R' Akiva Eiger. It is known that when he arrived in Warsaw, tens of thousands of Jews filled the streets to greet him. This great man — who at the time was short and hunchbacked — turned to his escort and asked, "Why have so many people come here? Could it be that they have never seen a hunchback?" Could it possibly be that he was unaware that he was the Torah leader of the time and that everyone came out in his honor?

Rav Shach replied that both Moshe Rabbeinu and R' Akiva Eiger certainly were aware of their own greatness. Rav Shach cited the famous dispute with the printers of Slavita as proof. The printers of Slavita, who were scions of a prominent family, were convinced that they were right, and they slandered R' Akiva Eiger by saying that his family perverted justice in the ruling against them. They were smitten by Divine wrath and as a result they sent a message to R' Akiva Eiger asking his pardon, stating that he had to pardon them in deference to their status, and out of honor for Torah. R' Akiva Eiger replied forcefully: "I represent honor for Torah in this generation!" In other words, by means of their slander, they impinged upon the honor of the Torah.

Rav Shach explained that R' Akiva Eiger knew that he was the greatest of his generation, but he decided that it was his obligation to mock the honor given him!

The Chazon Ish is cited as answering the question by explaining that modesty is a character trait that is independent of logic. In other words, just as conceit is a character trait, and a person can be conceited even if he has nothing to be conceited about, so too, the opposite can be true. A person can know that he has all the best qualities and still be modest.

עָנָו מְאֹד מִכֹּל הָאָדָם — *Exceedingly humble, more than any person* (12:3).

When R' Shraga Zeloshinsky studied in Ponevezh Yeshivah, he sat in the first row, opposite Rav Shach. One day he saw Rav Shach searching for a *siddur* near his seat, but, because of his poor vision, the *Rosh Yeshivah* could not find it. R' Zeloshinsky hastened to bring Rav Shach a *siddur.*

Rav Shach took the *siddur,* went back to the shelf where it belonged, and put it in its place — since he thought that he had been given the *siddur* to put away. And why not? Each day before the study session, wasn't he the one who put all the books away?

R' Shraga hurried to apologize, to explain that that was not his intention. Rav Shach, however, did not even understand why he was apologizing!

וַיֹּאמֶר שִׁמְעוּ־נָא דְבָרָי — *He said, "Please hear My words"* (12:6).

Bertinora derives from here that a wise man does not mix into the conversation of his friend, so as not to confuse him. For if Hashem commands, "Please hear My words," i.e., hold your response until I finish My words, this is certainly true for ordinary mortals!

Once, when Rav Shach began his lecture and attempted to present the basis of his thoughts, a heated argument arose regarding what he said, and he couldn't finish what he wanted to say. He said forgivingly,

"I can understand that everybody wants to talk, but since two opposing voices cannot be heard (see *Rosh Hashanah* 27a) we have to set an order. Well, I am the oldest here, so I have the right to speak first!"

He continued and once again a storm soon erupted. He said, "You are discussing my words and disagreeing with me without hearing me out to the end. This is not the proper way! If you take what I say out of context and discuss fragments of my ideas, you are liable to find yourselves arguing about the requirements of the 'commandment,' 'serve other gods and prostrate yourselves to them' (*Devarim* 11:16), instead of observing the prohibition, 'Do not serve other gods or prostrate yourselves before them.' "

קֵל נָא רְפָא נָא לָהּ — *Please, God, heal her now* (12:13).

A person came crying to Rav Shach about his brother who did not regain consciousness after a difficult operation. It had been 70 hours, and the doctors had given up on his chances to live.

The brother was afraid that this was the result of Rav Shach's displeasure with the brother, since he had once publicly and sharply expressed his opposition to Rav Shach.

Rav Shach replied with great feeling, "Did you really suspect me of being upset? Could I possibly agree to a Jew being sick on my account without wanting him to be fully cured? Now I am truly upset, because of your unjust suspicion!" Then he asked for the brother's name and the name of his mother so that he could immediately pray for his cure.

A half hour later, the family members called from the hospital to notify him that the brother had opened his eyes, asked for his family members, and returned to full consciousness!

קֵל נָא רְפָא נָא לָהּ — *Please, God, heal her now* (12:13).

R' Nosson Kamenetsky once visited Rav Shach, who asked him about the health of his father, R' Yaakov Kamenetsky. R' Nosson replied that he was very weak and it would be good to pray for him. Rav Shach gently told him, "*Zolst zein gesund!* — you should be well! I pray for him three times a day!"

שלח — Shelach

וַיֹּצִיאוּ דִּבַּת הָאָרֶץ אֲשֶׁר תָּרוּ אֹתָהּ — *They brought forth an evil report on the land that they had spied out* (13:32).

Rav Shach used to cite the words of *Mesillas Yesharim* (Chapter 11) that lengthily deprecates "honor," stating, "According to our Sages, the spies were responsible for bringing forth an evil report on the land, bringing death upon themselves and upon their whole generation. They were afraid that their honor would be diminished upon entering the land, for they would no longer be their leaders, and others would stand in their place."

In Rav Shach's advanced old age, as his weakness kept on increasing, he sat and made a spiritual accounting: What would he bring with him to the Heavenly Court?

R' Meir Heisler asked him, "What about the *Avi Ezri* that you wrote?"

"*Avi Ezri* is a good work," he replied, "but it has already brought me honor. You should know that that which brings honor in this world does not bring reward in the World to Come. It is like a used ticket!"

עַד־אָנָה יְנַאֲצֻנִי הָעָם הַזֶּה — *To what point will this people anger Me* (14:11).

R' Avraham Yitzchak Barzel recalls the time that he went to consult with Rav Shach concerning an important matter. Rav Shach heard his question, began answering, and fell asleep!

Rav Shach's family members explained to him that Rav Shach had not so much as closed his eyes for the past two nights. There had been some desecration of Hashem's Name that took place in the Knesset, and he had been too upset to sleep.

כִּי דְבַר־יהוה בָּזָה וְאֶת־מִצְוָתוֹ הֵפַר הִכָּרֵת תִּכָּרֵת הַנֶּפֶשׁ הַהִוא עֲוֹנָה בָהּ — *For he scorned the word of Hashem and broke His commandment; that soul will surely be cut off, its sin is within it* (15:31).

R' Nehorai says, "He who has the ability to study Torah and does not do so transgresses, 'For he scorned the word of Hashem' " (*Sanhedrin* 99a). Based on this statement of the Gemara, the author of a work encouraging Torah study wrote that he who wastes even one minute of Torah study desecrates the Name of Heaven and his soul deserves to be cut off in this world and in the World to Come, as Ramban says, "To be punished with eternal suffering along the lines of (*Yeshayahu* 66:24): 'For their decay will not cease and their fire will not be extinguished.' "

Rav Shach was not pleased that this was publicized, and he pointed to the commentary of Rashi here on "its sin is within it," who applies this only "at a time when its sin is within it, in that they did not repent." He added that although it is true that wasting Torah study time is the greatest desecration of Hashem's Name, Rabbeinu Yonah instilled in us (in *Shaarei Teshuvah* 4:16) that the atonement for the sin of desecrating Hashem's Name is constant Torah study and toil. He bases this on the words of the Sages (*Rosh Hashanah* 13a) which explain the verse (*I Shmuel* 3:14): "Therefore I have sworn concerning the house of Eli that the sin of the house of Eli would never be atoned for by sacrifice or offering" — it will never be atoned for by sacrifice or meal-offering, but it would be atoned for by Torah study, and this, despite the fact that the sin of the house of Eli involved desecration of the Holies, as stated there.

הִכָּרֵת תִּכָּרֵת הַנֶּפֶשׁ הַהִוא — *That soul will surely be cut off* (15:31).

"That soul will surely be cut off" is written in Hebrew with a double form of "cut off" ["hikares tikares" — translated here as "surely cut off"]. The Gemara (*Sanhedrin* 64b) explains that *hikares* refers to this world, whereas *tikares* refers to the World to Come. Rav Shach recalls that when the Brisker Rav, Rav Yitzchak Zev Soloveitchik, was sick and Rav Shach was sitting by his bedside, R' Yechezkel Sarna, the *rosh yeshivah* of Chevron Yeshivah, came to visit him. Rav Shach told them a marvelous exposition of the principle of reward and punishment and brought a proof to his idea. There was a rabbi there who disagreed, but R'

Yechezkel agreed and the Brisker Rav was greatly pleased, saying, "You have given me life!"

This is what Rav Shach said: "Everyone agrees that there is a God Who controls the world. This is something that one can see with his own eyes, and even gentiles admit to it. Now, one man arose, Hitler, may his name be blotted out, and waged a horrible world war. He destroyed kingdoms and was a mass murderer of six million of our brothers and many tens of millions of others. Ultimately, he brought ruination and desolation to his own nation, on whose behalf he ostensibly fought. He himself hid in a bunker deep underground and when he saw that the game was over, he committed suicide and was dead in a moment. Now, how could it be that the epitome of evil who caused such suffering, death, and loss should die such an easy death? Rather, it is apparent that there is punishment after death, and that is where he is suffering his gruesome punishment!"

וְלֹא תָתוּרוּ אַחֲרֵי לְבַבְכֶם וְאַחֲרֵי עֵינֵיכֶם אֲשֶׁר־אַתֶּם זֹנִים אַחֲרֵיהֶם
— *And you shall not explore after your heart and after your eyes after which you stray* (15:39).

Rav Shach would recount how when the Chofetz Chaim was a very old man approaching his 90th birthday, he included on his list of personal spiritual commitments the determination to keep on preserving the purity of what his eyes saw. Yet, the *Rosh Yeshivah* noted with amazement, today's youth are certain that they will not be harmed by what they see! Not only do they not understand the nature of their soul, but they ignore the verse which explicitly states "after which you stray" — that man's nature is to be influenced by what he sees.

Rav Shach would say that since "R' Yaakov" (the Steipler) does not receive women who come for blessings and advice, he must, although he would rather not, "Since someone must listen to to their crying and console them."

In this vein, R' Meir Heisler recalls that in 1972, just after Rav Shach underwent a difficult operation, he tried to go right back to lecturing, but he fainted, lost a lot of blood, and suffered from extreme weakness. R' Meir went to his house and found him by a table with his head down on a book.

He told Rav Shach, "The *Rosh Yeshivah* does not look well."

"I don't feel well," he replied. "I have no strength to talk."

"So why don't you go to the convalescent home?" suggested R' Heisler.

He whispered vehemently, "No! No!"

R' Heisler asked, "Can the *Rosh Yeshivah* learn Torah?"

"Certainly not," he replied. "I cannot even keep my head up!"

So again the question was asked: "Why not go to the convalescent home?"

He replied, "Try to understand. I cannot learn Torah, but I can sit here, and a student from nearby Me'or Chaim can come here and pour her heart out. I may not be able to help her — after all, I have no strength — but the very fact that she has someone to whom to pour her heart out, and she can see that I, too, cry with her over her misfortune, helps her a bit. That is why I do not get into bed. I sit here and wait. Perhaps a bitter soul will enter."

קרח — Korach

וַיִּשְׁמַע מֹשֶׁה וַיִּפֹּל עַל־פָּנָיו — *Moshe heard and fell on his face* (16:4).

When Moshe heard that he was suspected of self-exaltation, he examined himself and said to himself, "I do not seek to be king, nor do I seek that my brother Aharon be Kohen Gadol" (*Midrash Rabbah* 18:4).

A Torah scholar once disagreed vehemently with an approach used by Rav Shach in his *Avi Ezri*. He wrote Rav Shach a sharply worded letter attacking his approach. At the end of his sharp letter, he asked Rav Shach for permission to publish the section in question from *Avi Ezri* along with his letter, with the understanding that he would acknowledge having received this permission as well. Of course, the implication of publicizing Rav Shach's permission was that he was right and Rav Shach was wrong. The letter was sent right before Pesach. On one of the intermediate days (*Chol HaMoed*) of the festival, the letter-writer heard a knock on his door. It was Rav Shach, who entered the house with a smile. He said, "I reviewed the entire matter about which you wrote me. According to my approach, I am right. I cannot, however, prove that your approach is incorrect, and by that way of thinking, you are right. I therefore grant you permission to publish the letter."

לֹא חֲמוֹר אֶחָד מֵהֶם נָשָׂאתִי — *I have not taken a donkey of any one of them* (16:15).

Rashi explains that he always used his own donkey. When Rav Shach's wife was ill, he was constantly at her bedside in the hospital. This became known to R' Chaim Zaichik, who was his disciple back in the Luninetz Yeshivah. Rav Chaim asked his wife to prepare dinner for Rav Shach, certain that Rav Shach went for many hours without eating. She did as she was asked, and R' Chaim took the food and traveled on two buses to the hospital. Rav Shach displayed great pleasure upon seeing him, and greeted him warmly. When he told Rav Shach that he had brought some food with him, Rav Shach recited the blessing and took a taste. Then he returned the food and said, "Thank you and your wife, but I want neither you nor your wife to bother on my account. Nevertheless, since I did not want you to think that I won't eat because I don't trust your *kashrus*, I made sure to eat some of it. But now, please don't bring me any more."

וַיָּקָם מֹשֶׁה וַיֵּלֶךְ אֶל־דָּתָן וַאֲבִירָם — *So Moshe stood up and went to Dasan and Aviram* (16:25).

Rashi comments that Moshe was under the impression that they would treat him graciously, but they did not do so. *Ohr HaChaim* states that he experienced a "rising up" by going to them, in line with the Midrash (*Shemos Rabbah* 45:5) which states, "My degradation uplifts me," and in accordance with the verse (*Mishlei* 16:18): "Humility precedes honor."

Rav Shach never summoned anyone. At the very most, he would request that a person come to see him should he find himself in the neighborhood. R' Dan Segal relates that Rav Shach once found out that a young Torah scholar who lived in Givat Rokach needed help, so he immediately put on his coat, left his house, and began walking toward Givat Rokach — and he would not even hear of using a taxi that someone ordered for him. Instead, he went by foot, climbing up the stairs of the hill until he reached his destination. There are many other such stories about him.

It should also be mentioned here that when Rav Shach was well into his 80's, he heard that, for whatever reason, several youths could not be registered in any local school. He immediately "stood up and went" to the schools, spoke to the principals, and persuaded them to accept the youths. The *Rosh Yeshivah's* family members could not hide their astonishment: Could he not have accomplished the same thing by telephone?

Rav Shach explained, "Over the telephone, the principals would be able to use all sorts of excuses. If, however, they see that I bothered to come in person, they will realize how close the matter is to my heart, and they will fulfill my request."

וַיָּקָם מֹשֶׁה וַיֵּלֶךְ אֶל־דָּתָן וַאֲבִירָם — *So Moshe stood up and went to Dasan and Aviram (16:25).*

Ohr HaChaim states that he experienced a "rising up" by going to them, foregoing his honor, and regarding him it says, (*Mishlei* 16:18): "Humility precedes honor."

Two women once came to Ponevezh Yeshivah, asking to speak with Rav Shach. They explained that they were teachers from Yerushalayim, and they wanted to complain about the management of Bais Yaakov. Since Rav Shach was the president of *Chinuch Atzma'i*, which includes Bais Yaakov, they came to him. When the person with whom they spoke went to find Rav Shach, he found him surrounded by students, in the middle of a heated argument. He told Rav Shach that there were two Bais Yaakov teachers waiting downstairs, and he asked what time he could tell them would be good for Rav Shach to meet with them. No sooner did Rav Shach hear that there were two teachers waiting, than he immediately went to speak with them.

The person who told Rav Shach felt terrible, and as soon as Rav Shach returned, he asked for forgiveness for disturbing him.

Rav Shach did not understand why he was requesting forgiveness. "What did you expect?" he asked. "That I should invite them up to the *beis midrash* of the yeshivah? If they want to speak with me, I must go down to them!"

When told, "*Es pahst nisht* — it is not proper for the *Rosh Yeshivah* to bother himself," he asked, "What am I, a minister [using the English word in his *Yiddish* speech] locked up in his chamber who sees people by appointment only?"

וְלֹא־יִהְיֶה כְקֹרַח וְכַעֲדָתוֹ — *And he shall not be like Korach and his assembly (17:5).*

Our Sages (*Sanhedrin* 110a) learn from this that whoever maintains a dispute transgresses a negative commandment.

The Ponevezher Rav, R' Kahaneman, told Rav Shach that when the "progressives" of Radin wanted to take over the leadership of the community, they founded a new *chevrah kaddisha* (burial society) and a dispute burned wildly throughout the town. R' Yisrael Meir HaKohen, the Chofetz Chaim, called an emergency meeting of the whole town in the synagogue. At the meeting, he ascended the pulpit and said: "Dispute is a very serious matter, and it involves a Biblical prohibition. When you come before the Heavenly Court, you will be compelled to explain why you allowed a dispute to flare up and engulf the community. Then you will blame me and say, 'Yisrael Meir lived in our community and he did not protest.' I therefore have summoned you today to warn you again and again: Dispute is a very serious matter and is totally prohibited. Cease and desist immediately! If not, I demand that you sign with your own hand that you were warned, but that you refuse to heed my warning. I have enough with my own *pekele* — with my own package [of sins] that I will bring with me — and I refuse to be responsible for your sins as well!"

These heartfelt words served their purpose, and the dispute died down.

וְלֹא־יִהְיֶה כְקֹרַח וְכַעֲדָתוֹ — *And he shall not be like Korach and his assembly* (17:5).

Our Sages (*Sanhedrin* 110a) understood this verse to be teaching that whoever maintains a dispute transgresses a negative commandment. *Smag* (*Lo Saaseh* 157) and Rabbeinu Yonah include it in their listings of Biblical prohibitions. This is also the implication of *sefer Chofetz Chaim* (*Lavin* 12).

A Torah scholar once came to ask Rav Shach about a job offer for an important position abroad. He did not want to accept the position, because there was a serious dispute there and, he said, dispute brings Satan and the Angel of Death.

Rav Shach immediately replied, "Dispute brings Satan and the Angel of Death? Dispute *is* Satan and the Angel of Death!"

וּפְדוּיָו מִבֶּן־חֹדֶשׁ תִּפְדֶּה בְּעֶרְכְּךָ כֶּסֶף חֲמֵשֶׁת שְׁקָלִים — *And those that are to be redeemed, from one month shall you redeem according to the valuation, five silver shekalim* (18:16).

Rav Shach recalled that once he was discussing with R' Yitzchak Zev Soloveitchik, the Brisker Rav, whether one received any credit for performing half of a mitzvah, such as in the case of one who only has a half-measure of matzah to eat on the first night of Pesach.

The Brisker Rav said that apparently one could bring proof from the statement of Maharil (cited in *Rema, Yoreh Deah* 305:6) concerning redeeming the firstborn that, if one gives the Kohen an item worth less than the requisite five *sela'im*, the child is not considered "redeemed," but the Kohen can nevertheless keep it until the redeemer completes the requisite sum. "If there is no such thing as performing half of a mitzvah," asked the Brisker Rav, "why should the Kohen not return the item?"

"Nevertheless," concluded the Brisker Rav, "redeeming the firstborn may be different, since it is a debt owed to the Kohen. Just as a person must give whatever he has to repay a debt that is due, even if it does not equal the full amount, perhaps when one does not have the requisite five *sela'im* he must give whatever he has. This law may have no bearing, then, on the question of a half of a mitzvah." (See Rambam to *Avos* 4:2 concerning Moshe's setting aside three [out of six] cities of refuge, which he considers "half of a mitzvah.")

חקת — **Chukas**

וּנְתַתֶּם אֹתָהּ אֶל־אֶלְעָזָר הַכֹּהֵן — *You [plural] shall give it to Elazar the Kohen (19:3).*

Ramban explains that use of the plural form of "You" [u'nesa-tem], rather than the singular form [v'nasata], is to allow Aharon to share in the honor.

One of the yeshivah students once had a very powerful question on the subject matter being studied. He and his study partner went to Rav Shach and posed the question to him. It was a marvelous question, and it was Rav Shach's habit to build up the question before answering it, as well as increasing the honor of the one who asked the question. Meanwhile, two other students came to Rav Shach to discuss the subject with him. He said to them, "Listen carefully to the marvelous question that this young man is asking" — and he immediately corrected himself, "... that these young men are asking," thereby including the study partner as well.

זֹאת הַתּוֹרָה אָדָם כִּי־יָמוּת בְּאֹהֶל — *This is the teaching [lit. the Torah] regarding a man who would die in a tent (19:14).*

The Gemara (*Berachos* 63a) derives from here that Torah can only exist for one who gives his life in the "tents of Torah."

A Torah scholar once asked Rav Shach what to do: He was offered a job as Talmud teacher in a yeshivah, but a certain great rabbi opposed his appointment and wanted his own designee to get the position. Rav Shach was very emphatic in answering that he had to accept the position, because he was ideally suited for the job and he would have much to offer both the students and the yeshivah. Accordingly, he should ignore the other person's objections.

When he told Rav Shach that he was afraid to have that great person's anger directed at him, Rav Shach replied: "If that is what you fear, that is truly a concern. He is a great man, and his anger can harm you. Accordingly, you should say before each lecture, 'I am hereby prepared to give up my life for the sake of the Holy Torah!' "

זֹאת הַתּוֹרָה אָדָם כִּי־יָמוּת בְּאֹהֶל — *This is the teaching [lit. the Torah] regarding a man who would die in a tent* (19:14).

R' Shlomo Zalman Grossman once went into Rav Shach's study at midnight. He saw that Rav Shach was deeply engrossed in thought while standing at his desk, leaning on his hands, and studying a passage in *Nesivos HaMishpat*. R' Grossman did not want to disturb him, so he waited with other people in the outside room.

Suddenly, they heard a crash. They rushed inside and found Rav Shach on the floor, groaning in pain. It seems that while immersed in his thoughts he tried to sit down — but there was no chair behind him. He fell down, was in great pain, and he could not get up. They immediately lifted him and wanted to carry him to his bed, but he would not allow them to do so. He asked that they stand him at his desk so that he could finish studying! He could not even stand up, and he leaned half of his body on the desk, as he continued studying *Nesivos HaMishpat* for another half hour, until he felt that he had completed it to his satisfaction. Only then did he agree to be carried to his bed — for he was unable to walk — and to have a doctor summoned!

זֹאת הַתּוֹרָה אָדָם כִּי־יָמוּת בְּאֹהֶל — *This is the teaching [lit. the Torah] regarding a man who would die in a tent* (19:14).

The Gemara (*Shabbos* 83b) derives from here that a person should never hold himself back from the House of Study, nor from Torah study, not even as he is dying, for it says, "This is the teaching [lit. the Torah] regarding a man who would die in a tent" — even as he is dying he should be involved in Torah.

Besides his lectures in Ponevezh Yeshivah, Rav Shach would go once a week to Yeshivah Grodno in Ashdod (a branch of the Ponevezh Yeshivah) to give a lecture there. He continued this practice well into his old age, despite his weakness.

On one of his trips to Ashdod, Rav Shach's escort realized that the *Rosh Yeshivah* seemed to be burning with fever! He suggested that they return to Ponevezh. After all, Rav Shach always put all his energy into his lectures and, in his present state, it would be dangerous for him!

"True," responded Rav Shach, "but if my days are in fact over — how marvelous it would be to die while lecturing words of Torah!"

זֹאת הַתּוֹרָה אָדָם כִּי־יָמוּת בְּאֹהֶל — *This is the teaching [lit. the Torah] regarding a man who would die in a tent* (19:14).

Over the Sukkos holiday, Rav Shach's *sukkah* bustled with many visitors. There were Torah scholars, rabbis, and students, and they all came to greet their great rabbi during the festival. Once, toward the end of Rav Shach's life, when he was exceedingly weak, many visitors had come and Rav Shach was very tired. Because he was so exhausted, he fell asleep in his chair, and his grandson suggested that he go to rest, and return to his company after a short break.

Rav Shach told him, "And if I die during those 10 minutes, isn't it better to die while hosting guests and doing good deeds?"

שִׁמְעוּ־נָא הַמֹּרִים — *Listen now, rebels* (20:10).

After Rav Shach's opening lecture for the 1987 *Yarchei Kallah* (a popular vacation-period study program for laymen), he told those close to him that he had left out a part that he had wanted to say, a true insight into the "waters of strife" (see 20:13). This is the explanation:

The Gemara (*Sanhedrin* 111a) relates that when Moshe ascended to Heaven, he found the Holy One, Blessed is He, sitting and writing "slow to anger" (see *Bamidbar* 14:18). He said, "Master of the Universe, 'slow to anger' for the righteous?" Hashem replied, "For the wicked as well." Upon which Moshe said, "Let the wicked be destroyed." In other words, it is better for us that Hashem deal harshly with the wicked so that we may learn a lesson (see *Metzudos, Tehillim* 10:15). Hashem's response was that His Glory is magnified even more, however, when people see His unlimited beneficence and how He is good to both the righteous and the wicked.

Here, too, when the people fought with Moshe, the Holy One, Blessed is He, told Moshe to speak to the rock. Despite the people not being worthy, they would see His quality of beneficence, in that He is kind to the wicked as well as to the righteous. Our teacher Moshe, however, scolded them and said, "Listen now, rebels." As a result, thoughts of repentance filled them, and it was then that he gave them water. Because of their repentance, they saw only that Hashem is righteous. Thus, the sanctification of His Name was diminished. Accordingly, Hashem said to Moshe and Aharon (20:12): "Because you did not believe in Me to sanctify Me."

(The Midrash and the Rambam, *Shemoneh Perakim,* end of 4, cited in Ramban 20:8, explain that Hashem's complaint was that he said, "Listen now, *rebels.*")

וַיִּבְכּוּ אֶת־אַהֲרֹן שְׁלֹשִׁים יוֹם כֹּל בֵּית יִשְׂרָאֵל — *And they wept for Aharon thirty days, the entire House of Israel (20:29).*

Rashi explains that "the entire House of Israel" refers to men as well as women. For Aharon would pursue peace and bring love between disputants and between husband and wife.

Rav Shach's door was always open to any man or woman, boy or girl, any bitter soul who needed someone with whom to talk about his troubles, or any person who needed advice.

R' Shmuel Deutsch recalls that, in 1972, after Rav Shach underwent a difficult operation to remove a growth, he was extremely weak. Undergoing an operation is not easy at any age; certainly not in one's 70's Several days after the operation, he heard that a young man who had been his student was having marital problems, and he decided to speak with the student's wife. The couple lived in Yerushalayim, and Rav Shach got up and made the trip from Bnei Brak to Yerushalayim. The doctor told him that he must stop three times on the way, leave the car, and take in some fresh air. He brought along a portable easy chair and paused several times for a rest. He would rest a bit and, refreshed, he would continue his trip. And all for the sake of marital harmony!

עַל־כֵּן יֹאמְרוּ הַמֹּשְׁלִים בֹּאוּ חֶשְׁבּוֹן — *About this the poets [moshlim] would say: Come to Cheshbon (21:27).*

The Gemara (*Bava Basra* 78b) explains homiletically that "moshlim" (lit. those who rule) refers to those who rule over their inclination; "Come to Cheshbon" refers to making the Divine account (*cheshbon*) of the loss of a mitzvah versus its reward. *Mesillas Yesharim* (Chapter Three) discusses at length the requirement to constantly make a spiritual accounting and analyze one's deeds to make certain that there are no foreign motivations mixed in.

Rav Shach was among those who "ruled over his inclinations." He would constantly think about his actions, and all the more so when something would occur that he considered a Divine sign to make a spiritual accounting.

R' Chaim Bergman, Rav Shach's grandson, recalls the Purim morning several decades ago when there was a light and happy atmosphere surrounding everything. Several students of the yeshivah made their way to Rav Shach's apartment to share in the festivities with him. Much to their consternation, there was an uncharacteristically sad expression on his face. It was clear that something was bothering him. All he would do was sit quietly facing his students, as if he were hiding some terrible secret.

One of those present, a student who, in the spirit of the day, had a bit too much to drink, asked Rav Shach why he was so quiet. Rav Shach explained that it was because his wife, the Rebbetzin, had bought a chicken the day before which she intended to cook for the Purim meal. The butcher had told her that there was a minor question concerning the *kashrus* of the chicken, yet since it was the last chicken left in the store, he advised her to take the chicken home. The butcher promised that he would go to the rabbi, ask the question, and notify her as to the status of the chicken. The Rebbetzin took his advice and took the chicken home. At home, she cooked the chicken and prepared it for the festive meal. Meanwhile, the butcher came back with the rabbi's answer: The chicken was kosher, but not ideal and, if possible, it should not be used.

When Rav Shach finished the story, he added: "I was greatly disturbed about this. True, the soup and chicken were already cooked for the festive meal and we have eaten nothing (thereby permitting its use *post facto*), but nevertheless, all night long I sat and thought about why this happened to me. What did I do to deserve this? Suddenly I remembered an improper statement of mine. I remembered that last week I asked a question on the view of one of the more recent authorities, and I spoke about him in an improper manner.

"Perhaps," concluded Rav Shach, "that is the reason this happened to me."

"Does the *Rosh Yeshivah* take back the approach he used in the lecture?" asked the tipsy student.

"Heaven forbid," he replied. "I don't take back the content of what I said. I just think that I could have said it in a more respectful way."

עַל־כֵּן יֹאמְרוּ הַמֹּשְׁלִים בֹּאוּ חֶשְׁבּוֹן — *About this the poets [moshlim] would say: Come to Cheshbon* (21:27).

R av Shach always demanded of his disciples that they not be pulled along by whatever the herd does. Instead, they should always consider what the true Torah view is for each action. This especially applied to imagined "license" to waste Torah-study time "for the sake of" a mitzvah.

Once, Rav Shach was supposed to be the *sandak* at a circumcision for the son of one of his students. It was 9:30 a.m. (half an hour after the official beginning of the first study session for *kollel* young men) and, as he was about to enter, he saw a large group of young *kollel* men who were present to partake in the circumcision. Rav Shach was very bothered that these students were now wasting time from their official Torah study sessions. He turned to the father of the baby and decisively said: "I am not going inside until all the *kollel* men leave and go to *kollel*!"

בלק — Balak

אִם־יִתֶּן־לִי בָלָק מְלֹא בֵיתוֹ כֶּסֶף וְזָהָב לֹא אוּכַל לַעֲבֹר אֶת־פִּי
יְהוָה אֱלֹהָי — *If Balak were to give me his houseful of
silver and gold, I am unable to transgress the word
of Hashem, my God* (22:18).

Rav Shach related the following story: A group of rabbis once
met with the *maskilim* (proponents of "the enlightenment") who
wanted to introduce improper "innovations" into Jewish life.
Among the *maskilim* were those who clearly showed their
animosity to the Jewish religion, revealing their evil intentions. Others
presented themselves as moderates, who merely wanted some minor
concessions to the spirit of the times. One of the latter said apologeti-
cally, "Look, I have quite a bit of influence and if I really wanted to, I
could have all the yeshivahs closed down. Nevertheless, I respect the
Torah, and my only interest is the benefit of Judaism."

The Beis HaLevi (Rav Joseph Dov Soloveitchik) stood up and said,
"Wicked one! You are following the path of Bilam."

He proceeded to explain: "The wicked Bilam said, 'If Balak were to
give me his houseful of silver and gold, I am unable to transgress the
word of Hashem, my God'. Why, he seems so righteous and God-
fearing! Why, then, does the Gemara (*Sanhedrin* 90a) list him among
the most wicked of the gentiles? The answer is that when a person
says, 'If they would give me a 1,000 rubles I would not leave my
hometown,' it makes sense; he has the ability to move, but he chooses
to remain. When a person says, however, 'Even if they give me 1,000
rubles I will not stop the earth from rotating around the sun,' he is
considered a fool. For with or without receiving 1,000 rubles, the
rotation of the earth is beyond his control.

"That," continued the Beis HaLevi, "is why Bilam is considered so
wicked. When he said that even a lot of money could not convince him
to violate Hashem's will, he implied that he had the ability to violate

His will, but would not do so out of the goodness of his heart. That is pure wickedness. The same applies to you. You imply that in your opinion Torah can be extirpated from the Jewish people, and that it is possible to close down yeshivahs, but that out of the goodness of your heart you will allow them to stay open. You are just like Bilam!

"You should know," he concluded, "that just as Bilam erred, you too are mistaken. He did not have the ability to violate Hashem's will, and when he attempted to do so, the Midrash says that Hashem sent an angel to restrain him. Similarly, you do not have the power to close down yeshivahs, because Hashem is their protector!"

אִם־לִקְרֹא לְךָ בָּאוּ הָאֲנָשִׁים קוּם לֵךְ אִתָּם — *If the men came to summon you, arise and go with them* (22:20).

First Bilam was told (22:12), "You shall not go with them," yet now he is told, "Arise and go with them!" The Gemara (*Makkos* 10b) derives from this that a person is guided along the path that he chooses for himself.

There was an influential activist in community affairs who, for many years, was in and out of the *Rosh Yeshivah's* house. He would proudly tell people that everything he did was under the guidance of the *Rosh Yeshivah*. Actually, however, he would generally do the opposite. How so? He would ask for guidance in some matter, and the *Rosh Yeshivah* would give his opinion. The activist would then say, "But maybe we can do it differently?" The *Rosh Yeshivah* would shrug his shoulders and say, *"Nu nu."*

The activist would follow this *"Nu nu"* advice.

This would happen year after year, decade after decade. Although Rav Shach was fully aware of how he was being used, he never protested.

What great forbearance it must have taken to keep silent! (see *Gittin* 56b).

הֶן־עָם כְּלָבִיא יָקוּם וְכַאֲרִי יִתְנַשָּׂא — *Behold! The people will arise like a lion cub and raise itself like a lion* (23:24).

Rashi (ad loc.) interprets this as referring to the Jewish people who, "When they get up from their sleep in the morning, they exert themselves like a lion to seize commandments: to wear a *tallis* and to put on *tefillin*."

In his later years, Rav Shach would "seize" the commandments of the day as soon as their time would come. "I do not know where I will be in a few hours," he would tell his confidants. They, in turn, would tangibly sense the directive of the Sages (*Avos d'Rav Nassan* 15), "Repent one day before you die." For this reason, he would seize the earliest opportunity to *daven* Minchah (in the early afternoon), out of fear that an hour or two later he would be unable to *daven* or, Heaven forbid, he would be free from all the commandments.

Indeed, he once told R' Chaim Mordechai Ausband, "As soon as the time to recite *Shema* begins, I recite *Shema*. Who knows what might happen at the very next moment?"

מַה־טֹּבוּ אֹהָלֶיךָ יַעֲקֹב מִשְׁכְּנֹתֶיךָ יִשְׂרָאֵל — *How goodly are your tents, O Yaakov, your dwelling places, O Yisrael* (24:5).

The Gemara (*Sanhedrin* 105b) interprets this verse as referring to synagogues and study halls. Rav Shach commented that the study hall (*beis midrash*) was not limited to Torah scholars and those destined for greatness. Rather, every member of the Jewish people — the simple people, represented by "Yaakov" (see *Ohr HaChaim*, cited in the next story), as well as the leaders, represented by "Yisrael" — were frequent visitors, and the sounds of Torah loudly burst forth from the study halls.

The *Rosh Yeshivah* recounted that he heard from an old man that in the city of Minsk there was a study hall called, "R' Isserke's *cheder*" in which four hundred people would study Mishnah each Shabbos. The teacher would read each Mishnah and explain it, and then everybody would review it out loud three times. The group included youth, adults, and the elderly, yet none were ashamed to study Mishnah in the manner of children in *cheder*!

In the same city there was a study hall for water carriers. These people would walk around all day carrying heavy pails of water on their shoulders. In exchange for meager pennies, they would fill the water barrels in the homes. During the winter, they had to walk on paths that were slippery from the snow and ice, and in the summertime, their work was extremely difficult because of the oppressive heat. Nevertheless, they would gather in the study hall at the end of a day of backbreaking work, to hear a lecture from their teacher, R' Yehoshua Horodner Zymbalist.

The *Rosh Yeshivah* also recalled that the large study hall in Kletzk had eleven tables, each of which had a separate study group. These study groups ranged from those who studied *siddur* to those who studied complex sections of the Jerusalem Talmud in depth. The same could be said about Vilna, Kovna, Warsaw, Lublin, Cracow and many other places. There were study halls for tailors and shoemakers, for bakers and builders, and the sounds of Torah would loudly burst forth from them.

The Sages (*Sifri, Haazinu*) comment on the verse (*Zecharyah* 10:4), "From it the corner[stone], from it the foundation," that "from it" shall come the wise men, "from it" shall come the scribes. It was from all these study halls that the scholars and teachers would grow. When a person acquired a portion of the Torah, he would influence his friends and teach them.

מַה־טֹּבוּ אֹהָלֶיךָ יַעֲקֹב מִשְׁכְּנֹתֶיךָ יִשְׂרָאֵל — *How goodly are your tents, O Yaakov, your dwelling places, O Yisrael* (24:5).

*T*he Gemara (*Sanhedrin* 105b) interprets this verse as referring to synagogues and study halls. *Ohr HaChaim* explains the use of "Yaakov" in conjunction with "tents," because "Yaakov" refers to those who did not dedicate their entire lives to Torah study, and "tents" refers to something temporary. Accordingly, it refers to those who do not study Torah full time, but rather set specific times to study Torah in the synagogues and the study halls.

An American Jew once presented the following problem to the *Rosh Yeshivah*: Since he works all day long, returns home for a short while, and then goes to the study hall to study Torah, his wife hardly sees him. She therefore asked him to study at home. Should he agree to her request?

Rav Shach answered that it was clear to him that one has to study Torah in a study hall or a synagogue. True, this is difficult for his wife, but she should know that "According to the suffering is the reward" (*Avos* 5:22). Furthermore, the Gemara (*Berachos* 17a) asserts that women merit the World to Come for sending their husbands to study and waiting for them to return from their studies!

מַה־טֹּבוּ אֹהָלֶיךָ יַעֲקֹב מִשְׁכְּנֹתֶיךָ יִשְׂרָאֵל — *How goodly are your tents, O Yaakov, your dwelling places, O Yisrael* (24:5).

*T*he Gemara (*Sanhedrin* 105b) interprets this verse as referring to synagogues and study halls, for they are the tents and the dwelling places of a Jew; his house is merely a temporary abode.

In 1972, when Rav Shach was recovering from an operation to remove a growth, a private male nurse was hired to see to his comfort. The nurse tried to make him as comfortable as possible in his bed, and then asked him, "Is the Rav comfortable?"

Rav Shach responded, "I find it more comfortable on the hard wooden bench of the study hall!"

לְכָה אִיעָצְךָ אֲשֶׁר יַעֲשֶׂה הָעָם הַזֶּה לְעַמְּךָ — *Come, I will advise you what this people will do to your people* (24:14).

Rashi (ad loc.) explains that the advice was: "The God of these hates promiscuity — bring about their downfall through promiscuity."

Rav Shach insisted that the strongest standards of modesty be upheld in seminars aimed at *baalei teshuvah*. He ruled that single girls should not be allowed to attend seminars for families, and that they should have a seminar of their own. The organizers argued that single girls from such permissive and promiscuous backgrounds would never agree to spend an entire week at a seminar with only other girls for company. Rav Shach responded that we are not meant to be Hashem's negotiators, and that the ends do not justify the means. It is incumbent on us to do our part, and then Hashem does His part.

And so, registration opened for a week-long seminar for girls, with everybody involved certain that there would be minimal interest. To the surprise of all — other than Rav Shach — registration had to be closed early for lack of additional space. Since then, there were dozens of highly successful seminars for girls, and over 1,500 young women returned to Orthodox Judaism.

פנחס — Pinchas

וַתִּקְרַבְנָה בְּנוֹת צְלָפְחָד --*The daughters of Tzelofechad drew near* (27:1).

$\mathcal{T}$he Midrash (*Midrash Rabbah* 21:10) comments that in that generation, women would fix the breaches in observance that had been broken open by the men. This can be seen in the story of the Golden Calf, where Aharon told the people (*Shemos* 32:2), "Remove the golden rings that are in the ears of your wives," and the women refused, as indicated by the very next verse, "And the entire people had the golden rings that were in their ears removed." The women refused to have anything to do with the Golden Calf.

The daughters of Tzelofechad were another example of this principle. The men did not want to enter the land of Israel, as was seen in the story of the spies, whereas the women "drew near" to request a piece of land of their own. For this reason, this story follows the verse concerning the death of the generation of the Wilderness (*Bamidbar* 26:65), "And not a man was left of them, except for Calev son of Yefuneh, and Yehoshua son of Nun."

Rav Shach related that when the malady of the "enlightenment" swept through the town of Brisk, the leaders of the community decided to set up a choir to accompany the cantor during the High Holy Day prayers. When the choir rose to sing, the Brisker Rav, R' Yitzchak Zev Soloveitchik, saw it as a breach in the walls of religion, and he told the choir members to sit down. They followed his orders. Then the community leaders ordered them to get back up, and they fulfilled those orders. This continued until the Rav turned to the ladies' section and cried out, "*Yiddisher Frauen* [Jewish women]! They are trying to destroy the Torah, and you are keeping silent?" Immediately, the women bent over and reprimanded their husbands. As a result, the town leaders gave up, and the breach was closed.

וּבָנִים לֹא־הָיוּ לוֹ — *And he had no sons* (27:3).

Ohr HaChaim explains that the past tense (*had no sons*), rather than the present tense (*has no sons*), alludes to the Talmudic dictum (*Yevamos* 62b), "The sons of sons are like children." The Gemara (ibid.) applies this to the sons of daughters as well as the sons of sons. The daughters of Tzelofechad were thus, in effect, saying, "As of yet, he *had* no 'sons,' but we still hope that he will have 'sons' through his daughters" (see also Rabbeinu Chananel, cited in Rabbeinu Bachya, *Bereishis* 31:43).

People used to entrust Rav Shach with money to dispense to charity. His grandchildren relate that when they were at their neediest — studying Torah full time while having families to feed — he would never give them any of this money, although it was explicitly given to him to dispense as he saw fit. He would explain, "Giving my grandchildren is like taking for myself, and how could I possibly take any of this money for myself?" Instead, he would give them money from his salary, which was certainly his to do with as he saw fit!

One time, a married grandson, who was in a very difficult financial situation, bitterly complained to him, "Grandfather helps everyone else; how am I worse than a stranger?!"

Rav Shach went to his refrigerator and wrapped up all the food inside to give to his grandson, saying, "Don't you understand that my not giving is out of my love for you, for I consider you like my own son?!"

עֲצֶרֶת תִּהְיֶה לָכֶם — *It shall be a restraining for you* (29:35).

Rav Shach related that when he stayed in Vilna at the home of his teacher, R' Chaim Ozer Grodzinsky, he met a man by the name of Rabbi Wed. Rabbi Wed, a notable chassid of Gur, was in charge of publishing chassidic texts in the Vilna printing press. He was well-liked, as well as very learned — truly "good to Heaven and good to people" (*Kiddushin* 40a).

Before a certain holiday he told Rav Shach that his Rebbe, the saintly Imrei Emes of Gur, taught that on a holiday one can achieve the level of an angel.

When Rav Shach expressed his astonishment, the chassid explained: "The Gemara (*Pesachim* 68b) discusses the apparent contradiction between two verses in the Torah. One verse says, 'It shall be a restraining for you', and the other verse (*Devarim* 16:8) says, 'It shall be a restraining unto Hashem, your God.' The Gemara explains that the two verses together teach that the day should be divided: half for eating and drinking (*for you*) and half for the study hall (*unto Hashem, your God*).

"Now we find elsewhere a verse (*Shemos* 24:6) which says, 'Moshe took half the blood and placed it in basins and half the blood he sprinkled upon the altar.' Rashi cites the explanation of the Sages (*Vayikra Rabbah* 6:5) which asks, 'Who divided it [in half]? An angel came and divided it.' The reason for this explanation is that only an angel is capable of dividing precisely in half, with no excess whatsoever in either part. Accordingly, when we were commanded to divide the day half *unto Hashem, your G-d*, and half *for you*, precise division is beyond the capabilities of anyone other than an angel.

"We must therefore say," concluded the chassid, "that on the holidays a Jew ascends to the level of an angel."

וָאִוָּתֵר אֲנִי לְבַדִּי — *So that I alone have remained* (*Haftarah* of *Pinchas* [*I Melachim* 19:10]).

Once, in the midst of a complex communal battle, Rav Shach found himself taking a position against everybody else. He told his confidants the following story:

When he taught in the yeshivah of Kletzk, the *rosh yeshivah,* R' Aharon Kotler, was sent to Volozhin. His mission was to determine whether the Yeshivah of Kletzk could be moved into the quarters of the Volozhin Yeshivah which had been closed by the authorities. On his way, he decided to stop in Stutchin to seek advice from R' Yehudah Leib Chasman concerning how to deal with the issue.

When he arrived in Stutchin, he learned that R' Leib had traveled to Vilna for the funeral of his sister, and that he would be sitting *shivah* there. R' Aharon went to Vilna to pay a *shivah* call. When he came to the house, he was told that R' Leib was called out in the middle of his *shivah* to attend a meeting which had been convened in order to approve building a cultural center. R' Aharon went to the meeting and heard R' Leib's fiery protest in defense of R' Chaim Ozer Grodzinsky's honor, for R' Chaim Ozer was known to oppose the cultural center. As a result, the meeting adjourned without reaching a decision.

On the way home, R' Aharon told R' Leib the reason for his visit. R' Leib advised him not to go to Volozhin at all, and he invited him to remain for Shabbos.

After the Shabbos meal, R' Leib went out onto his porch and determinedly paced back and forth, all the while reciting *Tehillim* with pent-up feeling. When he reached the verse (*Tehillim* 14:3), "They have all gone aside, they have all together become filthy, there is none that does good, no, not one," he paused and enthusiastically told R' Aharon, "David HaMelech is complaining to Hashem that not a single one of his many friends remained with him to help him in time of need."

Rav Shach concluded, "That's the way I feel now. I remain alone, and no one comes to my aid."

מטות — Mattos

עֲבָדֶיךָ יַעֲשׂוּ כַּאֲשֶׁר אֲדֹנִי מְצַוֶּה —*Your servants shall do as my lord commands* (32:25)

*T*he Sforno (R' Ovadyah Sforno) reveals an argument implicit in these verses. The children of Gad and Reuven declared, "Your servants shall do as my lord commands," "And your servants shall cross... as my lord speaks" (32:27), "As Hashem has spoken to your servants, so shall we do" (ibid. v. 31), apparently fully accepting thereby the authority of Hashem and Moshe. Yet, whereas Moshe emphasized that only *after* fulfilling the condition will the land belong to them, they stressed, "We shall cross over... with the heritage of our inheritance" (ibid. v. 32), i.e., it shall be ours even as we cross over. Moshe, wanting to avoid dispute, acquiesces: "So Moshe gave to them... the land..." (ibid. v. 33).

Through the dialogue concealed in the subtext of these verses, we learn not to be misled by carefully worded declarations which imply the acceptance of authority, but to carefully "read between the lines" in every situation.

A person once wanted to take control of a certain institution. Rav Shach was displeased with that person, and through his counsel the take-over attempt was foiled. One day, that person came to Rav Shach and declared his intention to fully accept Rav Shach's authority as *daas Torah* (the opinion of the Torah), and to listen to his counsel in all matters.

Several days later, this person proposed a so-called compromise, whereby he would indirectly control the institution. The board of directors brought the proposal to Rav Shach. He smiled and said, "If this is the animal with which we are dealing — *trieb ihr ahrois mit shtekens* (force it out with sticks)."

Seeing their astonishment at this statement, he explained:

"When I studied in Slutzk, there was an old *shammos* who inherited his position from his father, who had had the merit of serving the Beis HaLevi (R' Yosef Dov Soloveitchik) during the short period of time during which he was Rabbi of that city. The *shammos* told me that they used to slaughter their animals in a neighboring town, and not in Slutzk itself, for a variety of *kashrus* reasons.

"When R' Soloveitchik became the Rabbi, each of the residents sent him *mishlo'ach manos* (the requisite gifts of food sent on Purim). One of the butchers sent him an exceptional gift — a milk cow.

"A few months later, that butcher went to the Rabbi and asked him sanctimoniously, 'How is it that we in Slutzk, a city of such importance and piety, rely on the slaughtering of others? Would it not be better to slaughter here, in our own city, under the watchful eye of our rabbi?'

" 'Aha!' exclaimed the Beis HaLevi, 'Now I understand the animal! Quickly! Drive it out of the barn with sticks!' Then he cleverly told the butcher: 'The situation is perfectly understandable. If over there — where we do not even know who does the slaughtering — you raise doubts about the acceptability of the slaughter, how much more concerned would we have to be here — where we do know the identity of the slaughterers, who will certainly be afraid of you and your cohorts!'"

"Here too," concluded Rav Shach, "at first I wondered why he came to express his subservience to me. Now I know; drive him out with sticks!"

מסעי — Masei

וְהִקְרִיתֶם לָכֶם עָרִים עָרֵי מִקְלָט תִּהְיֶינָה לָכֶם —*You shall arrange cities for yourselves, cities of refuge shall they be for you* (35:11).

*K*li Yakar, in his commentary to *Devarim* (4:41), compares the study hall to the cities of refuge. He cites the dictum of our Sages (*Avos* 4:8), "Exile yourself to a place of Torah," noting that one exiles oneself to a city of refuge as well. Just as the cities of refuge offer the ability to live, "He shall flee to one of these cities and live" (*Devarim* ibid.), so too the Torah and mitzvos give life, "And he shall live by them" (*Vayikra* 18:5). Similarly, just as one may not leave a city of refuge, so too, he may not leave the study hall, the house of Torah!

Rav Shach's sister, Mrs. Esther Singer, related that, in her youth, she did not know her brother. He was in a yeshivah in a different city, and when the First World War broke out, they were separated by a border between the two of them.

Their mother arranged with a neighbor whose son studied in the same yeshivah that they would write to their sons and arrange a meeting at the border fence. At this meeting, they would be able to speak to their sons as well as give them care packages, so desperately needed in those days of lack and famine. Rav Shach's sister accompanied them and anxiously awaited her first meeting with her brother who was so diligently studying Torah.

The three women — the mother, the daughter, and the neighbor — arrived at the prearranged meeting place near the fence, and saw that on the other side, only the neighbor's son was coming. He brought with him a letter from the young Rav Shach in which he apologized to his mother. He added that he was certain that his mother would understand, since she so wanted him to grow in Torah greatness, as indicated by her telling him when the war broke out that the safest place to be was within the walls of the study hall. He feared, however, that if he were to come to the meeting and see his recently-widowed mother, his emotions would get the better of him and interfere with his devotion to Torah study. Thus, he decided not to come and was sure that his mother would agree with his decision.

ספר דברים &

Devarim

דברים — **Devarim**

אֵיכָה אֶשָּׂא לְבַדִּי טָרְחֲכֶם וּמַשַּׂאֲכֶם וְרִיבְכֶם — *How can I alone carry your trouble and your burden and your quarrels* (1:12).

Rav Shach once introduced a couple who subsequently married. Years later, there were some marital problems and the couple was on the verge of divorce. For a two-year period, Rav Shach traveled fairly often from Bnei Brak to Jerusalem, and remained there for hours at a time, trying to make peace between the couple.

Anyone who knows how long and hard Rav Shach prepared his lessons, how much he devoted himself to working with his students, and how many important matters rested on his shoulders — to say nothing of being well into his 80's — can begin to understand the superhuman effort needed to travel regularly over a two-year period for this matter!

הָבוּ לָכֶם אֲנָשִׁים חֲכָמִים וּנְבֹנִים וִידֻעִים לְשִׁבְטֵיכֶם וַאֲשִׂימֵם בְּרָאשֵׁיכֶם — *Provide yourselves men who are wise and understanding and well known to your tribes, and I shall appoint them as your heads* (1:13).

Both *Ohr HaChaim* and *Kli Yakar* question the apparently superfluous *"yourselves."* Perhaps this alludes to a principle stated by R' Yisrael Salanter: Each person is in charge of himself, and he must judge everything he does according to the laws of the Torah.

Rav Shach used to recount the story of the young Torah scholar whose economic situation was so shaky that he felt compelled to leave the yeshivah and go to work. He went to R' Eliyahu Ragular of

Kalish (author of *Yad Eliyahu*) and told him that he had received a sum of money from his father-in-law as a dowry. This sum of money had been invested and it had provided a modest income. Now, however, he found the income insufficient for his needs, and he had decided to use that money to buy a store, so that he could earn a proper living.

"Very nice," replied R' Eliyahu. "But tell me, do you know how to run a store?"

"Is training required to run a store?" the young man wondered out loud.

R' Eliyahu explained his question: "Have you mastered the four books of the *Shulchan Aruch*? Don't you know that, to open a business, one must be well versed in all the books of the *Shulchan Aruch* as well as its commentaries?!"

After recounting the story, Rav Shach would note, "That is how R' Eliyahu followed the path blazed by his master, Rav Yisrael Salanter. R' Yisrael always insisted that knowledge of the laws of the *Shulchan Aruch* was not meant only for judges on the religious court. Each person must be his own judge in all his affairs, and he must know all the regulations concerning the most difficult matters of the home, as well as matters of business."

וָאֶקַּח אֶת־רָאשֵׁי שִׁבְטֵיכֶם אֲנָשִׁים חֲכָמִים וִידֻעִים... — *So I took the heads of your tribes, men who were wise and well known . . .* (1:15).

Rashi explains that Moshe said: "[I took] men who were wise and well known, but men who were "understanding" (see verse 13), I did not find." Rashi, in his commentary on that previous verse, cites the dialogue between Arios and R' Yose: "What is the difference between 'those who are wise' and 'those who are understanding'?" asked Arios. R' Yose answered, " 'One who is wise' is like a rich moneychanger. When they bring him *dinars* to examine, he examines. And when they do not bring him money to examine, he sits idly. 'One who is understanding' is like an enterprising moneychanger. When they bring him money to examine, he examines. And when they do not bring him money to examine, he goes about and brings in business of his own."

At first glance, it would appear that the only difference between the two moneychangers is in their degree of initiative and enterprise: Does he sit at home or does he go about seeking business? The Gra, however, explains in his commentary to the verse in *Mishlei* (1:5),

"One of understanding acquires strategies," that it is indeed a higher level of wisdom. According to him, one of understanding devises strategies to further his understanding.

R' Chaim Pfeffer recounts the following story from his days of study at the yeshivah: "Four of us decided that we were not making the most of our relationship with Rav Shach. True, we attended his lectures and enjoyed them immensely, but the lecture is the product of careful analysis and study. It was this process of analysis and study that we felt we were lacking — the method of approaching a new topic, the critical analysis of a hypothesis.

"We went up to the *Rosh Yeshivah's* apartment and expressed our desire to study together with him.

"Rav Shach considered our request and said, 'Each morning and each afternoon I study in the yeshivah and answer the questions of the students. Since I am obligated to be available to all the students at that time, I cannot study with you then. In the evening I work on my commentary, *Avi Ezri*. I am now working on *Pe'ah* [one of the agricultural "gifts" designated for the poor]. If you want, we can study that material together.'

"We happily agreed, and it was indeed marvelous. Nevertheless, it quickly became apparent that he had already thought through the material with all its ins and outs, and once again we found ourselves listening to completed lectures!

"We told him, 'We would like to learn how the *Rosh Yeshivah* approaches a new subject and *begins* its analysis.'

"So he set aside his work on *Avi Ezri*, stopped studying *Pe'ah*, and began studying with us *Maseches Sotah* from scratch!"

לֹא־תַכִּירוּ פָנִים בַּמִּשְׁפָּט — *You shall not show favoritism in judgment* (1:17).

R' Yechiel Michel Epstein, the author of the noted halachic work *Aruch HaShulchan*, told the following story to Rav Shach. The Rav of Bialystok, R' Moshe Zev Yaavetz, a noted Torah scholar who lived at the time of R' Chaim of Volozhin, was once called upon to adjudicate a monetary dispute between two well-known wealthy men. The two, R' Zimel Epstein and R' Kopel Heilprin, were the contractors hired by the Czar to build the highway between Moscow and Warsaw. In addition, they had many other businesses through which they had amassed great wealth and became so influential that government ministers would be frequent guests at their home. When their chariots arrived at the home of the rabbi, they sent a messenger to notify him that they had come for their hearing. He responded that they should come inside.

Much to their dismay, when they entered they saw the rabbi sitting in his seat, wearing a prayer shawl covering his whole face down to his shoulders. Without any words of greeting he asked, "Are the litigants here?" When they replied in the affirmative, he asked, "Who is the claimant?" R' Zimel replied, "Me." "Who is 'Me'?" asked the rabbi. "Me, Zimel Epstein," he replied. Said the rabbi, "Speak, Zimel." R' Zimel presented his claim. "And who is the defendant?" asked the Rabbi. "I, Kopel Heilprin," replied the other one. The rabbi all but spat out, "What have you got to answer, Kopel?" The two were astounded. Not only did he not accord them the honor to which they were accustomed, but he did not even address them by the polite common title of "Reb"! When they finished their claims and counter-claims, he stated his decision and asked, "Do you accept my adjudication?" "Yes," they replied. He then removed his prayer shawl and greeted them effusively. Furthermore, when they attempted to pay him for his time, he refused, saying that he never accepted payment for adjudication, not even when he was in great need of money.

When they requested that he explain his odd behavior, he replied, "Through not calling you by any honorific titles I fulfilled the dictum of our Sages (*Avos* 1:8), 'When litigants stand before you, they should be in your eyes like wicked people.' As to covering my face and not looking at you, I learned that from the verse (*Mishlei* 24:23), 'These words also belong to the wise: It is not good to show favoritism in judgment.' Gra explains that this cannot possibly refer to showing favoritism, since that is explicitly prohibited by the Torah (*Devarim* 1:17). Rather, the Hebrew phrase for showing favoritism, *haker panim*, literally means 'recognize the face.' Thus, the verse in *Mishlei* adds to the prohibition of showing favoritism that one should not even look at the face of the litigants!"

וְהַדָּבָר אֲשֶׁר יִקְשֶׁה מִכֶּם תַּקְרִבוּן אֵלַי וּשְׁמַעְתִּיו — *And the matter that is too difficult for you, you shall bring to me and I shall hear it* (1:17).

Rav Shach often said that a teacher of Torah must know how to say, "I don't know." He related the following story to prove his point: When Rav Shmuel Salant, the Rav of Jerusalem, passed away, the Elders of Jerusalem sought a suitable replacement. They asked Rav Chaim Soloveitchik of Brisk for his opinion about one of the candidates. He told them, "This candidate is indeed a Torah scholar. I am certain that he will prepare a masterful discourse to present in his first lecture. If, however, someone were to point out a flaw in his logic, I fear that he would not have the strength to admit to having erred. Accordingly, I cannot recommend him for this position."

Once, Rav Shach was discussing the good points of a Torah scholar who was appointed Rav of a community in Bnei Brak. "His best point," said Rav Shach, "is that when there is something he does not know, he says, 'I don't know!' "

וּבַמִּדְבָּר אֲשֶׁר רָאִיתָ אֲשֶׁר נְשָׂאֲךָ יְהוָה אֱלֹהֶיךָ כַּאֲשֶׁר יִשָּׂא־אִישׁ אֶת־בְּנוֹ — *And in the wilderness, as you have seen, that Hashem, your God, carried you as a man carries his son* (1:31).

When Rav Shach told R' Chaim Ozer Grodzinsky that he planned to settle in Israel, he told him, "What for? It is a barren wilderness!" As a leader of his generation, R' Chaim Ozer felt that it was imperative for teachers of Torah to stay with their flocks even — or perhaps especially — during the difficult period of the rise of Communism. Nevertheless, Rav Shach had already made up his mind, and he notified R' Chaim Ozer that he was indeed leaving.

When Rav Shach arrived in Israel, he had no way of earning a living. He was offered a job teaching in a Tel Aviv yeshivah, and his uncle, R' Isser Zalman Meltzer, advised him to accept the position. He began teaching there and the administration was pleased with his work. At that time, this yeshivah studied Torah only, with no secular subjects, and the students were serious about learning Torah. Nevertheless, it came to Rav Shach's attention that people were saying that it was not appropriate for him to teach in that institution. One day he went into the ladies' gallery of the Great Synagogue of Tel Aviv to study without disturbance. While there, he debated with himself whether he should continue teaching at that yeshivah. He told himself that the small Torah community of Jerusalem could not possibly provide decent jobs for all the Torah scholars coming to Israel. He even began to sadly think that R' Chaim Ozer was right in calling Israel a barren wilderness, and that a person could not be choosy in earning a living in the wilderness.

Suddenly, almost as a sign from Heaven, R' Avraham Farbstein came into the ladies' gallery so that he, too, could study without interruption. When he saw Rav Shach's distress, he asked him what was bothering him. When Rav Shach told him his dilemma, R' Farbstein exclaimed, "Why, the Chazon Ish lives in Bnei Brak!"

Rav Shach went directly to the Chazon Ish who told him, "We heard about you when you were still back in Europe, and we truly wondered what you were doing in that institution!" When Rav Shach asked him about earning a living, he replied, "If the Heavenly Court calls you to order for giving up a place in which you could earn a living, tell them that you have no interest in earning a living from such a place!"

"In the end," Rav Shach concludes the story, "you can see that I managed even in the 'wilderness'!"

רַב־לָכֶם סֹב אֶת־הָהָר הַזֶּה פְּנוּ לָכֶם צָפֹנָה — *Enough of your going around this mountain, turn yourselves northward* (2:3).

Rav Shach was generally against religious demonstrations, saying that while the harm they caused was certain, beneficial results were doubtful. There was spiritual harm to the demonstrators when arguing their position, and physical danger in fighting the police, as well as opponents. Furthermore, such demonstrations often caused a desecration of Hashem's Name and increased hatred, while only reinforcing the opponents' opposition.

He would base his position on the Midrash (*Devarim Rabbah* 1:19) on the verse, "Turn yourselves northward (*tzafonah*)." The Midrash states, "[It is as if Hashem says:] 'If you see Esav trying to pick a fight with you, hide (*hatzpinu*) yourselves from him until his time passes.' Israel replied, 'And to where shall we flee?' Said He, 'Flee to the Torah,' for we know that *tzafonah* refers to Torah, as it says (*Mishlei* 2:6), 'He lays up (*yitzpon*) sound wisdom to the righteous.' "

Rav Shach would conclude: "We learn two things from this. First, not to pick fights with those who rise up against us, but rather to hide ourselves and not invoke their hatred. Second, that we must flee to the Torah, for that is our answer to them — more Torah study, another yeshivah, another *kollel*. The more we increase the light, the more darkness is pushed away!"

ואתחנן — Va'eschanan

אֶעְבְּרָה־נָּא וְאֶרְאֶה אֶת־הָאָרֶץ הַטּוֹבָה — *Please let me cross and see the good land* (3:25).

The Midrash (*Devarim Rabbah* 11:6) relates Moshe's prayer to God: "Master of the Universe, if You do not bring me into the Land of Israel, allow me to be as the beasts of the field who eat grass, drink spring water, and see the world. Let my soul be like theirs." The Holy One, Blessed is He, replied, "It is too much for you!" (*Devarim* 3:26). Moshe then said, "Master of the Universe, if not, allow me to remain in this world like the birds who fly to all four corners of the earth, gathering their food each day, and returning to their nest in the evening. Let my soul be like theirs."

A certain family once came to Rav Shach for advice. The mother was sick and the doctors recommended a dangerous operation whose chance of success was small. In any case, they said that she would never return to her former self. The family was devastated, and their question was whether they should agree to the operation.

He told them, "The only relevant factor is prolonging life. Even if the quality of life will be reduced and there will be what appears to be unnecessary suffering, life is paramount. We find that our master, Moshe, asked to remain alive even as a bird! What value can life as a bird have — he cannot fulfill the mitzvos as a bird! Yet, one who knows that everything that Hashem created was created for His glory, and that each creature adds to the glory of Heaven in this world, knows the true value of each second of life, in whatever state!"

וְאַתֶּם הַדְּבֵקִים בַּיהוָה אֱלֹהֵיכֶם חַיִּים כֻּלְּכֶם הַיּוֹם — *But you who cling to Hashem, your God — you are all alive today* (4:4).

efesh HaChaim (*Shaar HaTorah*) explains at length that the true "clinging" to Hashem is involvement in His Torah. He states, "And when studying Torah, one should have the intention of clinging to the Holy One, Blessed is He. In other words, he should cling with all his might to the Word of Hashem and it is thus as if he actually clings to the Blessed One, for He and His Will are one."

Serious financial pressures once compelled a young married Torah scholar to consider leaving the yeshivah to go out to work. He approached Rav Shach and explained his problems. Rav Shach agreed that the young man's situation was quite difficult and that under the circumstances, he should go into a business.

The young man turned to leave, feeling relief upon resolving his doubt. On his way out, he heard a heartrending sigh; Rav Shach was murmuring to himself, "He must — but how can he?" How can one leave the *beis midrash*, the source of pure water, the wellsprings of Torah?

The young man went back and said to Rav Shach, "The *Rosh Yeshivah's* sigh tipped the scales. I am staying in the world of Torah!"

— רְאֵה לִמַּדְתִּי אֶתְכֶם חֻקִּים וּמִשְׁפָּטִים כַּאֲשֶׁר צִוַּנִי ה׳ אֱלֹקָי
See, I have taught you statutes and ordinances, as Hashem, my God, has commanded me (4:5).

he Gemara (*Nedarim* 37a) derives from this verse that Moshe told them, "Just as I was [commanded to teach] without payment, so too, you are [commanded to teach] without payment."

R' Simchah Zelig Rieger, the Rabbinical Judge of pre-war Brisk, asked R' Isser Zalman Meltzer, the *Rosh Yeshivah* of the Slutzk Yeshivah, to find a tutor for his 12-year-old son. R' Isser Zalman offered the position to the young Rav Shach, who was the top student of the yeshivah. In addition, he was very much in need of the remuneration that would come from the tutoring, as he received no money from home and he needed new clothes to replace his frayed shirt, worn pants, shoes whose soles had separated, and a hat that had lost its shape.

Rav Shach agreed to tutor the youth, studied with him diligently, and greatly raised the boy's level of learning. When R' Simchah Zelig came to the yeshivah, he approached Rav Shach to pay him for his services. Rav Shach refused to accept any money, saying that the youth really had no need for his services, and the reason he advanced was due to his own diligence and innate capabilities.

The disconcerted R' Simchah Zelig turned to R' Isser Zalman, but he, too, was unable to prevail upon Rav Shach to accept the money. R' Isser Zalman turned to his son-in-law, R' Aharon Kotler, for advice. R' Aharon came up with the following brilliant idea: If the youth indeed has such diligence and capabilities, as Rav Shach claimed, he should be asked to prepare on his own a particularly lengthy and complex *Tosafos,* on which he would then be tested.

Rav Shach told the youth to prepare that *Tosafos,* without telling him why. The boy diligently worked at it and indeed passed the test — and Rav Shach's great joy was quite evident!

כִּי הוּא חָכְמַתְכֶם וּבִינַתְכֶם לְעֵינֵי הָעַמִּים — *For it is your wisdom and understanding in the eyes of the peoples* (4:6).

*I*n his introduction to *Pe'as HaShulchan,* the author quotes his teacher, the Gra, as testifying that he had totally mastered all seven wisdoms of the world and knew that they all served merely to add flavor and spice to the holy Torah. The only wisdom that he had not mastered, he said, was medicine, because his father did not let him study it, saying that Torah study is more important than saving lives (see *Megillah* 16b), and if he knew medicine, he would be forced to stop his Torah study to save lives.

Rav Shach related that the Gra was asked when it was that he studied all the other wisdoms, being that a person is obligated to "think of it [Torah] day and night" (*Yehoshua* 1:8; see *Menachos* 99b). He replied by explaining the verse in *Mishlei* (31:24), "She makes a garment and sells it and gives a belt to the merchant." "Why," he asked, "Does the verse begin with selling and end with giving? The answer," explained the Gra, "emerges from a parable.

"A person once went into a wholesale outlet and saw a merchant buying a large quantity of merchandise, for which he paid. The seller had the merchandise packed well and securely tied. The seller then turned to the person watching and asked him how he could be helped. The person asked, 'Did that person pay for the rope used to tie the merchandise.'

"'No', answered the wholesaler, 'the rope was free.'

"'In that case,' said the observer, 'I'd like that quantity of rope.'

"'That will cost you such and such,' said the wholesaler.

"'But,' exclaimed the observer, 'you yourself just said that the rope was free!'

"'Of course,' said the wholesaler. 'A person who buys a large quantity of expensive merchandise gets the rope for free. However, a person who wants only the rope must pay full price for it!'

"This is what transpires in the verse," the Gra explained. "Once 'she makes a garment and sells it,' she then 'gives a belt to the merchant' for free. Similarly, whoever attempts to master the wisdoms must expend a great amount of time, effort, and study. Yet one who diligently plumbs the depths of the holy Torah and requires those wisdoms to add flavor and spice, Heaven teaches him and opens his eyes to see how all is hinted at and included in the Torah itself!"

Rav Shach would conclude this story by adding, "Now we have a new insight into the statement that the Gra refrained from studying medicine at the behest of his father. Not only did he not devote any time to its study, but the Holy One, Blessed is He, followed the wishes of his servant and did not enlighten the eyes of the Gra to find this wisdom in the Holy Torah!"

— וּשְׁמַרְתֶּם וַעֲשִׂיתֶם כִּי הוּא חָכְמַתְכֶם וּבִינַתְכֶם לְעֵינֵי הָעַמִּים
You shall safeguard and perform [them] for it is your wisdom and understanding in the eyes of the peoples (4:6).

Rav Shach related the following story:

A Jew once sued his friend in a gentile court. The plaintiff told the judge that Jews are bound by Torah law and he is willing to have the case judged before a Rabbinic court, and follow the ruling of the rabbi. The judge told him that although he did not know much about Torah law, he would be willing to have the rabbi appear before him so that he could analyze how the rabbi decides a case.

The plaintiff went to the rabbi, told him what the judge had said and the rabbi came before the judge.

The judge said to him, "This plaintiff insists on being judged by Torah law. If you can prove that Torah law is superior, I will allow you to adjudicate the case."

"Okay, your honor." said the rabbi. "How would your honor decide a case in which two people come before you, each holding onto half of a garment, each claiming that the garment is his?"

"I would rule that they should divide the garment between them," replied the judge.

"How can you believe them?" asked the rabbi. "Maybe one of them is lying?"

"I would make them swear that they were telling the truth," replied the judge.

"About what would they swear?"

"About their claim, of course," replied the judge. "Each would swear that the garment belongs fully to him!"

"But then," challenged the rabbi, "you are causing one of them to swear a false oath! If, in any case, we have no intention of giving either one the whole garment, why should either one swear about a half that he will not receive?"

"Good point," conceded the judge. "Well, then, we'll make each one swear that half the garment is his."

"But he claims that the entire garment is his!" the rabbi reminded him.

The judge had nothing more to say. The ruling of the Mishnah (*Bava Metzia* 2a), that each one swear that he owns no less than half the garment, never entered his mind. When the rabbi cited this ruling, the judge was so impressed that he had the litigants adjudicated by the rabbi, according to Torah Law!

כִּי מִי־גוֹי גָּדוֹל אֲשֶׁר־לוֹ אֱלֹהִים קְרֹבִים אֵלָיו כַּיהֹוָה אֱלֹהֵינוּ בְּכָל־קָרְאֵנוּ אֵלָיו — *For which is a great nation that has a God Who is close to it, as is Hashem, our God, whenever we call to Him* (4:7).

The Midrash (*Devarim Rabbah, Va'eschanan*) states that Scripture refers to prayer in ten ways, one of which is "calling." Based on this idea, the Gemara (*Rosh Hashanah* 18a) explains that "whenever we call to Him" refers to prayer with a congregation, whose sublime power is beyond description.

The following story, which Rav Shach recounted to R' Eliezer Kahaneman, gives us an inkling of what the congregational prayer of ordinary people was like in the preceding generation:

"In my youth, when I studied in the village of Ponevezh under the renowned R' Itzeleh of Ponevezh, we would pray in the local synagogue. R' Naftali Hertz, author of *Noam HaMitzvos,* prayed there, as did many ordinary local residents. One of these congregants was the wealthy owner of the local flour mill. One day, at the beginning of morning services, a local resident came in and excitedly told the mill owner that a fire had broken out in his mill. In those days, of course, there was no official fire department. If a fire broke out, all the residents of the city had to immediately go to the wells, fill up pails of water, and run to put out the fire.

"I looked at the owner," continued Rav Shach, "to see his reaction to this news. To my great surprise he just stood there with equanimity, as if nothing had happened, and he began the *Baruch She'amar* prayer with the same measured slowness of any other day. As he prayed with great devotion, more and more people came to tell him about the fire, but he just continued praying as usual.

"I thought that, as soon as he would finish the *Shemoneh Esrei*, he would take off his *tefillin* and go out to save his property. Yet, much to my surprise, he just stood there, carefully listening to each word of the *chazzan*'s repetition of the *Shemoneh Esrei*. At the end of this repetition, again people came in to get him to come and save his property, and yet, he would not move from his place of prayer. He carefully continued saying *Ashrei, U'va L'Tzion* and, even after saying *Aleinu* he did not rush out of the synagogue, but diligently said the psalm of the day and continued until the end of the service. Only then did he take off his *tefillin* and go to his property.

"I was dumbfounded," Rav Shach concluded. "This person could have lost everything in the fire and, nevertheless, he did not interrupt his prayers! But he understood that he was talking to the Holy One, Blessed is He; how could he interrupt?"

רַק הִשָּׁמֶר לְךָ וּשְׁמֹר נַפְשְׁךָ מְאֹד — *Only beware for yourself and greatly beware for your soul* (4:9).

Rambam (*Hil. Rotze'ach* 11:4) writes that this verse teaches us that we are obligated to get rid of a dangerous obstacle. He then writes, "Our Sages forbade many things because of the danger involved ...," and later (ibid. 11:6), "It is similarly prohibited to walk by a shaky wall ... and to stand near any other danger."

R' Eliezer Schlesinger was a student in Ponevezh Yeshivah in 1952. One day, he boarded a bus to Tel Aviv and saw Rav Shach already sitting there. He sat himself down next to Rav Shach.

When the bus passed what was then the uninhabited area of Wadi Musrarah, (later known as Nachal Ayalon and now the train station at the entrance to Tel Aviv,) R' Schlesinger saw Rav Shach's lips move. When he listened carefully, he heard Rav Shach saying *Tefillas HaDerech*, the wayfarer's prayer which is said when traveling on a dangerous journey.

The *Shulchan Aruch* (*Orach Chaim* 110:7) rules that this prayer is only recited in its entirety on a journey of a *parsah* (approximately

15,000 feet) away from the city; for less than that, one should stop before reaching Hashem's Name at the end of the blessing. *Mishnah Berurah* explains that journeys close to the city are generally not dangerous, and there is therefore no obligation to recite the full blessing. Accordingly, a short journey from Bnei Brak to Tel Aviv should not require saying the full blessing.

When Rav Shach completed the prayer, the student, wishing to learn from his mentor, asked him if he had said the prayer with the full blessing. When Rav Shach answered in the affirmative, the student asked him why this situation differed from the one discussed by the *Shulchan Aruch*. Rav Shach replied, "Today there are many dangers on the road" (and yet, he still would not recite the prayer until leaving the city, in accordance with the ruling of the *Shulchan Aruch*).

רַק הִשָּׁמֶר לְךָ וּשְׁמֹר נַפְשְׁךָ מְאֹד פֶּן־תִּשְׁכַּח אֶת־הַדְּבָרִים אֲשֶׁר־רָאוּ עֵינֶיךָ — *Only beware for yourself and greatly beware for your soul, lest you forget the things that your eyes have beheld* (4:9).

*T*he Mishnah in *Avos* (3:8) cites this verse as the basis for saying that whoever allows himself to forget that which he studied is considered as if he forfeits his soul.

R' Meir Hershkowitz tells the following story: "In 1986, I mentioned to Rav Shach that there was a young man who needed encouragement. He told me to send the youth in to him.

"One Friday, right after the Minchah service, I informed Rav Shach that the young man was planning to see him that afternoon, and I mentioned a few points that I felt should be raised in the conversation. Rav Shach said that he would discuss those points.

"On Friday night, when I said 'Good Shabbos' to Rav Shach, he mentioned to me that the young man never came. I told him that I was surprised, since the youth said he would go.

"When I ran into the young man, he turned to me excitedly and told me that he had gone to Rav Shach, that Rav Shach had spoken to him for 20 minutes, and that he felt he had gained a lot from the conversation. I understood from this that Rav Shach had apparently not connected him with the young man of whom I had spoken. Therefore I told Rav Shach that the young man had come to him yesterday along with another student and that they had spoken for 20 minutes. Rav Shach said, 'I don't remember a thing.'

"As long as I was talking with him, I continued, 'There is a difficult Rashi in the second chapter of Tractate *Sanhedrin* ...'

" 'You already asked me about that Rashi six weeks ago!' He immediately replied. "Torah matters ... even those from a while ago — were more clearly on his mind than more mundane events that had just occurred!"

וְהוֹדַעְתָּם לְבָנֶיךָ — *And make them known to your children* (4:9).

*I*t is a great responsibility to know the nature of children and how to behave toward them. The story is told that, in one of the new *charedi* neighborhoods, there were two Orthodox families who were having a bad influence on the neighborhood. The local rabbis decided to organize a gathering for prayer and repentance, and the rabbi spearheading the project went to get Rav Shach's approval for the undertaking.

To everyone's astonishment, he returned saying that Rav Shach was against their decision.

Why?

The rabbi explained that Rav Shach had asked him some questions: "Did anyone go to these two families to try and explain the situation? To try and be a good influence on them? Did anyone even smile at them, or even give them the right time of day?"

Then Rav Shach explained what the results of the "prayer gathering" may be: "Perhaps when they hear about the meeting, they will understand that it is about them and they will become embittered, feel rebuffed, and behave even worse. First, try and have some influence on them, and then, we'll see."

The rabbis undertook this warm and caring approach, and the families turned around and became fine and upstanding members of the community.

וְהוֹדַעְתָּם לְבָנֶיךָ וְלִבְנֵי בָנֶיךָ יוֹם אֲשֶׁר עָמַדְתָּ לִפְנֵי ה' אֱלֹקֶיךָ בְּחֹרֵב — *And make them known to your children and your children's children — the day that you stood before Hashem, your God, at Chorev* (4:9-10).

*T*he Gemara (*Berachos* 22a) derives from the juxtaposition in this verse that just as the Torah was received with awe, fear, shaking, and sweat (see *Shemos* 20:15 — Rashi), so too, Torah should be studied with awe, fear, shaking, and sweat. (Also see Rambam, Commentary to Mishnah, *Avos* 6:4.)

It is well known that R' Yechezkel Levinstein, *mashgiach* of the

Ponevezh Yeshivah, used to always sit erect in his chair, never leaning back in comfort. Similarly, Rav Shach's students noticed that when Rav Shach would learn in the yeshivah, he would sit on the front part of the chair, sitting erect and not leaning back. Once, when he was so immersed in thought that he was not paying attention, he leaned back — but as soon as he realized it he hurried to sit erect, so that his studies would be with awe and fear, and not in a princely manner of comfort.

As Rambam (ibid., end of Chapter 5) writes: "For the only wisdom that remains is that learned with toil and difficulty, but restful joy-reading will not last and is of no benefit."

וְיָדַעְתָּ הַיּוֹם וַהֲשֵׁבֹתָ אֶל־לְבָבֶךָ כִּי ה' הוּא הָאֱלֹקִים — *You shall know this day and take to your heart that Hashem, He is the God* (4:39).

Rabbeinu Yonah (*Shaarei Teshuvah* 3:17) writes, "Know that the exalted virtues were given to us as positive commandments, such as the virtue of Torah study ... and the virtue of pondering the greatness of God, as it says, 'You shall know this day and take to your heart that Hashem, He is the God.' "

In the Book of *Tehillim*, David HaMelech teaches us how to instill in our hearts the exalted virtue of faith by saying (116:10), "I believed for I speak," which the early commentators explain to mean that I instilled faith through speaking matters of belief.

R' Shmuel HaLevi Wosner, the chief rabbi of Zichron Meir, relates that when he went to visit Rav Shach and he saw him sitting by the bedside of his wife at the peak of her illness, his lips were moving. R' Wosner assumed that he was praying and did not want to disturb him.

Rav Shach turned to him and said, "I can't concentrate enough now to study Torah in the proper fashion. Instead I am repeating verses of faith, thereby fulfilling two mitzvos simultaneously: Torah study and strengthening faith!"

וְנָס אֶל־אַחַת מִן־הֶעָרִים הָאֵל וָחָי — *Then he shall flee to one of these cities and live* (4:42).

Rambam (*Hil. Rotze'ach* 7:1) rules that when a student is exiled to one of the cities of refuge, his rebbi is exiled along with him, for it says *and live*, "and life without study, for those who have wisdom [in Torah] an7d those who seek it, is considered like death."

Rabbi Mordechai Reinhold recounts the time, some thirty years ago, when Rav Shach suffered great pains and required a difficult operation. R' Reinhold was asked to stay with him in the hospital and see to it that he would not be disturbed.

Rav Shach stood by his bed — his pains were too great to allow him to be able to lie in bed. He leaned on the bed with two hands, and between the two hands was an open Gemara!

His suffering was so great that he could not even lie in bed — but not to study would be even greater suffering — it would be considered like death!

"Fourteen years later," continued R' Reinhold, "a relative of mine had the same illness and was treated by the same doctor, Dr. Bank. He complained to the doctor about the terrible pain, and the professor said, 'You should just know that Rav Shach's suffering was much greater, and yet, he did not cease his studies for a moment.' "

וּלְמַדְתֶּם אֹתָם וּשְׁמַרְתֶּם לַעֲשֹׂתָם — *Learn them and be careful to perform them* (5:1).

*A*group of soldiers came for a tour of Bnei Brak. They heard a lecture on Judaism and went to visit the Ponevezh Yeshivah. They were greatly impressed by the hundreds of students enthusiastically studying Torah and were intrigued by the antique gilded *aron kodesh*.

One of the soldiers stood at the entrance, enchanted by what he saw. His eyes moved from bench to bench and from study group to study group. A new world opened up in front of his eyes, and he found it hard to digest.

Suddenly, he saw an old man with a white beard, sitting alone, deeply immersed in his studies. He did not know that he was looking at the rabbi who was the leader of the Jewish people, Rav Shach. He wondered to himself, "Is there no limit to how long Torah is studied?"

He went over to Rav Shach and interrupted him, asking, "Excuse me, how long have you been studying here?"

Rav Shach looked at him with his kind eyes and responded, "Over thirty years."

"And do you find yourself still progressing in your studies?"

Rav Shach thought for a moment and replied, "I think that I am, thank God."

שָׁמוֹר אֶת־יוֹם הַשַּׁבָּת לְקַדְּשׁוֹ — *Guard the Sabbath day to sanctify it* (5:12).

A young man once asked Rav Shach for advice regarding treatment for his cancer-ridden mother. The cancer was spreading, and the doctors felt it necessary to operate as soon as possible. On the other hand, it was in the midst of the three weeks of mourning, between the seventeenth of Tammuz and Tishah B'Av, a time considered inauspicious. The fellow wanted to know whether surgery should be postponed until after Tishah B'Av.

Rav Shach was shocked by the question and he emphatically ruled, "They should operate immediately, the sooner the better! If such an operation supersedes the prohibitions of Shabbos, it certainly supersedes the three weeks!"

The young man persisted, "But maybe there is a difference between Shabbos and the three weeks. Shabbos involves a prohibition, and danger to life supersedes a prohibition. The three weeks, however, are a time of danger, and as a result, the operation may not succeed, Heaven forbid."

"You are mistaken," replied Rav Shach. "Desecrating Shabbos involves more than a prohibition. The verse explicitly says, 'Guard the Sabbath day — to sanctify it.' One who desecrates Shabbos defiles the sanctity of of the day. To start up with Shabbos is in itself dangerous. And if operations nevertheless supersede Shabbos, they certainly supersede the three weeks!"

שָׁמוֹר אֶת־יוֹם הַשַּׁבָּת לְקַדְּשׁוֹ — *Guard the Sabbath day to sanctify it* (5:12).

A community rabbi from South Africa brought three old Lithuanian Jews to visit Rav Shach. They sat together and reminisced about their youth.

At the end of the conversation, Rav Shach asked the three, "And are you Sabbath-observant?"

There was only silence.

He asked again, "Do you keep Shabbos?"

Again silence.

He asked a third time, "Do you keep Shabbos?"

When there was again no answer, he said, "Look, I am almost 100 years old, and I have kept Shabbos my entire life. Give me your word that you will keep Shabbos."

There was an embarrassed silence until one of them gathered the courage to nod and say, "We thank the rabbi for his hospitality."

Rav Shach replied, "In my village, there was a young man who was not completely normal, but he had a heart of gold. He would help everyone and when they would thank him, he would say, 'I don't need your thanks — I want you to remember me.'"

Rav Shach came to a powerful finish, "I, too, do not need your thanks — I want you to remember me!"

One by one they gave their word that they would keep Shabbos.

כַּבֵּד אֶת־אָבִיךָ וְאֶת־אִמֶּךָ ... וּלְמַעַן יִיטַב לָךְ — *Honor your father and your mother ... and so that it will be good for you* (5:16).

When parents would bring their children to be blessed by Rav Shach, he would beam at the children and give each one candies. He would always give the youngest first, and would bless them all, saying, "If you listen to your parents, you will be blessed with all the blessings in the world!"

וְזֹאת הַמִּצְוָה הַחֻקִּים וְהַמִּשְׁפָּטִים אֲשֶׁר צִוָּה ה' אֱלֹקֵיכֶם ... לְמַעַן תִּירָא אֶת ה' אֱלֹקֶיךָ — *This is the commandment, and the statutes, and the ordinances that Hashem, your God, commanded to teach you ... in order that you will fear Hashem, your God* (6:1-2).

The Torah is also referred to as "fear." The Gemara (*Bava Basra* 16:1) explains that the verse (*Iyov* 15:4), "You too cast off fear," refers to casting off Torah, which is the antidote for the evil inclination. Similarly, the Sages say (*Avos* 3:17): "If there is no (Torah) wisdom there is no fear."

Rav Shach once rushed into the yeshivah with an extremely difficult Talmudic question on his mind. Prior to presenting it he said that Rabbeinu Yonah writes (*Shaarei Teshuvah* 3:16) that one must engage his thoughts so as to constantly ponder fear of Hashem. He then continued, "Do you know the meaning of 'engage his thoughts'? It means like the 'engagements' (*Maarachos*) of R' Akiva Eiger!" — extremely well-reasoned questions and answers of great depth on Talmudic subjects.

One *erev Yom Kippur*, Rav Shach entered the *beis midrash* of the yeshivah all dressed in white, wrapped in his prayer shawl, and looking just like a Heavenly angel. He gathered the students around him and asked them a very difficult question and then said, "Ponder this over Yom Kippur until you come up with the answer!"

שְׁמַע יִשְׂרָאֵל — *Hear, O Israel* (6:4).

*A*person once told Rav Shach that he heard a sermon from the Chofetz Chaim which shook him to the foundations of his soul, and he still remembered it verbatim. Rav Shach asked him to recount what he had heard, and the person demurred, saying that although he could repeat the words — and even use the same tune — he was certain that it wouldn't have the same effect. Rav Shach begged him to repeat it nevertheless. The person closed his eyes and began reciting the *Shema*, speaking slowly and carefully, as if he were counting gold coins. "What can I tell you?" concluded Rav Shach. "It was a sermon that touched me to the bottom of my heart!"

וְאָהַבְתָּ אֵת יְהוָה אֱלֹהֶיךָ בְּכָל־לְבָבְךָ וּבְכָל־נַפְשְׁךָ — *You should love Hashem, your God, with all your heart, with all your soul* (6:5).

*T*he Gemara (*Pesachim* 25a) derives from here that one may not be cured, even from a life-threatening illness, through idolatry. (For other reasons, it is also prohibited to cure by means of murder or sexual immorality.)

Rav Shach related that R' Chaim Soloveitchik of Brisk was asked whether, in order to avoid being drafted into the Polish Army, it was permitted to work in a factory that operates on Shabbos. Rav Chaim responded that it was certainly permitted, because the draftees could be sent to the front lines and get killed, and even the possibility of danger to life supersedes Shabbos.

R' Chaim was then asked if it was permitted to register in the Gymnasia (the Polish high school), whose students were freed from the draft. He replied that it certainly was not, because they taught apostasy there and "One may be cured by all means other than idolatry!"

וּבְכָל־מְאֹדֶךָ — *And with all me'odecha* (6:5).

*A*mong the definitions for the unusual word *me'odecha* is the one cited by Rashi which relates the word to the Hebrew *middah*, measure; one is obligated to love Hashem with whatever measure He metes out to him, whether it be goodness or punishment. Similarly, the Gemara (*Berachos* 60b) derives from this verse that one must recite a blessing over bad news with the same feeling of joy that he feels when reciting a blessing over good news.

When R' Shlomo Zalman Auerbach's brother, R' Rephael David, passed away, Rav Shach went to R' Shlomo Zalman to pay him a condolence call. R' Shlomo Zalman told him that the Chasam Sofer writes that when his rebbi, R' Nassan Adler, lost his only daughter at the age of 14, he recited the requisite blessing (*Dayan HaEmes*) with the kind of joy seen on him only on Simchas Torah!

R' Shlomo Zalman added, "Although we are not on that level, we must know that such a level exists!"

וְשִׁנַּנְתָּם — *You shall teach them* (6:7).

The Gemara (*Kiddushin* 30b) derives from the Torah's use of the word *v'shinantam* that the words of Torah should be *meshunanim*, well versed on your lips, so that if a person asks you something, you will not hesitate and you will be able to immediately answer him.

One Shabbos, Rav Shach asked some students to open the book *Shev Shmaatsa* to a certain question that he wanted to discuss with them. The book is divided into seven sections, each of which has subchapters, and they asked him in which section and which chapter that question could be found. His face darkened and he said, "Students your age should know the location of every question in the *Shev Shmaatsa!*"

וְשִׁנַּנְתָּם לְבָנֶיךָ — *You shall teach them to your sons* (6:7).

There was a period in which Rav Shach was unable to go to the yeshivah, and instead, the yeshivah would send boys to his house to "talk in learning" — discuss the subjects they were learning — with him. He had difficulty seeing, and the students were in awe of him. Rav Shach did most of the speaking and the students would listen and feel themselves transformed. One day, Rav Shach called over one of the other rabbis and told him that two boys had been to see him that day and he told the rabbi their names. He then continued, "The first was okay, but there is something bothering the other one. What is it?" Understanding the question as an order, the rabbi checked and found out that the the boy needed a suitable study partner. A while later, Rav Shach told the rabbi, "Today he came to me and he looks much better."

In his moving will he wrote, "I also gave my soul to see to it that you [my students] succeeded in your studies." Indeed, he gave his soul to watch over all the needs of his students.

וְשִׁנַּנְתָּם לְבָנֶיךָ — *You shall teach them to your sons* (6:7).

Rav Shach used to offer a silent prayer before any lecture or public address. R' Aharon Waldman says that he heard him reciting Psalm 20 before each lecture. Immediately before the lecture, he heard him say the verse (*Mishlei* 2:6), "For Hashem gives wisdom, from His lips [comes] knowledge and understanding," followed by (ibid. 16:1), "The thoughts of the heart are man's, but from Hashem comes the utterance of the tongue."

Once, when Rav Shach was leaving his apartment to go to the yeshivah, Rabbi Dovid Zimmerman heard him whisper to himself, "I am hereby prepared to fulfill the mitzvah of 'You shall teach them to your sons.'"

וְשִׁנַּנְתָּם לְבָנֶיךָ — *You shall teach them to your sons* (6:7).

One Shabbos morning at the yeshivah, Rav Shach asked R' Shlomo Hirshler a difficult question concerning the topic then being studied at the yeshivah.

R' Shlomo thought about it and said, "It is a very difficult question, I do not know the answer."

Rav Shach said, "Fine, but what shall I tell the students when they ask?"

וְשִׁנַּנְתָּם לְבָנֶיךָ — *You shall teach them to your sons* (6:7).

Rav Shach used to say that just as defining students as sons obligates the "father" to love them as his own children, there is no less an obligation for the students to see themselves as sons who are dependent on their father and deferential to him.

He related that once, when R' Chaim Soloveitchik of Brisk was preparing his lecture in the presence of a group of select students, they told him that they do not agree with the basics of his lecture, and that they do not understand what compels him to adopt the approach he was using in explaining the Talmudic passage. He looked at them and asked, "Do you know the thoughts and intentions of the Kohen Gadol (high priest) when he entered the Holy of Holies on Yom Kippur?"

A bit astonished, they said that they did not.

"Right," said R' Chaim. "There is no reason that you should know. Everyone depended upon the Kohen Gadol to properly do his holy work. By the very same token, there is no reason that you should understand my intentions. All you have to do is to listen to what I say and nothing else."

Rav Shach explained that R' Chaim wanted to instill in them the knowledge that, as a result of awe of the rebbi and subservience to him, the student can acquire his method of analysis and understand it. If, however, he sets himself up as the judge of his rebbi, he will never transcend his limited understanding.

Apparently, R' Chaim understood that their question was the result of a lack of subservience to their rebbi.

וְשִׁנַּנְתָּם לְבָנֶיךָ וְדִבַּרְתָּ בָּם — *You shall teach them to your sons and you shall speak of them* (6:7).

*I*n the yeshivah, various tractates of the Talmud are studied in a repeated cycle. When R' Yaakov Adler studied in the yeshivah, they were beginning *Maseches Sanhedrin* for what would have been his second time. He asked Rav Shach for permission to study *Maseches Shevuos* instead. Permission was granted, on condition that he come each morning to discuss in depth what he was learning. R' Adler indeed came each morning, and Rav Shach discussed that tractate with him in depth without any preparation, as if he had just studied that tractate.

On the other hand, R' Zvi Garboz would sit near Rav Shach and study *Maseches Yoma*, which was not the tractate studied by the yeshivah. Whenever he had any difficulties, he would ask Rav Shach. After several days of this, Rav Shach asked him to please stop asking questions from that *maseches*, for even after responding, the *Rosh Yeshivah* would continue to think about the matter. As a result, he could not properly concentrate on the questions that others asked him on the tractate being studied in the yeshivah.

וְשִׁנַּנְתָּם לְבָנֶיךָ וְדִבַּרְתָּ בָּם — *You shall teach them to your sons and you shall speak of them* (6:7).

*R*av Shach once told a certain *rosh yeshivah* that a rabbi must seclude himself several hours a day to study — both to learn in depth and to learn in order to cover ground. He added that even a milk cow cannot give milk all day long. Rather, it must take a break to eat and to rest to revivify itself.

וְדִבַּרְתָּ בָּם — *And you shall speak of them* (6:7).

"*A*nd you shall speak of them," emphasizes the Gemara (*Yoma* 19b), "but not in matters of no consequence." Rav Shach was once told that R' Zelmeleh of Vilna questioned whether the prohibition against speaking matters of no consequence was absolute, or just a byproduct of the obligation to study Torah. The difference between the two possibilities applies to someone in a bathhouse, where speaking words of Torah is prohibited. If the prohibition against speaking matters of no consequence is absolute, it applies in a bathhouse as well. If, however, it is a byproduct of the obligation to study Torah, it should be permitted in a bathhouse.

Rav Shach's reaction: "The question is quite nice, but any way you look at it, the difference mentioned is incorrect. If things that need to be said are said in the bathhouse, then they are not matters of no consequence. And if unnecessary things are said, then that is foolish, and the greatest prohibition of them all is to do foolish things."

וְדִבַּרְתָּ בָּם — *And you shall speak of them* (6:7).

"*A*nd you shall speak of them," emphasizes the Gemara (*Yoma* 19b), "But not in matters of no consequence." A youth once came to Rav Shach and asked him for guidance in Torah study. Rav Shach told him, "If you really and truly want to ascend in Torah, the very first thing you must do is to give me your solemn word that you will not read newspapers" — and he was not referring to the secular newspapers which one is forbidden to read!

וְדִבַּרְתָּ בָּם בְּשִׁבְתְּךָ בְּבֵיתֶךָ — *And you shall speak of them while you sit in your home* (6:7).

*S*forno explains that by constantly speaking of them you will always remember them. Rav Shach once wanted to instill in his pupil the importance of review. He asked him, "Do you know *Maseches Bava Kamma*?"

"Yes," the pupil replied, "I reviewed it twice!"

Rav Shach told him, "I studied that tractate one hundred times — and I am not exaggerating, I actually counted — yet I still do not know it. And you know it after two times?"

וְדִבַּרְתָּ בָּם בְּשִׁבְתְּךָ בְּבֵיתֶךָ וּבְלֶכְתְּךָ בַדֶּרֶךְ וּבְשָׁכְבְּךָ וּבְקוּמֶךָ —
And you shall speak of them while you sit in your home and while you walk on the way, when you lie down and when you rise (6:7)

Haamek Davar cites the above-mentioned Gemara in *Yoma* ("But not in matters of no consequence") and adds that by speaking of Torah in all these situations, you will never pull yourself away from Torah study, and as a result, you will come to loving [Hashem] and cleaving to Him.

In early 1990, R' Mordechai Mann returned from a meeting of the Council of Torah Sages, visibly moved, and he committed to writing what he had seen: The council was discussing the forthcoming *Degel HaTorah* convention in Tel Aviv. The discussion revolved around how the convention could be held while simultaneously minimizing, as much as possible, interference with Torah study. A date was agreed upon, and they all waited for Rav Shach's approval.

His face darkened and he motioned with his hands as if to say, "We have no choice!"

His mouth could not utter a word of approval for a plan that would interfere in any way with Torah study!

וּבְלֶכְתְּךָ בַדֶּרֶךְ — *And while you walk on the way* (6:7).

After an important meeting in Jerusalem, several of the participants wanted to join Rav Shach in the car taking him back to Bnei Brak. Rav Shach was concerned that these people might want to engage him in conversation and waste his precious time. On the other hand, he did not want to insult them. So he replied, "With pleasure! You should know that I love traveling on the road. I have prepared some of my best lectures while traveling!"

They took the hint and allowed Rav Shach to sink deep into his thoughts.

וּבְלֶכְתְּךָ בַדֶּרֶךְ — *And while you walk on the way* (6:7).

O ne day, Rav Shach came into the yeshivah from his house on Wasserman Street with a little boy holding his hand. When asked who the boy was, he looked down at the boy and cried out, "*Oy vey!* He asked me to help him across the street!"

The Rav was so engrossed in his thoughts of Torah as he was walking on the way, that he did not realize that he did not do what the child had asked of him!

On another occasion, he arrived at the yeshivah *without* a child:

He had just finished his Shabbos lunch. He turned to his little grandson and said, "Come, let's go to the *beis midrash* and we will learn together." He lovingly put his hand around the boy's shoulders and started walking with him to the yeshivah. Somewhere along the way, the boy snuck out from under his grandfather's arm and ran to play. Rav Shach was so engrossed in his learning that he realized nothing, and he entered the yeshivah with his arm still outstretched!

וּבְלֶכְתְּךָ בַדֶּרֶךְ — *And while you walk on the way* (6:7).

A former student of Rav Shach sent his son to the yeshivah. The son was very successful in his studies, and the father went to Rav Shach to inquire about his progress. Rav Shach praised him and said that, in his opinion, the young man was ready to look for marriage prospects. He had already built himself up in his understanding of Torah, and he could continue his studies in a *kollel* for married students.

The father said, "With a millstone around his neck, can he study Torah?" (see *Kiddushin* 29b). "Better that he continue his progress in the yeshivah. If I knew that he would be as engrossed in his studies after his wedding as the *Rosh Yeshivah* was, then I would agree.

"I can testify," he added, that once the *Rosh Yeshivah* bought a bag of cucumbers and began walking home. The bag had a hole in it and the cucumbers fell out, one at a time. By chance, I was walking behind him and I bent down to pick up each cucumber. The *Rosh Yeshivah* came home with an empty bag in his hand, and was surprised when I handed him all the cucumbers that had fallen. He hadn't realized a thing!

"If my son were thus engrossed in his learning," concluded the father, "I would certainly agree to allow him get married now!"

וּבְשָׁכְבְּךָ וּבְקוּמֶךָ — *When you lie down and when you rise* (6:7).

*R*av Shach once said: "The Jewish home should be suffused with the awe of Heaven and the fear of sin. I remember the way my parents raised me. I was taught that when the yarmulke falls off one's head it is appropriate to cry in sorrow. Such education has a long-term effect. I remember waking up once as a child after the time limit set by *Magen Avraham* for reciting *Shema* [the first of two time limits for the morning recitation of the daily *Shema*] and bursting into tears. It took me a full day to be consoled!"

Ninety years later, during the yeshivah intersession, Rav Shach's weakness got the better of him and he woke up a bit late. He looked at his watch and cried out, *"Oy vey!* For the second time in my life I have missed *Magen Avraham*'s time limit for reciting *Shema!*"

וְדִבַּרְתָּ בָּם ... וּקְשַׁרְתָּם — *And you shall speak of them ... Bind them (6:7-8).*

*R*av Shach once said that any practicing Jew will not let a day pass without donning *tefillin*. The fear of being "a head upon which *tefillin* was not placed" (see *Rosh Hashanah* 17a) is so strong, that he will not be at peace with himself unless he dons *tefillin* daily. All the more so, however, a person who does not study Torah one day should not be at peace with himself until he "repays his debt at night" (see *Eruvin* 65a), so that he not be a "head that did not study Torah!"

אֶת־יְהוָה אֱלֹהֶיךָ תִּירָא — *Hashem, your God, shall you fear (6:13).*

*T*he Gemara (*Bava Kamma* 41b) cites Rabbi Akiva who states that the unspecific "*es*" that precedes "Hashem, your God," comes to include Torah scholars. *Tosafos* (ad loc.) explain that this refers to the Rav from whom one learned most of his wisdom — regarding whom one is instructed: "The fear of your Rav should be like the fear of Heaven" (*Avos* 4:12) — and to the leading Rav of the generation who is considered everyone's individual rabbi.

Torah giants were always careful and did not practice stringencies in the presence of other Torah giants who did not observe those stringencies.

Rav Shach related that R' Baruch Ber Leibowitz of Kaminetz used to pray wearing a *gartel* (a special black ropelike belt) during prayer services, for extra piety (see *Mishnah Berurah* 91:4). Once he went to pray in the presence of R' Chaim Ozer Grodzinsky, wearing his *gartel*, as usual. When he saw that R' Chaim Ozer was not wearing a *gartel*, he immediately removed his own.

כִּי־יִשְׁאָלְךָ בִנְךָ מָחָר לֵאמֹר מָה הָעֵדֹת ... — *When your son will ask you tomorrow, saying, "What are the testimonies ..."* (6:20).

Our Sages (*Mechilta, Parashas Bo*, also cited in the Pesach Haggadah) cite this as one of the verses from which they derive that the Torah speaks of four types of sons: "the wise, the evil, the simple, and the one who does not know how to ask."

Apparently, it should have said, "The righteous," as distinct from "the evil" rather than "the wise." However, said Rav Shach, the first thing demanded of a Torah student is to be wise. He must understand everything properly, weigh it carefully in the balance scales of his brain, and not be swayed like a fool by shallow appearances!

וּמְשַׁלֵּם לְשֹׂנְאָיו אֶל־פָּנָיו לְהַאֲבִידוֹ — *And He repays those who hate Him to his face, to make him perish* (7:10).

Rav Shach was once asked to explain how the wicked could be repaid in this world for their good deeds. The Mishnah tells us that one hour of enjoyment in the World to Come is more pleasurable than the entire life on this world (*Avos* 4:17), so how can an entire lifetime even repay one mitzvah?

Rav Shach answered in his pleasant way, "That Mishnah also says that one hour of performing mitzvos and good deeds in this world is greater than the entire life in the World to Come. Accordingly, if a wicked person's life is increased even for one hour, he can utilize the time by pondering faith in Hashem and His personal attention to everything in this world. This itself is more precious than all of life in the World to Come. So you see, there can be no greater reward than an hour of life!"

וְשָׁמַרְתָּ אֶת־הַמִּצְוָה וְאֶת־הַחֻקִּים וְאֶת־הַמִּשְׁפָּטִים אֲשֶׁר אָנֹכִי מְצַוְּךָ הַיּוֹם לַעֲשֹׂתָם — *You shall observe the commandment, and the statutes and the ordinances that I command you today, to perform them* (7:11).

*R*ashi explains: "Today, to perform them, and tomorrow to receive reward for them." *Mesillas Yesharim* explains this idea at length in his first chapter: A person's ultimate purpose is to enjoy the pleasure of the Divine Countenance in the World to Come. The means of achieving this is through living a life of Torah and mitzvos in this world.

Rav Shach once had a theological discussion with Professor Blumenthal, the director of the Opthalmology department at Asuta Hospital, who was a secular Jew. He told the professor, "A secular Jew lives 70 to 80 years and then dies like a donkey. He is buried in the ground, worms eat his flesh, and nothing is left other than mold and worms."

"I don't understand," the professor countered. "Why, when a religious Jew dies, ultimately he too is buried in the ground, and the worms come to him as well!"

Rav Shach smiled and said, "No, no! Let me give you an example. When a person rides on a donkey and, suddenly, the donkey dies, what does he do? He gets up off the donkey and continues on his way, He lets nature takes its course and assumes that the vultures and hyenas will come to eat the donkey carcass — he does not concern himself with the details.

"Do you understand?" concluded Rav Shach. "The main thing is the soul. It collects mitzvos and good deeds all the years that it is connected with the body. When the body dies, the soul ascends to Heaven and continues its journey, to the World to Come and to its ultimate reward. However, those who relate only to the physical world, the body, once the person dies and the physical body disintegrates, with what are you left?"

עקב — Eikev

וַיַּאֲכִלְךָ אֶת-הַמָּן — *Then he fed you the manna* (8:3).

Our Sages went to great lengths to praise those who ate the manna and could thus be considered "those who ate food from the Heavenly table." They went so far as to say that "the Torah could be given only to those who ate the manna."

After the Rebbetzin passed away, one of Rav Shach's students came into his house and saw him eating a piece of bread for breakfast. The student said, "Let me prepare a salad; I'll fry an omelet." Rav Shach replied, "And what is wrong with bread accompanied by Rambam?"

וְיָדַעְתָּ עִם-לְבָבֶךָ כִּי כַּאֲשֶׁר יְיַסֵּר אִישׁ אֶת-בְּנוֹ ה' אֱלֹקֶיךָ מְיַסְּרֶךָ — *You should know in your heart that just as a father will chastise his son, so Hashem, your God, chastises you* (8:5).

Rabbeinu Yonah (*Shaarei Teshuvah* 2:4) writes: "And when a person accepts God's reproof and improves his ways and deeds, it is proper for him to take joy in his suffering, for it helped him achieve exalted benefits. He should thus thank Hashem for them as he would for the rest of his successes."

Rav Shach used to recount a story told in the introduction to the book *Maalos HaTorah*: When the Gra's brother, R' Avraham, was stricken with his final illness, he was afflicted with severe suffering and his body was covered with festering bedsores. Nevertheless, not so much as a sigh was heard from him.

His son, R' Eliyahu, saw the terrible state that he was in and tearfully said, "Woe is me for seeing you in such a state."

R' Avraham said to his son, "Why are you crying about this great gift that Hashem has granted me? If I only had the strength, I would dance and sing with musical accompaniment about the great benefit that God has given me in this pain, and you are crying?" He did not stop expressing joy and enthusiasm about his state until his soul departed from his body!

When Rav Shach was 80 years old, he suffered greatly from a kidney ailment and required an operation. An iron tube was inserted into his body and when the tube would move as little as a millimeter, he would suffer from terrible pain. Rav Shach would cry out when the pain became unbearable, "Master of the Universe! Suffering is good — but give me the wisdom for suffering, so that I may accept it with love!"

וְאָכַלְתָּ וְשָׂבָעְתָּ וּבֵרַכְתָּ אֶת־ה׳ אֱלֹקֶיךָ — *You will eat, and you will be satisfied, and you will bless Hashem, your God* (8:10).

*I*n Rav Shach's waning days, he was no longer able to swallow food and he required feeding through a tube. When he was first told the news, he burst into tears. Such tears were understandable, of course. He had just been told that he could not eat naturally, and this was just one more sign of his deteriorating health.

Nevertheless, his grandchildren tried to mollify him. They asked him, "Why is *Zaide* crying?"

"Because of the terrible news," he replied. "From now on I will not be able to recite blessings on food!"

וְזָכַרְתָּ אֶת־ה׳ אֱלֹקֶיךָ כִּי הוּא הַנֹּתֵן לְךָ כֹּחַ לַעֲשׂוֹת חָיִל — *Then you shall remember Hashem, your God: that it was He Who gave you strength to make wealth* (8:18).

*R*abbeinu Yonah (*Shaarei Teshuvah* 3:15) explains that remembering God's benevolence and pondering it is one of the most exalted states which we are obligated to achieve.

One wintry morning, Rav Shach told R' Chaim Berman that he had not slept a wink the night before, and he had sat at his desk studying Torah.

"Do you know why?" asked Rav Shach. "Because there was a thunderstorm and it was pouring. I thought to myself, 'Mortal man, if you would now be lying in your grave with the rain pouring down and soaking the earth around you, would that be good for you? So thank Hashem that you are alive and sitting in a protected warm room — go sit and learn!' "

מַמְרִים הֱיִיתֶם עִם־ה' מִיּוֹם דַּעְתִּי אֶתְכֶם — *You have been rebels against Hashem from the day that I knew you* (9:24).

Our Sages explain that Moshe, in his great modesty, blamed himself for the weaknesses of the people of Israel, his flock. He felt that if only they would have had a better leader, they could have been stronger and better.

That is how the true leaders of Israel react to the shortcomings of the populance.

One of Rav Shach's students was sick in his bed at home. He was greatly surprised when Rav Shach come to his house to visit him.

Rav Shach turned to his student and said, "When you are not in the yeshivah, I can feel that you are missing. Apparently, it is because of my sins that you had to miss yeshivah — so it is I who must repent, so that you can become well and speedily return to the yeshivah!"

מָה ה' אֱלֹקֶיךָ שֹׁאֵל מֵעִמָּךְ כִּי אִם־לְיִרְאָה אֶת־ה' אֱלֹקֶיךָ... — *What does Hashem, your God, ask of you but to fear Hashem, your God* (10:12).

Rav Shach explained, "The Gemara (*Berachos* 33b) derives from this verse that all is up to Heaven, other than the fear of Heaven. Accordingly," he noted, "since this is man's only task, achieving such fear should involve constant effort. This is why a person's fear of Heaven weakens with time and requires constant renewal. We are commanded to read the *Shema* each morning and evening to constantly accept upon ourselves the yoke of Heaven and the yoke of mitzvos (the former is the subject of the first section of *Shema* and the latter is the subject of the second section — see *Mishnah, Berachos* 13a). This is also what is meant by the verse at the end of *Koheles* (12:13), 'The sum of the matter when all has been considered: Fear God and keep His commandments, for that is all of man.' Just as there is not a moment in which a person is free of the yoke of mitzvos, and he must constantly perform them — with Torah study being the equivalent of the others — so too, there is never a moment in which a person is free of the obligation to work hard at refreshing his fear of God!"

"And," concluded Rav Shach, "whoever does not know this may dress as piously as he wants, and perform mitzvos according to the highest of standards, and yet be missing the main thing!"

וַאֲהַבְתֶּם אֶת־הַגֵּר — *You shall love the convert* (10:19).

A Jewish man once married a gentile woman and they had a daughter. When the daughter was 6 years old, the father returned to Torah observance and she and the mother converted. The daughter studied in *charedi* schools and was a top student. When the time for marriage came, she was suggested as a prospective spouse for a top yeshivah boy. The young man asked Rav Shach for advice.

Rav Shach replied, "There is absolutely nothing wrong with marrying a convert; a convert is also a kosher Jew. Quite the contrary, we are commanded, 'You shall love the convert.' "

The young man followed Rav Shach's advice and he and his wife together built a Jewish home worthy of pride!

אֶת־יְהוָה אֱלֹהֶיךָ תִּירָא — *Hashem, your God, shall you fear* (10:20).

T he Gemara (*Bava Kamma* 41b) cites Rabbi Akiva who states that the unspecific "*es*" that precedes "Hashem, your God," comes to include Torah scholars.
The Brisker Rav, Rav Yitzchak Zev Soloveitchik, once presented a marvelously innovative exposition to Rav Shach. Afterwards, Rav Shach wanted to hear it again, but his fear and awe of his teacher was like his fear and awe of Heaven. So what did he do? He knew that the Rav was expecting an important visitor, and he assumed that the Rav would repeat the exposition. However, he considered it disrespectful to wait around in the Rav's house until the guest's arrival. So he left the house and waited outside on a cold wintry night for that person to arrive. Then he re-entered the Rav's house, along with the guest, so that he could once again hear the exposition!

וְהָיָה אִם־שָׁמֹעַ תִּשְׁמְעוּ — *And it will be that if listening, you will listen (11:13).*

R ashi indicates that the two-verb construction, "listening" and "listen" teaches that if you listen to the old, you will listen to [or "hear"] the new.
In the spring of 1996, someone who had been close to Rav Shach came to visit. Rav Shach's eyesight was already weak and he was quite hard of hearing. When the person introduced himself,

Rav Shach did not understand him. Even when his grandson repeated the name, he did not respond. He just stuck his hand out and greeted the guest.

The guest posed a complex Talmudic question, to which Rav Shach immediately responded, citing three proofs to support his contention. Afterwards, Rav Shach asked his grandson who had asked the question, but to everyone's amazement he could not hear the answer. He was only able to hear the words of Torah spoken.

וּלְעָבְדוֹ בְּכָל־לְבַבְכֶם — *And to serve Him with all your heart* (11:13).

*R*av Shach's uncle, R' Isser Zalman Meltzer, once sent him to ask a certain question of the Chofetz Chaim. Rav Shach wanted to use the opportunity to observe the great man standing in prayer before his Maker. Accordingly, he himself made sure to pray earlier. ("How could I possibly observe any person — however great he may be — when I myself am standing in prayer before my Maker?" he explained.) When the Chofetz Chaim prayed, Rav Shach stood nearby and watched him carefully.

"What can I tell you?" said Rav Shach years later. "I did not see a thing! And yet, everyone knows the awsome power his prayers had. All he had to do was pray and his prayers were answered! I began to understand what the Sages meant when they said (*Sifrei, Eikev*), 'What is *service of the heart*? It is prayer.' Indeed, prayer is the obligation of the heart, not of the external limbs. There is no need to see anything external, neither shaking nor any other movement!"

וּלְעָבְדוֹ בְּכָל־לְבַבְכֶם — *And to serve Him with all your heart* (11:13).

*R*av Shach said that it was false to say that R' Chaim Soloveitchik of Brisk was against studying *mussar*. Based on the testimony of R' Yisrael Salanter, it is obvious that it is impossible to change from good to bad without *mussar*, just as it is impossible to see without eyes or to walk without feet!

Rather, there is no greater *mussar* work than the *siddur* itself, and the greatest study of *mussar* is praying. The essence of *mussar* lies in saying, "Forgive us, our Father, for we have sinned," or, "Return us, our Father, to Your Torah." There can be such great outpouring of the soul in prayer. One can achieve such closeness to Hashem! Indeed, our

Sages (*Sifrei, Eikev*) say: How does one serve Him with all his heart? Through prayer. Furthermore, it is not for naught that the Chazon Ish once commented that he toiled at prayer more than he toiled at studying Torah — and everyone knows how the Chazon Ish toiled at studying Torah!

וּלְעָבְדוֹ בְּכָל־לְבַבְכֶם — *And to serve Him with all your heart* (11:13).

Rashi explains that the service of the heart is prayer.

In his advanced old age, Rav Shach was prescribed sleeping pills and was directed to take two a night. Every night he would take them at bedtime but on Fridays, because of the stringency of Shabbos, he would take them before Shabbos set in.

Right after taking the sleeping pills he would go to the yeshivah for the *Kabbalas Shabbos* services. Immediately after *Kabbalas Shabbos,* during the study break before *Maariv,* he would start to doze off. Each time he would wake up, he would try to ask a question having to do with his studies, or try to answer questions that he was asked, but his sleepiness got the better of him and he would doze off again. He would try to offset his sleepiness by standing up and leaning on his *shtender,* but he would even fall asleep while standing.

But as soon as they would start the *Maariv* service, his fatigue would seem to dissipate and he would pray with all his might without dozing off at all.

This would last until after reciting *Kiddush* over wine — when he would doze off again!

וְאָסַפְתָּ דְגָנֶךָ וְתִירֹשְׁךָ וְיִצְהָרֶךָ — *And you shall bring in your grain, your wine, and your oil* (11:14).

The Gemara (*Berachos* 35b) notes that were it not for this verse one would have thought that everyone is obigated to follow the verse (*Yehoshua* 1:8), "This Book of the Torah shall not leave your lips," i.e., that a person may do nothing except study Torah. This verse, however, teaches that one can follow the Torah's dictates even as he involves himself in worldly affairs.

A Gemara teacher once came to Rav Shach and told him that he wanted to leave his position and return to *kollel.* When Rav Shach asked why, the man explained that he yearned to study other tractates besides those tractates traditionally taught in yeshivah.

"And how will you earn a living?" asked Rav Shach.

He confidently answered, "God will provide."

Rav Shach gave him a long look and pointed at him, "You should know that the requirement to make an effort to earn a living is from the Torah, and this should not be lightly forfeited!"

וְאָסַפְתָּ דְגָנֶךָ וְתִירשְׁךָ וְיִצְהָרֶךָ — *And you shall bring in your grain, your wine, and your oil* (11:14).

Were it not for this verse, we would think (*Yehoshua* 1:8) "... you shall ponder it day and night," that we are prohibited from engaging in commerce or other efforts to earn a living (see *Berachos* 35b).

A young lady came to Rav Shach asking for a blessing that she find an appropriate mate, and that she be worthy of marrying a *ben Torah* [someone devoted to Torah]. She later returned to Rav Shach saying that someone had suggested that she meet a young man who worked for a living, but set aside time each day for Torah study. Her question was whether he could be considered a *ben Torah*.

Rav Shach told her, "*Ben Torah* is a concept, similar to bar mitzvah. A bar mitzvah is one who is obligated in the mitzvos and fulfills them, always having them in mind. Thus, even if he is asleep or in middle of his work he is still a bar mitzvah, because when a mitzvah does come his way he happily fulfills it. So, too, a *ben Torah*. Even when he is involved in earning a living, or in a mitzvah that no one else can fulfill, he has Torah in mind, and as soon as he has the chance he returns to his studies. That is a *ben Torah*.

"On the other hand," concluded Rav Shach, "a person can be a *kollel* fellow or even a teacher of Talmud. However, if in his free time he takes Torah out of his mind and gets involved in mundane matters, he cannot be considered a *ben Torah*!"

הִשָּׁמְרוּ לָכֶם פֶּן־יִפְתֶּה לְבַבְכֶם וְסַרְתֶּם וַעֲבַדְתֶּם אֱלֹהִים אֲחֵרִים — *Beware for yourselves, lest your heart be seduced and you will turn astray and you will serve gods of others* (11:16).

Rashi explains that "you will turn astray" by parting from the Torah, and as a result of this, "you will serve gods of others," for, once a person parts from the Torah, he goes and attaches himself to idolatry.

Rav Shach cited R' Yitzchak Zev Soloveitchik of Brisk as saying:

"Know that when a person strays from the true path, he continues to travel straight — the path onto which he has strayed. This continues day after day, and this person is certain that he is walking on the straight path. In fact, the path is straight — straight off the true path. Each day he veers further and further from the true path. Only by looking at where he went astray — slight as it may have been — can he see how he deviated from the straight path!"

וְלִמַּדְתֶּם אֹתָם אֶת־בְּנֵיכֶם — *You shall teach them to your children* (11:19).

A young man came to Rav Shach to discuss the subject he was studying. In the course of the discussion, Rav Shach asked him an intricate question, so that the young man could test his powers of analysis, as he tried to answer it. While the fellow was pondering the question other young men entered the room. Rav Shach wanted to bring them into the discussion, so he told the first young man to repeat the question for them. The young man said, "The *Rosh Yeshivah* asked such and such on the position of *Tosafos*."

Rav Shach smiled and said, "*Oy!* By now you should know how to ask a question!"

At the sight of the young man's astonishment, Rav Shach said, "How many years have you been asking the Four Questions on the *Seder* night?"

The young man's astonishment only increased; what possible connection could the Four Questions have to the matter at hand?

Rav Shach explained, "Note that when we ask the Four Questions, we do not begin by asking why on this night we eat only matzah. First we mention that on all other nights we eat bread or matzah, and only then we ask why on this night we eat only matzah. This teaches us that we should not begin with a question, but first explain the background. The same applies here. You must first explain the position of *Tosafos*, and only then present the question on the position."

לְדַבֵּר בָּם בְּשִׁבְתְּךָ בְּבֵיתֶךָ וּבְלֶכְתְּךָ בַדֶּרֶךְ — *To speak in them while you sit in your home, while you walk on the way* (11:19).

A Torah scroll was to be brought into the study hall of a new yeshivah as part of a gala dedication ceremony, and the administration invited Rav Shach and other dignitaries to grace the ceremony with their presence. When Rav Shach entered, one of the famous elder *roshei yeshivah* came over to greet him. Rav Shach took his outstretched hand with both of his own and passionately said, "Ah! You should not have come! Why, you study Torah day and night. What a pity you stopped your studies to come!"

The *rosh yeshivah* of the new yeshivah, who had invited Rav Shach and the others, asked the disciple who had accompanied Rav Shach to explain this last remark. After all, Rav Shach also studied Torah day and night and yet, he came to help give honor and lend his name to the new yeshivah!

The disciple whispered in reply, "I can testify that throughout the trip, Rav Shach did not stop learning for even a moment!"

לְדַבֵּר בָּם בְּשִׁבְתְּךָ בְּבֵיתֶךָ ... וּבְשָׁכְבְּךָ — *To speak in them while you sit in your home ... when you retire* (11:19).

The Gra used to say that each person wants to merit a place in the World to Come, in which he will take pleasure in God's shining Countenance. Yet how can a person know if he will indeed enter the World to Come? To answer this question, he cited the Gemara (*Berachos* 57b) which states that sleep is one-sixtieth of death. Accordingly, a person could see where he "is" in his sleep, and from there he can deduce where he will be after his death.

Everyone knows where Rav Shach was in his sleep. Once, when he was being wheeled into the recovery room after a difficult operation, he was seen moving his hands with great feeling, while muttering about a Talmudic topic. The tubes came out of his arms, and the doctors were forced to tie his arms down!

At the time, R' Dovid Povarski said, "We knew that he was immersed in his studies — but not to such a degree that even under anesthesia he thinks about Torah!"

וּבְלֶכְתְּךָ בַדֶּרֶךְ — *While you walk on the way* (11:19).

An elderly Torah scholar had a heart condition, and he complained to Rav Shach that his apartment was on a high floor and his condition made it almost impossible for him to climb the stairs. Each step required unbearable exertion!

Rav Shach told him, "Let me give you a simple piece of advice. Before going up the stairs, think of a question about the topic you just studied. Before you know it, you will find yourself in your apartment. You won't even realize that you went up the stairs! I must tell you that this is guaranteed to work. I, too, have difficulty going up to the yeshivah, but I think of some commentary of Rashba and I do not feel the difficulty!"

ראה — Re'eh

וּפֶן־תִּדְרֹשׁ לֵאלֹהֵיהֶם לֵאמֹר אֵיכָה יַעַבְדוּ הַגּוֹיִם הָאֵלֶּה אֶת־
אֱלֹהֵיהֶם וְאֶעֱשֶׂה־כֵּן גַּם־אָנִי — *And lest you seek out their gods, saying, "How did these nations worship their gods and even I will do the same"* (12:30).

S hortly after Rav Shach began serving as *Rosh Yeshivah* of Ponevezh Yeshivah, the then Prime Minister of Israel gave a very arrogant speech saturated with the sense that success is the result of human effort and power, rather than Divine intervention. Among other things, he said that the era of subservience to gentiles had ended; the era in which the *poritz* forced the Jew to dance before him and sing his praises was over. "Now," he said, "we are independent, and no one can tell us what to do!"

The absurdity is manifest. A nation that is dependent militarily, economically, and politically on the good will of foreign countries, a nation that could never have gotten off the ground without reparations payments, is not "independent." Such talk is merely sabre-rattling to show courage.

Rav Shach attacked the speech from a different angle. He said, "The *galus* (exile) Jew, when the *poritz* forced him to dance and sing his praises, felt nothing but disdain for the *poritz*. Maybe his feet were forced to dance, but in his heart he would say, '*Aleinu l'shabe'ach* ... — We must praise the Master of the Universe ... Who did not make us like the other nations....' To him, the *poritz* had the misfortune of having neither the pleasure of Shabbos nor the light of Torah. His heart would sing, 'Blessed is our God Who created us for His glory, separated us from the other nations, gave us the Torah of truth, and implanted within us eternal life!'

"Today, however, even if we do not have to actually dance, and even if we would be truly independent, with no need for aid, our people study foreign cultures. Even just studying their culture begins to draw me to follow them and become subservient to them. Rambam (*Hil. Avodas Kochavim* 2:2) explains that you should not inquire how the foreign gods were worshiped, even if you have no intention of serving them, for the inquiry itself causes one to be drawn after them and to do as their worshipers do.

"How much more so," concluded Rav Shach, "when people study alien cultures, intending to follow them. Are they not making themselves subservient to gentile culture? So, I ask you, who is better? The one who dances with his feet and feels disdain in his heart, or the one who expresses disdain but in his heart is subservient?"

וְלֹא־תַחְמֹל וְלֹא־תְכַסֶּה עָלָיו — *You shall not be compassionate and you shall not cover up for him* (13:9).

Rashi explains that this means that one may overturn the verdict if one finds a mitigating circumstance which benefits the inciter.

Rav Shach recounted how R' Chaim Soloveitchik of Brisk once said that the *Haskalah,* the "enlightenment" movement, was *treif* — absolutely not kosher. The *Maskilim* brazenly asked him how he could say such a thing, since he never issued halachic rulings; he referred all questions to Brisk's rabbinical judge.

R' Chaim replied: "It is true that I am afraid to issue halachic rulings. But that is only when there is any sort of doubt, no matter how remote. When there is no doubt whatsoever, though, I clearly rule that it is *treif*!"

וְלֹא־תַחְמֹל וְלֹא־תְכַסֶּה עָלָיו — *You shall not be compassionate and you shall not cover up for him* (13:9).

Rav Shach used to point out that the revered Chofetz Chaim took great care never to speak ill of a Jew, whomever he might be. There was one exception — the leader of the *Maskilim* in Vilna, Adam HaKohen Sherry, to whose name the Chofetz Chaim would add *yemach shemo* (may his name be erased). And why? Because when the Chofetz Chaim studied in Vilna in his youth, he became well known as a very bright young man who held great promise as a future Torah giant. Adam HaKohen himself came to him and tried to convince him to abandon his studies. The Chofetz Chaim shut out his arguments and moved to another city to escape the incitement.

The Chofetz Chaim used to marvel, "A Jew who believes in Hashem wants to bring merit to his friend by having him do a mitzvah. But why would a non-religious Jew go out of his way to make his friend sin? What can he possibly gain? The answer can only be that he serves the purpose of Satan. If so, then just as we ask for wickedness to be wiped out and for the powers of evil to be wiped out, so too, we should say of such a person, *yemach shemo!*"

בָּנִים אַתֶּם לַה׳ אֱלֹקֵיכֶם לֹא תִתְגֹּדְדוּ וְלֹא־תָשִׂימוּ קָרְחָה בֵּין עֵינֵיכֶם לָמֵת — *You are children to Hashem, your God — you shall not cut yourselves and you shall not make a bald spot between your eyes for a dead person* (14:1).

Rav Shach went to pay a condolence call to a man who had lost his wife. The man was broken and he tearfully said to Rav Shach, "Now I am all alone; what will become of me?!"

Rav Shach told him, "A Jew is never alone." Then he told him the story cited in the Midrash (*Devarim Rabbah* 2:16) about a Jew who was aboard a ship that came to port. The other travelers asked the Jew to go into town and buy provisions for them. He told them that he was a stranger there and all alone, and how would he manage? They told him that a Jew is never alone, for wherever he goes his God is with him; and they cited the verse (*Devarim* 4:7), "For which is a great nation that has a God Who is close to it as is Hashem, our God, whenever we call to Him?"

Rav Shach continued by citing the verse, "You are children to Hashem, your God — you shall not cut yourselves and you shall not make a bald spot between your eyes for a dead person." He then cited the explanation of Sforno — that since we are children to Hashem, we are never alone and we must not overly express great sorrow for any dead person. He finished by citing the Midrash (*Shemos Rabbah* 1:8) which states that although Yosef and his brothers died, their God did not die!

Finally, the widower was consoled.

וְכֹל שֶׁרֶץ הָעוֹף טָמֵא הוּא לָכֶם לֹא יֵאָכֵלוּ — *And every flying creeping creature is impure to you, they shall not be eaten* (14:19).

*I*n Rav Shach's later years, his grandson used to bring him his meals. One day, the grandson brought the meal as usual, but Rav Shach said he did not want to eat and he began crying. In response to his grandson asking why, he explained that since it was a very hot day, he was certain that bugs had fallen into the food, and since he could not check for them he did not want to eat.

The grandson offered to check the food, but Rav Shach refused. Finally, he agreed to eat on condition that his grandson sit right beside him and check each spoonful before he would put it into his mouth, to ascertain that there indeed were no bugs!

דֵי מַחְסֹרוֹ אֲשֶׁר יֶחְסַר לוֹ — *His requirement, whatever is lacking to him* (15:8).

*R*av Shach related that in the synagogue in Vilna in which R' Meir Michel Rabinowitz was the rabbi, there was a rich man who was generally called up to the Torah for *shishi* [the sixth person to be called up to the Torah], which is considered a great honor. This person would respond to the honor with generous donations for the upkeep of the synagogue. In the course of time, he lost his money and could no longer afford to donate money for the upkeep of the synagogue. Because of the need for money to maintain the synagogue, the officials wanted to call up others, who were still wealthy, for the honor of *Shishi*. R' Meir Michel insisted that they continue to accord the accustomed honor to the formerly wealthy man. His basis for this ruling was the Gemara (*Kesubos* 67b) which explains that "his requirement, whatever is lacking to him" teaches that if a formerly-wealthy poor person is now lacking a horse to ride on or a servant to run before him, that, too, should be granted him. The Gemara then cites the example of Hillel the elder, who used to make sure that a formerly-wealthy poor person had a horse to ride upon and a servant to run before him. One day, Hillel could not find a servant to run before this person, so he himself ran three *mil* before the poor person. R' Meir Michel explained that it is understandable that a horse is considered a "lack." It would be difficult for the person to walk everywhere. What "lack" is there, however, when there is no servant to run before him? The answer, he explained, was that for one who is accustomed to honor, honor is a need as well. Accordingly, when it is taken away he feels a real "lack."

Since this man had become accustomed to the honor of *shishi*, it becomes "his requirement which is lacking for him," and they must continue calling him up for *shishi*.

— וְשָׂמַחְתָּ בְּחַגֶּךָ אַתָּה וּבִנְךָ ... וְהַיָּתוֹם וְהָאַלְמָנָה אֲשֶׁר בִּשְׁעָרֶיךָ
*You shall rejoice on your festival — you, your son,
... the orphan and the widow who are in your cities*
(16:14).

*R*ambam (*Hil. Yom Tov* 6:17-18) writes: "A person must be happy in them and good-hearted; he, his children, wife, grandchildren, and all who accompany him, as it says, 'You shall rejoice on your festival...,' each as is fitting for him ... He should buy for the women nice clothing and jewelry ... and when he eats and drinks, he should make sure to feed the convert, the orphan, and the widow."

Once, right before Pesach, a time in which there are so many time-consuming preparations for the upcoming holiday, a major public-policy debate erupted. Rav Shach's house was a hub of activity; public figures came to give and receive advice, rumors abounded, and messengers came and went. In the midst of all this, Rav Shach said, "Please ask Mrs. So-and-so to come to me if she can."

Mrs. So-and-so was a widow who worked at a local school and was raising her only son all by herself. From time to time, she would come to Rav Shach's home for advice regarding her problems or to discuss one of the students under her charge.

She hurriedly came to Rav Shach's house on the hectic day before the holiday and stood at the door. The room was filled with people who surrounded Rav Shach.

As soon as he saw her, he quickly took her to a second room, handed her a respectable sum of money, and said, "Please, do me a favor and buy yourself some new clothes for the holiday."

שופטים — Shoftim

כִּי הַשֹּׁחַד יְעַוֵּר עֵינֵי חֲכָמִים — *For the bribe will blind the eyes of the wise* (16:19).

The Chazon Ish (*Emunah U'Bitachon*) writes that our Sages were above personal interests. The Talmudic statement (cited in *Tosafos, Chullin 5b, s.v. Tzaddikim*) that the "early ones were like angels" can be applied to those of the Talmudic period as well. If so, how could a bribe "blind the eyes of the wise and make righteous words crooked"? The Chazon Ish explains that this is a decree of the Torah, and since Hashem created the world according to the blueprint of the Torah, it was implanted in the nature of every person.

Rav Shach recounted the story of R' Shlomo Eiger, the renowned son of the great R' Akiva Eiger. His wife's grandfather, R' Hirsch, was quite wealthy, and in his will he left a fortune to the father of the first child in the family to carry his name. A son was born to R' Shlomo Eiger, and he was named Hirsch, in accordance with the will. The happiness was short-lived, however, for the baby died in its first month. Soon afterwards, another grandchild had a son and he, too, was named Hirsch. Each side now claimed the money. They went to the rabbi of Warsaw, the author of *Chemdas Shlomo*, to adjudicate the dispute. The rabbi asked for several days to decide the matter.

Now R' Shlomo Eiger was a brilliant Torah scholar. Certain of the rectitude of his claim, he wrote a thorough, well-reasoned responsum proving that the bequest should belong to him. Much to his consternation, the rabbi ruled in favor of the opposing side. Indignantly, he exclaimed, "I am certain that if such a case would come before my father he would rule differently!"

The Rabbi calmly replied, "And why do you think I pushed off my decision?" He then handed R' Shlomo a responsum written by his father, R' Akiva Eiger, in which the latter ruled exactly as the *Chemdas*

Shlomoh had. The Rabbi wisely realized that one cannot be objective enough to rule against oneself, and that R' Shlomo, certain of the rectitude of his claim, would appeal a decision that went against him. Therefore, he pushed off his decision until he could send the question to R' Akiva Eiger in Posen, and receive his answer — which was identical to his own — and only then stated his decision.

וְאֶל־הַשֹּׁפֵט אֲשֶׁר יִהְיֶה בַּיָּמִים הָהֵם — *And to the judge who will be in those days* (17:9).

Rashi explains: *In those days,* even if he is not as great as the other judges who preceded him, you must listen to him, for you have none but the judge who is in your days. The Gemara (*Rosh Hashanah* 25b) expresses this idea also as, "Yiftach [one of the lesser judges in the period of Judges] in his generation is like Shmuel [the greatest of the judges] in his generation."

R' Nosson Wachtfogel, the late *mashgiach* of Lakewood Yeshivah, was once discussing a problem with Rav Shach. Rav Shach said, "For such a problem, we need a Chofetz Chaim to decide!"

R' Nosson's son, R' Eliyahu Ber, who was present at the discussion, said, "Yiftach in his generation is like Shmuel in his generation."

Rav Shach responded, "*Nit kein Yiftach und nit kein dor* — There is no Yiftach and there is no generation!"

וְדָרַשְׁתָּ וְהִגִּידוּ לְךָ אֵת דְּבַר הַמִּשְׁפָּט — *You shall inquire and they will tell you the word of judgment* (17:9).

It does not say, "and they will tell you the judgment," but rather, "the word of judgment." The Netziv explains that this indicates that it is not sufficient to just state a ruling. Rather, they must inquire and investigate until they reach the truth. This is "the word of judgment."

The late R' Shimshon Pincus and R' Yaakov Horowitz once consulted Rav Shach concerning a delicate matter. Rav Shach considered the issue and carefully weighed the two sides of the question before issuing his decision.

When they had left, someone there asked Rav Shach, "Wasn't this same question asked several days ago, and didn't you rule the same way then?"

"I never rule based on yesterday's ruling," he replied.

When R' Chaim Kanievsky heard this story, he pointed out the

Gemara (*Yevamos* 109b) which states, "Whoever says, 'I only have Torah,' does not even have Torah, like one who gives his hand for a matter of law." Rashi explains that this refers to one who relies upon his recollection of the law.

לַעֲמֹד לְשָׁרֵת בְּשֵׁם־ה' — *To stand to minister in the name of Hashem* (18:5).

Rashi (based on the Gemara, *Zevachim* 23b) derives from this verse that ministering is done while standing.

Rav Shach once taught for three months at Yeshivah Beis Yosef in Jerusalem. Many years later, R' Perkowitz, an elderly Torah scholar who attended the yeshivah at that time, was asked if he knew Rav Shach. "Certainly," he replied, "I studied under him for three months." When asked if he could tell anything about Rav Shach, he answered, "What is there to tell — he never stopped learning!" He thought for a moment and added, "One thing I can say. In all those three months I never saw him sit! He stood by the *shtender,* stood near the *bimah* (central lectern), stood in prayer, and stood talking to the students. I did not see him sit for all three months!"

וְעָמְדוּ שְׁנֵי־הָאֲנָשִׁים — *Then the two men ... shall stand* (19:17).

Rashi (above 16:19) explains that this teaches that one should not stand while another person sits.

R' Asher Weiss recalls the time that he went to Rav Shach to "talk in learning." Rav Shach rose to greet him warmly — much to R' Weiss' consternation. He felt that it was not proper for the *Rosh Yeshivah,* at such an advanced age, to come to greet him. He quickly went over to Rav Shach's desk, but since he did not dare to sit down, he spoke to him while standing. Rav Shach continued standing, asking and answering, discussing and analyzing.

A member of the household approached R' Weiss and asked him to sit down. "Until you sit down," he said, "the *Rosh Yeshivah* will remain standing."

Another time, a student at the yeshivah approached Rav Shach's seat at the front of the study hall to ask him a question. Rav Shach smiled at him and said, "Please sit down next to me, because I feel weak and it is hard for me to get up."

The student was flustered, and Rav Shach repeated his request.

Finally, the student said, "It is unthinkable for me to sit in front, facing everyone else!"

Rav Shach waved disdainfully with his hand and said, "Front! Why we both know that there is no difference between front and back! But I'm sure you understand that it would be unthinkabe for you to stand and me to sit. It would be inappropriate!"

וְנִגְּשׁוּ הַכֹּהֲנִים בְּנֵי לֵוִי כִּי בָם בָּחַר ה'... וְעַל־פִּיהֶם יִהְיֶה כָּל־רִיב וְכָל־נָגַע — *The Kohanim, the offspring of Levi, shall approach, for them has Hashem ... chosen ... and according to their word shall be every dispute and every plague (21:5).*

The Netziv of Volozhin explains this verse based on the Gemara which states that a Torah scholar is responsible for his entire city. Therefore, Kohanim, the offspring of Levi, are responsible for all that occurs in the cities of Israel!

The rabbi of a city once came for a holiday visit to Rav Shach. Rav Shach asked him about the affairs of his city. The rabbi complained that the city *mikveh* was broken and the religious council was doing nothing to fix it. Rav Shach suggested that he build a private *mikveh* and the *Rosh Yeshivah* then placed a large sum of money on the table to be used for that purpose, informing the rabbi that he should be responsible for collecting the rest of the funds needed to build the *mikveh*. The rabbi apologized, saying that he was incapable of such fund-raising.

Rav Shach did not say a thing.

All the next day, the phone in the religious council chairman's office rang off the hook. Influential people were calling to complain to him about the irresponsible neglect in not fixing the *mikveh*. One of the callers inadvertently mentioned that it was Rav Shach who had asked that he call.

That very day, funds were "discovered" and the *mikveh* was beautifully refurbished.

And all because of a holiday visit — one of hundreds of visitors that day!

כי תצא — Ki Seitzei

וְלֹא־יִלְבַּשׁ גֶּבֶר שִׂמְלַת אִשָּׁה כִּי תוֹעֲבַת יְהֹוָה אֱלֹהֶיךָ כָּל־עֹשֵׂה אֵלֶּה — *Nor shall a man wear a woman's garment, for anyone who does so is an abomination of Hashem (22:5).*

Based on this prohibition, the *Shulchan Aruch* (*Yoreh Deah* 156:2) rules that a man may not look at his reflection in a mirror except for specific instances.

In one of Rav Shach's public campaigns to champion Torah *hashkafah*, a detailed article appeared in an American Yiddish-language newspaper. When Rav Shach was told about it, he asked to see the article so he could see whether his motives and message were clear.

Also in that issue of the newspaper was a memorial article regarding R' Reuven Grozovsky. While leafing through the newspaper, Rav Shach noticed R' Reuven's picture and immediately identified it, mentioning that they had met during the First World War. Then he found the article about his campaign, which had a picture of him. Rav Shach looked at the picture and, obviously puzzled, asked, "Who is this — maybe R' Yaakov Yitzchak Ruderman? It is not a good picture of him!"

לֹא תִלְבַּשׁ שַׁעַטְנֵז צֶמֶר וּפִשְׁתִּים יַחְדָּו — *You shall not wear combined fibers, wool and linen together (22:11).*

A student who had studied under Rav Shach's former students while he was at Kletzk Yeshivah in Rechovot relates that, in the middle of a lecture, one of those present blurted out that there was a question about *shaatnez*, a prohibited combination of wool and linen, in one of Rav Shach's garments. To the astonishment of the students, Rav Shach immediately rose and removed the garment!

וְשָׂם לָהּ עֲלִילֹת דְּבָרִים וְהוֹצִא עָלֶיהָ שֵׁם רָע — *And he makes a wanton accusation against her, spreading libel against her* (22:14).

*A*t the height of the First World War, with the death toll constantly rising and fear an ever-present companion of combatants and civilians alike, R' Isser Zalman Meltzer took Rav Shach under his wing and asked him to sleep in his house. R' Isser Zalman said that hosting a Torah scholar who toils at his Torah study is better for protecting one's home than any amulet.

Rav Shach, when retelling this story, would marvel at the modesty of R' Isser Zalman. After all, he was the prince of Torah and yet, he did not value his Torah study and righteousness but required a yeshivah student as an "amulet." As an example of how to develop a close relationship with a student, Rav Shach would recount how R' Isser Zalman would always look at the commentary that Rav Shach was writing, and add comments of his own.

Once, R' Isser Zalman saw what Rav Shach had written regarding the Rambam's ruling based on this verse (*Hil. Naarah Besulah* 3:3): "It is only judged in the presence of the Temple and in a court of twenty-three, because this law of libel involves capital law, since if what he says is true, she is put to death." Rav Shach was bothered by the fact that there seemed to be no source for saying that this is only judged in the presence of the Temple. As a result, he remarked in the margin: "But when the Temple is not present, it may be judged by a court of three since there is no capital punishment then." In conclusion, he wrote, "And I am surprised that none of the commentaries mention this."

When R' Isser Zalman saw this, he told Rav Shach, "This is unquestionably true. You have brought to light a point that even the early commentaries seem to have missed. Every person has his portion of Torah, and this comment is your portion. Indeed, we are taught that the Torah Moshe received at Sinai included even the questions a prize student was destined to ask."

לֹא-יָבֹא עַמּוֹנִי וּמוֹאָבִי בִּקְהַל יְהוָה — *An Ammonite or Moabite shall not enter the congregation of Hashem* (23:4).

The Gemara (*Yevamos* 76b) relates that Doeg attempted to disqualify David from being considered a Jew in good standing, since David was the offspring of Ruth the Moabite. Avner told him, "The verse [which prohibits marrying descendants of Ammon and Moab] says ... *Moavi*, in the masculine form from which we can infer, 'but not a *Moavis*, a female Moabite.' " Doeg persisted. "Does that mean that when the Torah says *mamzer* (ibid. 23:3) in masculine form only a male *mamzer* is prohibited, and when it speaks of an Egyptian (ibid. 23:8) in the masculine form, does it mean only a male Egyptian is prohibited?" "The case of Ammon and Moab is different, for Scripture itself gives the reason [for the law] — because they did not greet you with bread and water." It is generally the males who go out to greet people, not the females," replied Avner. "The men could have greeted men and the women could have greeted women," Doeg challenged.

Avner had no answer. King Shaul said, "If the law is not clear, go ask in the study hall." They told him, "... *Moabite* is said in the masculine form to exclude females." Doeg presented his questions, and they had no answer. They were about to declare David unfit when Amasa put on his sword and declared, "Whoever does not listen to this law shall be stabbed with the sword. This is the tradition received from the court of Shmuel of Ramah: ... *Moabite* is said in the masculine form to exclude females."

The Brisker Rav, R' Yitzchak Zev Soloveitchik, said that this was the mistake made by the "redeemer" who refused to marry Ruth "lest I imperil my own inheritance" (*Ruth* 4:6). He was afraid that a subsequent court would arise and rule, in accordance with Doeg, that a female Moabite is disqualified. He thought that the law was a derivation and was unaware that it was actually a law handed to Moshe at Sinai (*Halachah L'Moshe MiSinai*).

When the Brisker Rav said this, those present reacted coolly. Seeing this, he said, "Soon, R' Leizer [Rav Eliezer Shach] will be here, you will see his joy when he hears this novel point!"

Indeed, the Brisker Rav used to say, "I present every novel idea I come up with to R' Leizer first, because he knows how to extract the essence of the novel point, and how to be impressed by it. The Sages (*Shir HaShirim Rabbah* 4:23) explain the verse (*Shir HaShirim* 4:11), 'honey and milk beneath your tongue,' — 'if one says words of Torah in public that are not as tasty as milk and honey, it would be better for him never to have said them!' Thus you see that appreciation of the thought is a prerequisite for honoring the Torah. This condition I find only by R' Leizer!"

לֹא־יָבֹא עַמּוֹנִי וּמוֹאָבִי בִּקְהַל ה׳ . . . עַל־דְּבַר אֲשֶׁר לֹא־קִדְּמוּ אֶתְכֶם בַּלֶּחֶם וּבַמָּיִם — *An Ammonite or Moabite shall not enter the congregation of Hashem . . . because of the fact that they did not greet you with bread and water* (23:4-5).

amban explains that Scripture instructs us to distance these two nations, descendants of brothers, for Avraham had done kindness with them when he saved their ancestors from the sword and from prison (see *Bereishis* 14:16). Furthermore, it was in Avraham's merit that they were saved from the fate of Sodom (see ibid. 19:29).

Accordingly, they were obligated to repay Israel with kindness instead of the malevolence they exhibited. One of them (the Moabites) hired Bilam to curse them, and the other (the Ammonites) did not greet them with bread and water when they came nearby (above, 2:18). Ramban concludes that the sin of Ammon was greater than the sin of Moav, and thus they are mentioned first in the verse.

The implications are astounding! According to Ramban, Moav did greet Israel with bread and water, but they hired Bilam to curse them and bring about their utter destruction. If their plan would not have been thwarted by Hashem, they would have succeeded in their nefarious plot (see *Berachos* 7a). On the other hand, Israel did not really need Ammon's bread and water — the manna fell each day. Wells provided them with water. Yet Ammon's sin is considered worse! We can deduce from this that the greatest form of ingratitude is not paying attention to another being!

Once Rav Shach had to travel to Jerusalem for a meeting of the board of *Chinuch Atzma'i*. He would generally travel with Rabbi Shraga Grossbard, Director of *Chinuch Atzma'i*, but the latter was abroad at the time. Someone who knew Rav Shach sent a message that he had to be in Jerusalem in any case, and that he would be happy to take the *Rosh Yeshivah*, but Rav Shach firmly refused his offer.

The *Rosh Yeshivah* was asked to explain the reason for his refusal. "After all," they told him, "you will save so much time! If you don't take the ride, you will have to take a bus to Tel Aviv, another bus to Jerusalem, and then a local bus in Jerusalem."

"Don't you understand?" he asked. "If I travel with that man, I am indebted to him. As a result, I will have to carry on a conversation with him, and express interest in all his affairs. I will be wasting time for the entire length of the trip, time that could otherwise be used to study Torah. If I travel by bus, however, I can learn Torah on the way to Tel Aviv, learn on the way to Jerusalem, and learn in Jerusalem."

עַל־דְּבַר אֲשֶׁר לֹא־קִדְּמוּ אֶתְכֶם בַּלֶּחֶם וּבַמַּיִם — *Because of the fact that they did not greet you with bread and water* (23:5).

R' Simchah Kook, the chief rabbi of Rechovot, relates the following story: Rav Shach was once scheduled to speak at a gathering of *roshei yeshivah* of Torah high schools. However, the *Rosh Yeshivah* was feeling so weak that he had to cancel the appointment. That day he received no visitors.

Despite his infirmity, he gathered whatever remaining strength he had to pay a condolence call to the Kook family on the loss of R' Simchah's mother, Rebbetzin Kook of Tiberias. When asked about this, the *Rosh Yeshivah* explained that the obligation to show gratitude supersedes all other considerations.

And why did he feel so obligated to show gratitude? Because someone in the Soloveitchik family used to bother R' Yitzchak Zev Soloveitchik, the Brisker Rav, and Rebbetzin Kook took this person under her wing and devotedly took care of him. As a result, a burden was lifted off the Brisker Rav.

As a result of the Rebbetzin's kindness, the Brisker Rav was more available to discuss Torah with Rav Shach. For this, Rav Shach felt boundless gratitude.

לֹא־תְתַעֵב מִצְרִי כִּי־גֵר הָיִיתָ בְאַרְצוֹ — *You shall not abhor an Egyptian, for you were a sojourner in his land* (23:8).

Rav Shach often mentioned the Gemara (*Bava Kamma* 92b) which teaches the extent of the obligation to show gratitude, by stating, "What is the basis for the folk expression, 'Do not throw stones in the well from which you drink'? The verse, 'You shall not abhor an Egyptian, for you were a sojourner in his land.'"

One time, Rav Shach called one of his confidants and asked him to find a *kollel* fellow to study with a certain young man in the Nachalas Yaakov Yeshivah, to help him advance in his studies. He told the confidant to come to him on the first of each Hebrew month for money to pay the tutor.

The confidant did as he was asked, found an excellent tutor, set the price, and paid him each month. One month, he came to Rav Shach's house on the first, but could not get in because there was an important meeting going on. The next day, Rav Shach sought him out and asked him why he did not come. He replied that he had come but could not get in. Rav Shach apologized for his trouble and gave him the money. Meanwhile, the confidant felt that this was the perfect time to ask why Rav Shach was so concerned about this young man.

"In my youth," began Rav Shach, "I had only one shirt. Each week I would secretly wash it, and I would freeze in the bitter winds while it dried. Eventually, as a result of constant wear and tear, the shirt wore out and a large hole tore open in its back. I used to rush to be first in the *beis midrash*, and for hours on end I would not get up from my seat so that the back of the chair should hide the tear. One of the local women found out, and she sent me two shirts! That was my salvation: I could stand up while I learned and could go at will to the library, and when I washed one shirt I could wear the other.

"This young man," concluded Rav Shach, "is the grandson of that woman."

כִּי־יִקַּח אִישׁ אִשָּׁה — *If a man marries a woman* (24:1).

Just about every night in the month of Elul 5739 (1979) there was a wedding of one of the students of the Ponevezh Yeshivah and, as a result, the evening session was poorly attended, making it difficult for those who did attend to concentrate on their studies. The month of Elul, which precedes the High Holy Days, is traditionally the month during which spiritual preparation for the High Holy Days takes place, and Rav Shach was greatly distressed by the situation. He got up to speak before the yeshivah and said, "Perhaps you will make fun of an old man like me — who needs God's mercy each and every day — talking about next year. Nevertheless, I feel that I cannot keep silent. I am warning you and letting you know in advance that next year, not a single student will attend a single wedding in the month of Elul. This is an absolute ruling, with no excuses and no exceptions."

Afterwards, he was asked how any reason, good as it might be, could be sufficient to supersede the mitzvah of getting married. This mitzvah is derived from the Torah — "If a man marries a woman," and is listed by Rambam (*Mitzvah* 213).

Rav Shach replied, "If you would have paid attention to what I said, you would have seen that there is no question. I did not say that it is *forbidden* to get married in the month of Elul. Of course it is permitted. I only said that the yeshivah students would not attend the wedding!"

נָקִי יִהְיֶה לְבֵיתוֹ שָׁנָה אֶחָת וְשִׂמַּח אֶת־אִשְׁתּוֹ אֲשֶׁר־לָקָח — *He shall be free for his house for one year, and he shall gladden the wife whom he has married (24:5).*

In his younger years in Lithuania, Rav Shach studied in the Slobodka Yeshivah for two years, and considered its *mashgiach*, known as the Alter of Slobodka, to be his rabbi and mentor.

Rav Shach recalled that the Alter once chastised a young man before his wedding day, using the verse, "He shall be free for his house...." In Rav Shach's words: "I do not remember exactly what happened, but I noted one thing: The Alter's emphasis was on 'free' (*naki* in Hebrew, which generally connotes cleanliness and purity), not on 'he shall gladden.'"

כי תבא — Ki Savo

וּבָאתָ אֶל־הַכֹּהֵן אֲשֶׁר יִהְיֶה בַּיָּמִים הָהֵם וְאָמַרְתָּ אֵלָיו — *You* — *shall come to the Kohen who shall be in those days, and you shall say to him (26:3).*

Rashi cites *Sifrei*: " 'And you shall say to him' — that you are not unappreciative." Rav Shach, in his discourses — and even more so through his own behavior — taught how important it is to acquire this quality of appreciation.

One of many examples: When Rav Shach lived in Jerusalem, his landlord was R' Alter Shub. Many years passed. He had long since moved to Bnei Brak, become the *Rosh Yeshivah* and the leader of the generation. R' Avraham Kahaneman saw him on his way somewhere and asked him, "Where is the *Rosh Yeshivah* going?" Rav Shach replied that he was on his way to an engagement party.

"What is your connection to the *chasan* (groom)?" he asked.

Rav Shach answered simply, "The brother of the *chasan* is married to the granddaughter of my landlord!"

הִגַּדְתִּי הַיּוֹם לַה' אֱלֹקֶיךָ כִּי־בָאתִי אֶל־הָאָרֶץ — *I declare* — *today to Hashem, your God, that I have come to the Land (26:3).*

Rav Shach asked: "A Jew has two trees and their fruit ripens. He takes a basket, adorns it, and ascends to Jerusalem to show appreciation. He comes to the Temple and gives thanks to his God. For what? 'You shall come to the Kohen who shall be in those days, and you shall say to him: I declare today to Hashem, your God, that I have come to the Land that Hashem swore to our forefathers to give us.' Though his family has been living in the Land for generations, he says 'I have come,' " Rav Shach noted, "because he is declaring his appreciation for his forefathers having inherited it."

"And there is even more that he says," Rav Shach continued. " 'An Aramean would have destroyed my father, and he descended to Egypt ... Hashem took us out of Egypt with a strong hand and with an outstretched arm, with great awesomeness, and with signs and with wonders ... and now, behold! I have brought the first fruit of the ground that you have given me, O Hashem!' While one can understand the last part, where he expresses gratitude for the fruit, but why does he start with ancient history?

"This teaches us," answered Rav Shach, "what a true expression of gratitude should be. It was my uncle, R' Isser Zalman Meltzer, who taught me this idea. He noted that King David, in his Psalm for the inauguration of the Temple (30), did not go right into thanks for its inauguration. Instead, he began by saying, 'I will exalt you, Hashem, for You have drawn me up, and not let my foes rejoice over me. Hashem, You have raised up my soul from the lower world; You have preserved me from my descent to the pit ... You have transformed my lament into dancing for me. You undid my sackcloth and girded me with gladness.' This teaches us that it is not sufficient to just give thanks for the most recent salvation. Rather, one must give thanks for every single favor Hashem — or a person — has done for us, all along the way."

וַנִּצְעַק אֶל־ה׳ אֱלֹקֵי אֲבֹתֵינוּ — *Then we cried out to Hashem the God of our forefathers* (26:6).

The Midrash (*Devarim Rabbah, Va'eschanan*) lists ten names used by the Torah for prayer, including צְעָקָה, *crying out*.

Rav Shach was very impressed by the following story that he heard from his good friend, the Rebbe of Strikov: A Karliner chassid once went on a business trip to Vienna and had to stay there over the weekend. He decided that he would attend the synagogue of the Chortkover Rebbe for the Shabbos prayers. On Wednesday, he went in with great awe to request that the Rebbe give him a blessing, and to ask the Rebbe the following question: Since it is the custom of Karliner chassidim to shout their prayers, would the Rebbe mind if he prayed this way in the Chortkover synagogue? The Rebbe responded very critically, "What kind of way is that, to shout the prayers? Why, you are standing before the King, and you should pray quietly and with awe! That is our custom and it shall not be changed!"

"Well, I guess I won't be able to pray there!" the chassid said to himself. But when Shabbos came, however, he had found no better place to pray, so he attended the Chortkover synagogue, doing his best to damp down his enthusiasm and to control his feelings. When he reached *Nishmas kol chai,* however, all the dams burst — he was no longer able to control himself and he cried out with all his might.

After the services, he was mortified that he defied the Rebbe's express wishes. He immediately approached the Rebbe to apologize.

The Rebbe was puzzled. "Why are you apologizing?" he asked. "Quite the contrary; crying out is one of the ten forms of prayer, and crying out while praying is preferable to a cold prayer."

The chassid was dumfounded, "Didn't the Rebbe say ..." he stammered.

The Rebbe smiled and explained, "Don't you understand? When a Jew comes on Wednesday and says that he intends to cry out on Shabbos, it is incumbent on me to notify him that that is not the normal way of prayer, nor its desired form. When he is in the midst of prayer, however, and his heart bursts forth with a cry, why, there can be nothing more wonderful and praiseworthy!"

וְשָׂמַחְתָּ בְכָל־הַטּוֹב — *You shall rejoice with all the goodness* (26:11).

Ohr HaChaim writes: " 'With all the goodness' hints also at the Torah, as our Sages say (*Avodah Zarah* 19b), 'Goodness refers to Torah.' If only people would feel the sweetness and pleasantness of the Torah's goodness, they would lose all control and would pursue it, for the Torah includes all the goodness in the world."

One Purim, the yeshivah students went to Rav Shach's house and the atmoshere was quite festive.

Suddenly, Rav Shach asked a question, "Who can tell me why nowadays people do not learn?"

An atmosphere of seriousness descended on the room. Nobody had any idea what to say.

So Rav Shach answered his own question: "People do not learn nowadays because people do not learn ..."

And he explained, "If people would learn the way they should, they would discover the incredible sweetness of the Torah, and they would not be able to break themselves away from it!"

אָרוּר אֲשֶׁר לֹא־יָקִים אֶת־דִּבְרֵי הַתּוֹרָה־הַזֹּאת — *Accursed is one who will not uphold the words of this Torah* (27:26).

amban cites *Yerushalmi* (*Sotah* 7:4), that a person who learns and teaches, keeps the Torah and does [its mitzvos], but has the opportunity to support it and does not, is included in this curse.

Rav Shach related that, once, when the Chofetz Chaim was in his advanced old age, they carried him into the *Vaad HaYeshivos* meeting in Bialystok, and he said, "Believe me, my dear brothers, I am so weak that I would not come here for a hundred pieces of gold. Why do I say, 'a hundred pieces of gold'? I am so weak that I would not even come for a hundred mitzvos! But for the sake of strengthening Torah, I just had to come."

Rav Shach would add, "Do you have any idea what a mitzvah was worth to the Chofetz Chaim? Why, our Sages (*Makkos* 10a) say that the verse (*Koheles* 5:9), 'One who loves money will never be satisfied with money' refers to Moshe who would not relinquish the opportunity to perform even half of a mitzvah — setting up the three Cities of Rrefuge located in trans-Jordan, even though they wold not be effective until the three Cities of Refuge in Eretz Yisrael would be set up. A whole mitzvah is obviously more valuable — and the Chofetz Chaim was so weak that he would forego a hundred mitzvos! How weak he must have been! And yet, Torah is a different matter entirely! For the sake of Torah, the Chofetz Chaim felt compelled to come."

In Rav Shach's own advanced old age, he once returned from a wedding totally exhausted and said to the grandson who had accompanied him, "Believe me, I would not have gone to the wedding for 10,000 pieces of gold but what could I do? The family supports Torah and I could not refuse!"

וְהָיִיתָ מְשֻׁגָּע מִמַּרְאֵה עֵינֶיךָ אֲשֶׁר תִּרְאֶה — *You will go mad from the sight of your eyes that you will see* (28:34).

Avraham Yitzchak Kook recalls the time when he traveled by taxi to Bnei Brak, one Chol HaMoed, to pay a holiday visit to Rav Shach. He noticed that the streets were unusually empty. The taxi driver said to him, "Everybody is at home either watching or listening to the soccer finals that the Israeli team is now playing. Actually, I, too, wanted very much to watch it, and it was only out of my great respect for you that I agreed to this trip." He turned on the radio to listen to the news and was ecstatic when he heard that the Israeli national team had won!

When R' Kook arrived, he went into Rav Shach's room. Instead of the warm *shalom aleichem* to which he had become accustomed, Rav Shach greeted him bitterly by saying, "Aha! We won! The whole country is celebrating!"

A few minutes later, Rav Shach said in a voice filled with pain, "If not for the fact that it is Chol HaMoed, it would be proper to declare a public fast!"

R' Kook did not understand what disturbed him so much, and his bafflement must have been apparent.

"Look," said Rav Shach, "this is worse than sinning. They have totally perverted the concept and significance of man. The important part of man is the 'image of God' in which he is created — the ability to reason and think logically. They have turned it all upside down, measuring the importance and success of a person by how well he kicks."

"I pity them," commented R' Kook.

"Them?" asked Rav Shach. "I would not declare a public fast for *them*. The pity is on *us*, for it is beginning to affect our people. And don't tell me that it has no effect, because I can prove to you that it already has had an effect: Tell me, the truth; do you view these people as if they are mad or insane? If not, you too have been affected!"

תַּחַת אֲשֶׁר לֹא־עָבַדְתָּ אֶת־יְהֹוָה אֱלֹהֶיךָ בְּשִׂמְחָה וּבְטוּב לֵבָב —
Because you did not serve Hashem, your God, with gladness and with goodness of heart (28:47).

R' Yaakov Katz brought his son with him to visit Rav Shach, and asked for guidance on how to lead his son to be successful in his Torah studies, and make the most of his abilities.

Rav Shach replied, "The main way to grow in Torah learning is by doing everything with joy and enthusiasm. The most important thing is to make sure that everything is done with enthusiasm. It is forbidden to torture oneself with deprivation of food or sleep, for that has a negative effect on one's joy of life. A youth should feel tremendous satisfaction from reviewing his weekly studies each Friday and summarizing them. In addition, he should study the book *Ketzos Ha-Choshen* every Shabbos to increase his joy and enthusiasm for learning. The only way to guarantee that he will become great in Torah is to make sure that everything is always with joy."

Another time, Rav Shach reprimanded a young man in his 20's and said, "Why do you have such a scowl on your face? Why do you look so upset?" The young man replied that he was in a bad mood.

"That's impossible!" exclaimed Rav Shach. "Why, the Gemara is open right in front of you. It brings one such great joy!"

גּוֹי אֲשֶׁר לֹא־תִשְׁמַע לְשֹׁנוֹ — *A nation whose language you will not understand* (28:49).

A young man was once discussing a Torah subject with Rav Shach, and he was being very illogical. Rav Shach fondly gave the fellow a slap on the back and smilingly told him, "You are talking like a Turkish drunkard."

The young man looked at Rav Shach quizzically.

Rav Shach smiled and explained, "This is not my expression. I heard it from my uncle, R' Isser Zalman Meltzer. A drunkard has no idea of what he is saying, but those who hear him can understand the foolish things he says. A Turkish drunkard, however, whose language is not understood by those around him, is different. He has no idea of what he is saying and those who hear him do not understand a word either!"

נצבים — Nitzavim

עַל־מֶה עָשָׂה יְהוָה כָּכָה לָאָרֶץ הַזֹּאת — *For what reason did Hashem do so to this Land?* (29:23).

*I*n *Pirkei Avos* (3:1) we are exhorted to be aware of the fact that we will one day have to give a דִּין וְחֶשְׁבּוֹן, an "accounting and reckoning," of all our deeds, before God. The Gaon of Vilna explains that the words "accounting" and "reckoning" refer to two distinct items to which we will have to respond: "Accounting" refers to responding for actually committing the sin, while "reckoning" relates to the fact that the time and effort expended in committing the sin could have been directed instead toward doing a *good* deed. Thus, when a person sins, he has, in effect, committed a double misdeed — (1) he has transgressed, and (2) he has squandered an opportunity to do a mitzvah.

The Brisker Rav noted, however, that any time one fails to do a mitzvah he is effectively committing a sin, and is subject to punishment for his inaction. This being the case, both "accounting" and "reckoning" still refer to the commission of a sin.

Rav Shach resolved this problem as follows: A person who refrains from doing a mitzva can ordinarily offer the excuse that he just did not have the strength, time, capability, etc. to do *anything* at that time. Once a person commits a transgression, however, he can no longer use this argument, for if he had the capability to engage in sin, he could just as well have channeled those resources toward doing a mitzvah instead.

The *Rosh Yeshivah* also offered an entirely different explanation for the Mishnah's use of the dual expression "accounting and reckoning." Besides the actual "accounting" for the sin per se, there are all sorts of indirect consequences brought about by the sin.

For instance, if a pious person — one who is looked up to and respected by the public — commits a misdeed, and is punished for his sin, there is an element of *chillul Hashem* involved, for when people see misfortune befalling a pious person, their faith in Divine justice is shaken. *Pirkei Avos* (4:4) teaches that one is held accountable for causing a *chillul Hashem* whether he did so deliberately or unintentionally. Therefore, in addition to the punishment meted out for the sin itself, God makes a "reckoning" for the *chillul Hashem* that was indirectly brought about by the sin.

Rav Shach's grandson pointed out to him that according to this reasoning, a wicked person who is inflicted with punishment for a sin should be credited with having brought about a *kiddush Hashem,* for serving as an illustration of Divine justice. The *Rosh Yeshivah* agreed that this would indeed be a logical corollary of his explanation.

וְשַׁבְתָּ עַד־יְהֹוָה אֱלֹהֶיךָ — *And you will return unto Hashem, your God* (30:2).

The Rambam writes (*Hil. Teshuvah* 4:5): "Although repentance and prayer are always desirable, during the ten days between Rosh Hashanah and Yom Kippur they are especially desirable, and are accepted immediately."

Rav Shach lived all his life paying constant attention to the principles of repentance and soul-searching, and markedly so when the days of repentance — Elul and the High Holy Days — arrived. Whoever spoke to him or was in his presence during those times could detect a fear of these Days of Judgment in everything the *Rosh Yeshivah* said and did. He exhorted the yeshivah students, as well, to take advantage of these awesome days.

The *Rosh Yeshivah's* grandson, Rav Isser Zalman Bergman, relates: "A few years ago I held a bar mitzvah celebration for one of my sons during the Ten Days of Repentance. When I went over to my grandfather to invite him to the festivities, he became upset and protested, 'How can one make a bar mitzvah party during the Ten Days of Repentance?! It is a totally inappropriate time for a celebration!'

"Only after I apologized profusely and explained that the invitations had already been sent out did he agree — grudgingly — to allow the bar mitzvah to take place. The awe of judgment-time so pervaded his mindset during Elul that he could not fathom how anyone would ever dream of making a bar mitzvah party during these days!"

כִּי־קָרוֹב אֵלֶיךָ הַדָּבָר מְאֹד — *The matter is very near to you* (30:14).

*I*n 5746 (1986) the *Rosh Yeshivah* delivered an address at the yeshivah *Tiferes HaTalmud*, where he said, among other things:

"When a person becomes old, he sometimes wants to rip out his hair in aggravation over all the time he now realizes that he had wasted on foolish things during his lifetime! You are still young! Utilize your time and energies properly, so that you will not have regrets later!

"Torah learning can be compared to studying medicine. If one wants to work in the field of medicine, he can do so in many different capacities — as an orderly, a nurse, a paramedic, a physician's assistant, an physician, a surgeon, and so on. It all depends on how much time and effort he invests in his training. So it is with Torah as well; the level one attains is in proportion to his efforts. But there is this difference: in medicine there is no guarantee that if one toils he will succeed, while in Torah study we are told that it is impossible for one to toil without seeing results (*Megillah* 6b). The Torah itself testifies that 'It (the Torah) is very near to you, it is in your mouth and in your heart to achieve it.'

"I heard that when someone told the Vilna Gaon that he was known far and wide as 'the Vilner Gaon (*Gaon of Vilna*),' he replied, 'Well, there is truth in that statement: *Vill nor — if you really want (in Yiddish) — you will be a Gaon!*'

"It is all in your hands. Don't pass up this opportunity!"

כִּי הוּא חַיֶּיךָ — *For He is your life and the length of your days* (30:20).

*A*s is well known, R' Chaim Ozer Grodzinsk dedicated himself selflessly and ceaselessly to the needs of the community; in a sense, he was the "father of all of Israel."

One time, after many long hours of dealing with community matters, followed by several more hours of receiving visitors seeking guidance, advice, assistance, and counsel, Rav Chaim Ozer turned to Rav Shach and said, "Up to now I have been devoting myself to 'Other-Worldly' affairs. Now it is time to enjoy a little of 'This World'!" Whereupon the two of them began to delve into lengthy, learned discussions of Torah topics!

וילך — Vayeilech

וּבְנֵיהֶם אֲשֶׁר לֹא־יָדְעוּ יִשְׁמְעוּ וְלָמְדוּ — *And their children who do not know — they shall hear and learn* (31:13).

n the aftermath of a spate of *charedi* vandalism against bus shelters that carried obscene advertisements, and the subsequent uproar this caused in secular Israeli circles, a certain popular rabbi active in the *teshuvah* movement was approached by the media to be interviewed about this topic. Since the incidents in which bus shelters were totally destroyed were generating a great deal of resentment against *charedi* Jews in general, the rabbi agreed to the interview, hoping that he might somehow be able to dispel the hostile atmosphere.

He called his mentor and guide Rav Shach for advice as to what message he should seek to convey to the television audience. The *Rosh Yeshivah* responded, "My friend, go out there and tell them that the main thing is to learn Torah!"

The rabbi was somewhat baffled by Rav Shach's answer. How would this response satisfy the relentless questions of an aggressive interviewer? He suspected that perhaps Rav Shach was not a great expert on the subject of television interviews — and indeed how should he be? Nevertheless, he accepted the counsel of his rabbi without question, and went for the interview.

Each time the interviewer asked a question, the rabbi replied with the answer supplied to him by Rav Shach: "The main thing is to learn Torah!" The interviewer, who had viewed his guest as "easy prey," given the vulgarity and the tremendous unpopularity of the acts that this rabbi was supposed to defend, soon became flustered by the seemingly evasive answer that was repeated again and again. He tried several times to steer the rabbi away from his repetitious message about the importance of learning Torah, but in the end he was forced to give up and bring the interview to a close.

"Today," that rabbi relates, "the video of that interview is used in journalism school, as a prime example of how to keep one's cool while under verbal assault during an interview, and how not to allow oneself to be 'led like a lamb to the slaughter' by a hostile, superiorly skilled interviewer! And it was all because I listened to Rav Shach's advice!"

האזינו — Haazinu

יַעֲרֹף כַּמָּטָר לִקְחִי — *Let my teaching drip like the rain* (32:2).

*I*n this verse, the Torah's teachings are compared to rain, a metaphor explained on many levels. *Ohr HaChaim* writes, "Just as lack of rain can bring death to people, so the lack of Torah can cause death (יַעֲרֹף also means beheading) to a person."

Rav Shach's devotion to Torah learning was apparent to all those who knew him. A close student of the *Rosh Yeshivah* relates: "One Shabbos moring after prayers, Rav Shach approached me and asked, 'Do you know what the suffering of Gehinnom is like?'

" 'Not really,' I answered to the puzzling question.

" 'Imagine that you have thought of a way to understand a difficult statement of the Rambam, and you want to check out the text to see if the interpretation fits into his words. But it is late Friday night, and all you have is a dim oil lamp, burning high up on the wall. You appoint a 'watchman' to make sure you don't adjust the lamp on Shabbos (as is required by halachah when reading by the light of an adjustable flame), take a Rambam, and go next to the lamp. It's still too dark to see, so you climb up on a chair to get closer — but you still can't make out the words. You jump up with the book to try to get a bit closer, but it doesn't help. Now, that's Gehinnom!' "

"I thought to myself, 'okay, if that's Gehinnom, I think I can handle it!' But I wondered why the *Rosh Yeshivah* suddenly decided to share this thought with me. On the way out of shul I met the *Rosh Yeshivah's* grandson who told me, 'I don't know what came over my grandfather last night. He woke up in the middle of the night and said to me, "Be a watchman for me!" Then he groped in the dark until he pulled a book off the shelf. He opened it and stood on top of a chair. Then he pulled over a table and climbed on top of *that*. Then — the strangest part of it all — he started to jump up and down toward the lamp over the cupboard! So strange!' "

כִּי שֵׁם יְהוָה אֶקְרָא הָבוּ גֹדֶל לֵאלֹהֵינוּ — *When I call out the Name of Hashem, ascribe greatness to our God* (32:3).

The *Sifrei* derives from here that after hearing someone utter a blessing to God, he should "ascribe greatness to Him" by answering, "Amen!" (See also Rashi on *Berachos* 21a.)

Rav Shach related that when Graf (Count) Potocki, the well-known convert, was executed *al kiddush Hashem* in the 18th century for the crime of converting to Judaism, R' Alexander Ziskind of Horodna (the author of *Yesod V'Shoresh HaAvodah*) made a supreme effort to be present — even concealing his identity, for no Jews were allowed to witness the execution. He did so, he said, in order to have the rare, tremendous privilege of being able to hear the blessing recited by a Jew when he is martyred for his faith: "Blessed is Hashem, Who has sanctified us with His commandments and commanded us to sanctify the Name of Heaven," and to answer "Amen" to it.

אֵל אֱמוּנָה וְאֵין עָוֶל צַדִּיק וְיָשָׁר הוּא — *A faithful God without iniquity, righteous and fair is He* (32:4).

When Rav Shach would pay a condolence call, he would sometimes recount to the mourners the following story. It involved the Rav who taught R' Chaim Brisker (Soloveitchic), R' David Blinder ("the Blind one)," who was given that appellation because he controlled his sight so absolutely that he never extended his gaze beyond his immediate vicinity.

When R' David's brother was deathly ill, he went to visit and comfort him. He saw that in addition to suffering from excruciating physical pain, his brother was in a state of great mental anguish as well. The brother explained to R' David that, like the great R' Yochanan ben Zakkai before him, he was terrified of the judgment that he would soon have to face: "There are two paths before me — one to Gan Eden and the other to Gehinnom — and I don't know down which one I will be led!" (*Berachos* 28b).

"Don't worry about that," R' David consoled him. "Who do you think will be sitting in judgment over you? Thieves and criminals? Heaven forbid! Every bit of Torah that you studied, every mitzvah that you performed throughout your lifetime, will stand to your merit. As for the sins you may have committed — you have repented for them, and even those sins for which mere repentance is insufficient (see *Yoma* 86a) are now achieving atonement, through physical suffering. You can rest assured that you will receive a fair trial and be granted your just reward! You have nothing to worry about!"

שְׁאַל אָבִיךָ וְיַגֵּדְךָ זְקֵנֶיךָ וְיֹאמְרוּ לָךְ — *Ask your father and he will tell you, your elders and they will relate it to you* (32:7).

There was once an American boy whose parents were seeking an intensive, Torah-only education for their son, and sent him to study in an Israeli yeshivah for boys of high-school age. The boy had trouble adjusting to the yeshivah, however, and the administration suggested to his father that he be removed from the school. The father came to Israel to get his son, but the boy insisted on staying in the yeshivah. Unsure of what to do, the father was advised by a relative to ask Rav Shach for guidance.

The *Rosh Yeshivah* received the father and son and heard the two sides of the issue — that of the father, who agreed with the yeshivah administration that his son return home, and that of the son, who insisted on staying. After both sides presented their cases, Rav Shach turned to the boy and said, "Do you commit yourself to following the advice that I will give you?"

The boy agreed, and Rav Shach extended his hand for a handshake to "seal the deal." Then he told him, "Look, I don't know you or your father. I have never met either of you before, and most probably I will never see you again after today. But you should know that I never issue any opinion or advice off the top of my head. Everything is based on the wisdom of the Torah!

"The Torah says, 'Ask your father and he will tell you.' Now, it is quite obvious that not every single Jewish child has a father who is a great Torah scholar, blessed with the insight of Torah wisdom. Nevertheless, the Torah commands each and every son to listen to his father's words. If a father's intentions are proper and based on considerations of fear of God and of his son's best interests, he is granted assistance from Above in providing his son the best possible advice — all with God's help.

"Now, from what I have heard here, it seems to me that your father is concerned only for your best interest, and does not have any other interest. After all, what difference would it make to him if you stay here or not? It is for *your* sake that he seeks your return home! Therefore, under these circumstances the Torah obligates you to listen to him — and if you do so, you will be granted success!"

The son honored his word and followed the *Rosh Yeshivah's* advice. He went back to America, but several years later he returned to Israel to study in a *yeshiva gedolah* (for older boys). This time he succeeded admirably and went on to raise a fine, upstanding Jewish family.

שְׁאַל אָבִיךָ וְיַגֵּדְךָ זְקֵנֶיךָ וְיֹאמְרוּ לָךְ — *Ask your father and he will tell you, your elders and they will relate it to you* (32:7).

Rav Shach related an example of the great wisdom and refined character of his uncle, R' Isser Zalman Meltzer.

R' Isser Zalman was once sitting with one of the great Torah scholars of the time when a young married Torah student approached him and began presenting an approach to resolving a powerful, well-known, question on a Talmudic topic. The Torah scholar who was with R' Isser Zalman grimaced in pain as he heard the fellow expound on his thesis, which was totally without basis. To his surprise, however, R' Isser Zalman listened attentively and his eyes lit up. He told the *avrech*, "What a wonderful idea that is! You know, according to your thesis, there is a clear answer to the question posed by R' Akiva Eiger in such-and-such a place, as well as the difficulty posed by the *Ketzos HaChoshen* in such-and-such a section. Furthermore, the objection of the *Nesivos* falls away in light of your idea! And the *Beis Meir's* question falls away as well!"

The *avrech* was delighted. He had approached R' Isser Zalman to suggest a simple answer to a question, and came away with a whole exposition to his credit!

After the *avrech* left, the Torah scholar turned to R' Isser Zalman and said, "I am amazed at you! Do you really agree with the nonsense that fellow was spewing?"

"Of course not!" objected R' Isser Zalman. "How could you suspect me of that?!"

"If so," asked the scholar, even more confused than before, "why did you go along with him — and even encourage him?!"

"I did nothing of the sort!" exclaimed R' Isser Zalman. "On the contrary, I reprimanded him and proved to him the error of his thinking several times over! If he has any sense at all he will realize that if, according to his line of reasoning, R' Akiva Eiger, the *Ketzos* and *Nesivos*, and the *Beis Meir* all asked baseless questions, then his line of reasoning must be completely wrong. Surely he doesn't think that he outsmarted all those great Sages!"

כִּי לֹא־דָבָר רֵק הוּא מִכֶּם — *For it is not an empty thing for you* (lit. *from you*) (32:47).

The *Yerushalmi* interprets this verse as follows: "*It is not an empty thing.* And if you do find it empty — it is *from you* (i.e., it is your own fault), for you have not sufficiently toiled to understand it."

Rav Shach related that the Brisker Rav told him that his father (R' Chaim Brisker) once called him over to tell him a novel approach to a Talmudic topic, and asked him to record it in writing. However, he objected to his father that he did not understand the fine distinction that his father was drawing, and could therefore not commit the ideas to writing. R' Chaim explained it to him again, but once again he declared that he did not comprehend the distinctions being made, and could not write the thesis down.

The Brisker Rav commented to Rav Shach that now, many years later, he looks back at that incident and feels tremendous regret. He did not regret not having written down his father's words, for it is indeed impossible to commit to writing something that someone does not fully understand. Rather, he felt bad that he had not tried harder to contemplate and understand the concept put forth by his father, so that he *would* be able to write it down!

כִּי־הוּא חַיֵּיכֶם — *For it* (the Torah) *is your life* (32:47).

A certain *bachur* in Ponevezh Yeshivah was feeling a bit down and was looking for some compassion and concern. He went to the *Rosh Yeshivah* and told him that he was depressed. He felt that he did not understand the *shiurim*, and felt that perhaps the yeshivah was not for him. He thought that the *Rosh Yeshivah* might encourage him with some warm words of comfort. To his surprise, however, Rav Shach's response was brusque and to the point. "If you don't understand the *shiurim* in Level 2, perhaps you should be moved to Level 1!"

The *bachur* was insulted by that suggestion. Did the *Rosh Yeshivah* really think he deserved to be "put back a grade"?!

Rav Shach continued along the same lines. "And if you can't understand the Level 1 *shiur* either, perhaps you should go to *shiur* only twice a week and spend the rest of your time reviewing those two lessons."

The *bachur* was even more taken aback now.

"And if that is also too hard for you, perhaps you should consider sitting and learning yourself — *bekius* (covering ground, but not with the usual depth and analysis), with just Rashi and *Tosafos*. And if that is also too hard, you could skip the *Tosafos*!"

The boy was totally outraged by now. "What does the *Rosh Yeshivah* take me for? Some young kid from *cheder* (elementary school)?"

But the *Rosh Yeshivah* just continued. "And if that, too, is difficult for you, there is always *Mishnayos*.

"The idea I am trying to get across is," concluded the *Rosh Yeshivah*, "that besides learning Torah there is nothing else in the world. There can be no life without Torah. If you are having difficulty with your present learning circumstances, change them. But 'you do not have the option of excusing yourself from the task' (*Avos* 2:16).

"The Torah is life. When a person is in good health, he is fortunate. If he becomes sick, he suffers in pain. If his condition worsens, he suffers more. But no matter how badly he suffers, it is better than being dead! Life, no matter how miserable, is superior to death. The same goes for Torah! Any form of learning at all is better than nothing!"

The *bachur* later related that this tough talk from Rav Shach actually jarred him sufficiently to realize that he did in fact have the capability to understand the *shiur*, if he only applied himself. He went on to become one of the best students in the yeshivah.

וזאת הברכה — Vezos Haberachah

יְהוָה מִסִּינַי בָּא וְזָרַח מִשֵּׂעִיר לָמוֹ — *Hashem came from Sinai — having shone forth to them from Seir, having appeared from Mount Paran (33:2).*

The Midrash (see Rashi) explains this verse to mean that God first approached the descendants of Edom (who live in Seir) and of Yishmael (who live in Paran) to offer the Torah to them, before giving it to Israel at Mount Sinai. The Edomites asked, "What is written in this Torah?" When they were told that one of the commandments was, "You shall not kill," they rejected the offer. The Yishmaelites asked the same question, and turned down the Torah when they learned that it included the prohibition against stealing. When God told the Jews about the Torah, however, they responded, "We will do it; [then] we will hear" (*Shemos* 24:7) — no questions asked, no reservations expressed.

R' Yosef Sheinin recounts: "One time, during Rav Shach's daily *shiur*, we came upon an Aggadic section of Talmud. Many *ramim* (teachers of Talmud) skip over such non-halachic sections, focusing instead on the more challenging and difficult halachic passages. But Rav Shach read the Gemara and explained each aphorism with his usual lucid, pleasant delivery. He often cited the words of the Rambam (in his Mishnah Commentary) in this regard: 'I try, whenever matters of faith are brought up in the [Mishnah] text, to offer some words of explanation for, in my eyes, it is more important to clarify a principle of faith and religion than anything else.'

"On that occasion, one of the *bachurim* in the *shiur* had the nerve to ask the *Rosh Yeshivah*, 'Why are we doing this? Why don't we skip the Aggadic sections?'

"In his great modesty, Rav Shach — rather than address the boy's impertinence — simply told him, 'We are not descendants of Edom or

Yishmael, who asked God, "What is written in it?" We accept lovingly and study *whatever* is written!'"

וְהֵם תֻּכּוּ לְרַגְלֶךָ — *They planted themselves at Your feet* (33:3).

*I*n a play on the word תֻּכּוּ, *planted themselves*, the Sages comment, "This refers to Torah scholars who scrape (מכתת) their feet traveling to distant cities and countries to study Torah" (*Bava Basra* 8a).

An American yeshivah *bachur* who had traveled to Lithuania to study in its famous yeshivahs related to Rav Shach that he had once gone to Radin to visit the Chofetz Chaim, who told him, "You American *bachurim* will get more reward for your learning than the local boys. For you have all the comforts of life in your home country, yet you willingly 'exile yourselves to a place of Torah' (*Avos* 4:14) despite all the hardships this entails."

As Rav Shach explained, the poverty in Eastern Europe at that time was such that although the yeshivahs served barely more than meager rations of stale bread, one could suspect a *bachur* who went to learn in yeshivah of going just to get the free food — for in his own house he did not even get *that* much! The American *bachurim*, however, could not, by any stretch of the imagination, be suspected of coming to Lithuania to improve their standard of living! Their total dedication to Torah study for its own sake was beyond question.

שְׂמַח זְבוּלֻן בְּצֵאתֶךָ וְיִשָּׂשכָר בְּאֹהָלֶיךָ — *Rejoice, O Zevulun, in your excursions, and Yissachar in your tents* (33:18).

*T*he arrangement between these two brother-tribes is well known: The Zevulunites would engage in commerce and use their wealth to support the Yissacharites, who were thus freed from the burden of earning a livelihood and could completely devote themselves to learning Torah. The Zevulunites were then accorded a share in Yissachar's Torah study, which they had facilitated.

Rav Shach was, at one time, the *rosh yeshivah* of the Karliner yeshivah in Luninetz. When he first arrived there, there was no *mashgiach*, so he personally assumed that role until R' Zalman Brizel arrived to become the official *mashgiach* of the yeshivah.

Many years later R' Zalman joked to his grandson, "You must treat me with respect! You know, even Rav Shach stood up for me!"

In response to the young boy's wonderment, R' Zalman explained the background of his comment. "Yes, that's right. I was also surprised when it happened. And in fact I protested that it was an improper gesture, and that I was undeserving of such an honor. But he said to me, 'I am not standing up out of respect for you, but out of respect for your Torah!'

"'If I myself am not fitting for honor, then certainly my Torah is not either!' I declared.

"Rav Shach then explained himself. 'Before you came here, I had to spend my time going around to the *bachurim's* quarters, waking them up or urging them to get to the *beis midrash*, etc. Now that you have come, you have spared me this effort, and I am able to spend that time learning. Since you are the one who enabled that extra Torah study, you, no less than Zevulun, are entitled to receive credit yourself for that learning. It is therefore indeed fitting that I should rise for you!'"

וַיִּשְׁמְעוּ אֵלָיו בְּנֵי־יִשְׂרָאֵל — *And the Children of Israel accepted his teachings* (34:9, Onkelos).

Rav Shach was once discussing the greatness of the *Shaagas Aryeh* and the Vilna Gaon.

One of the students was puzzled about the comparison between these two great Torah personalities. "Wasn't the Vilna Gaon much greater than all others of his time, including the *Shaagas Aryeh*?" he asked.

"I'll have you know," responded Rav Shach, "that it was actually the *Shaagas Aryeh* who 'discovered' the Gaon's greatness and revealed it to the public!"

He then proceeded to explain this curious assertion. "In Vilna, people used to refer to the Gaon as 'the Chassid (saint), R' Eliyahu,' for he was known to all for his great piety. One day the *Shaagas Aryeh* had a difficult question, which he brought before R' Abele Fassweller, the rabbi of Vilna, to discuss. The *Shaagas Aryeh*, however, was not fully satisfied with R' Abele's answer, and he thought he might as well try putting the question to R' Eliyahu, who lived on the other side of town, although he did not expect much to come of this attempt. R' Eliyahu, to his surprise, gave a brilliant, lucid answer, the absolute truth of which was immediately evident. The *Shaagas Aryeh* was overjoyed to have his problem solved so ingeniously and thoroughly, and he told the people in town, 'You are mistaken in your appellation that you apply to this man. He is not simply "the Chassid R' Eliyahu," but "*the Gaon and* the Chassid R' Eliyahu!" The difference between his genius and scholarship and those of the Vilna rabbi,' he added, 'is as great as the distance between his house and that of the rabbi!'

"From that incident on, until this very day," concluded Rav Shach, "R Eliyahu was referred to as 'the Vilna Gaon'!"

וְהָגִיתָ בּוֹ יוֹמָם וָלַיְלָה — *And you shall meditate on it by day and by night* (Haftarah).

Rav Shach recounted that when he studied in Slobodka during the First World War, all the students fled the yeshivah to avoid being conscripted into the Czar's army. Rav Shach was the only one who stayed in the yeshivah. He had the privilege of eating twice a week in the home of the father of the "*Afikei Yam*" (R' Yechiel Michel Rabinowitz). In those days, Rav Shach recalled, he sat and learned in the freezing cold *beis midrash*, not having any warm clothing to wear or with which to cover himself. He remarked that if he was able to find a few pieces of wood that he could pile up next to the furnace to lie down upon, he considered himself fortunate to have found such a fine "pillow"!

As he reminisced, he began to cry and declared, in his great modesty, "I have been granted the opportunity to learn Torah out of great deprivation. But it is a shame that I did not learn more!"

From Rav Shach's reaction as he recounted this story — as from all of his words and actions — one could quite clearly sense that the only "possession" he considered to be of any value was his toil in the study of Torah. This was the path that he followed throughout his long life, as the fire of Torah burned unceasingly within his soul, from start to finish.